CHRISTIANITY
AND RUSSIAN CULTURE
IN SOVIET SOCIETY

Published in cooperation with
the Center for Contemporary Russian Studies,
Monterey Institute of International Studies

CCRS SERIES ON
CHANGE IN CONTEMPORARY SOVIET SOCIETY
Nicolai N. Petro, Series Editor

Christianity and Russian Culture in Soviet Society, edited by Nicolai N. Petro

Self-Government and Freedom in Russia, Sergei Pushkarev, with an Introduction by Nicholas V. Riasanovsky

Christianity and Government in Russia and the Soviet Union: Reflections on the Millennium, Sergei Pushkarev, Vladimir Rusak, and Gleb Yakunin

CHRISTIANITY AND RUSSIAN CULTURE IN SOVIET SOCIETY

edited by
Nicolai N. Petro

Westview Press
BOULDER, SAN FRANCISCO, & LONDON

CCRS Series on Change in Contemporary Soviet Society

Published in 1990 in the United States of America by Westview Press, Inc., 5500 Central Avenue, Boulder, Colorado 80301, and in the United Kingdom by Westview Press, Inc., 13 Brunswick Centre, London WC1N 1AF, England

Library of Congress Cataloging-in-Publication Data
Christianity and Russian culture in Soviet society / edited by Nicolai
  N. Petro.
     p.   cm.—(CCRS series on change in contemporary Soviet
society)
   ISBN 0-8133-7742-0
   1. Christianity—Soviet Union. 2. Soviet Union—
Civilization—20th century. 3. Christianity and culture.
4. Soviet Union—Church history—1917-   . 5. Church and state—Soviet
Union—History—20th century. I. Petro, Nicolai N. II. Series.
BR936.C49 1990
274.7'.082—dc20   89-49774
                                                                                         CIP

Printed and bound in the United States of America

∞ The paper used in this publication meets the requirements of the American National
    Standard for Permanence of Paper for Printed Library Materials Z39.48-1984.

10   9   8   7   6   5   4   3   2

Contents

Part Two: Christianity and Soviet Russian Culture

Preface

This volume is the product of a three-day conference organized by the Center for Contemporary Russian Studies at the Monterey Institute of International Studies, January 17-20, 1988. Sixty leading scholars of religion and politics from Israel, Canada, Germany, Holland, England, the United States, and the Soviet Union came to Monterey, California, to exchange views on church-state relations in the Soviet Union and the prospects for change. The Soviet delegation was headed by the Archbishop of Ivano-Frankovsk, Makarii, and included lecturers from the Moscow and Leningrad Spiritual Academies. In addition, through the auspices of Keston College, ten papers were prepared for the conference by unofficial religious activists in the Soviet Union, two of which were read *in absentia*.

Two themes that emerged during the course of the conference are reflected in this book. One is the tension between the expression of Christian beliefs and the legal restrictions imposed by the Soviet State on professions of faith. The other is the growing importance of Christian culture to the process of *perestroika*. Indeed, it is in recognition of the latter that the regime is now adopting a somewhat more tolerant attitude toward religious belief.

Soviet legislators have been slowly trying to resolve the contradiction between the official policy of separation of church and state and the *de facto* control which state officials exercise over religious appointments to this day. Added to this are the increasingly frequent independent initiatives of parishioners wishing to restore their run-down churches and monasteries, or to become involved in charitable activities. These contradictions in the current legal position of religious believers are reflected in the differing assessments by the authors in this volume. The confusion has changed little in the two years since this conference was held.

At the beginning of 1988, it was not yet clear how the Orthodox Church would be permitted to celebrate the millennium of the baptism of Rus'. In retrospect, the unprecedented amount of media coverage given to the clergy during this national celebration marks a turning point in official attitudes toward religion. Not only did the government sanction a more visible social role for the church and restore to it previously sequestered properties such as the monastery at Tolgsk and sections of the Kiev Monastery of the Caves, but the church for its part increasingly asserted its importance to the process of social restructuring of Soviet society. The culmination of this new attitude came when five clergymen were elected to the newly formed Congress of People's Deputies. These positive developments in church-state relations are discussed in the contributions by Archbishop Makarii and Philip Walters.

Last year's millennium celebrations, however, also highlighted the fundamental inequality that still characterizes the status of religious believers in an atheist state. These inequalities are graphically discussed in Vladimir Al'brekht's and A. Bessmertnyi-Anzimirov's *samizdat* contributions received from the Soviet Union, and by Gleb Rahr, a long-time observer of church affairs. Such concerns linger because the regime appears unable or unwilling to relinquish its ideological hostility toward religion, as evidenced by articles in the Party press critical of the church's claim to any social role,[1] and by the recent unceremonious removal of Konstantin Kharchev from the chairmanship of the Council on Religious Affairs of the U.S.S.R. Council of Ministers. Increasingly, Kharchev had been seen as critical of the restrictive measures imposed on religion during the 1930s, and as an advocate of legal reform equalizing the status of atheists and religious believers. Douglas Durasoff and Philip Walters trace the ebbs and flows in official policy on religion and offer preliminary criteria for gauging the success of the reforms in this area.

The second theme of the conference is the growing influence of Christian culture in the Soviet Union. Today there is unanimous agreement among Soviet government officials and regime critics about the low cultural level of society and its impact on civic affairs. But while the official response has been to emphasize the restoration of communist ideals and the revitalization of Marxism-Leninism, others in society have reached the conclusion that today's social problems can only be addressed through a return to religious values. For them the root cause of social apathy and low civic culture lies in the loss of the people's ties to Christian culture and Russian history.

The close connection of the Christian cultural tradition with Russian national identity was underscored by several speakers at the recent Congress of People's Deputies, most notably by writer Valentin Rasputin, and by the vice-chairman of the Soviet Cultural Fund, Sergei Averintsev.[2] In the present volume, Mikhail Agursky and Libor Brom discuss the evolution of two prominent Soviet intellectual figures, Maksim Gorky and Alexander Zinoviev, away from materialism. Valery Petrochenkov, Dmitry Shlapentokh, and Oskar Gruenwald then highlight the prominent place Christian themes occupy in contemporary Soviet Russian culture. Mikhail Heifetz traces the impact of the Christian revival - and the closely associated Russian national revival - on Russian-Jewish relations, while Nicolai Petro examines the legacy of Russian religious philosophy, and its impact among contemporary Soviet intellectuals.

Among the many crises the regime faces as it seeks to revitalize Soviet society, none is more profound than the crisis of faith in socialism. This crisis has led many Soviet intellectuals to search for less transient values. The consensus of the conference participants was that any alternative to socialism would probably draw from the national and religious heritages suppressed by the regime. To be sure, religion and nationalism are a highly volatile mixture, prone to excesses, but it is worth noting that many liberally-minded reformers also look to the cultural and religious heritage of the past for inspiration. They see pre-revolutionary Russia as offering a higher cultural vantage point than Soviet society today. In their eyes, the restoration of cultural tolerance is an imperative of perestroika since, as Academician Dmitrii S. Likhachev put it, "Persons of high culture are not aggressive, they are not hostile to other nationalities, or to differing opinions."[3]

Today one can easily discern the feeling among Soviet intellectuals that social engineering has failed. What is needed instead, as one scientist recently put it, is "the realization and consistent introduction into life of spiritual-moral values. . ."[4] Abandoning the past means, in the words of writer Iurii Bondarev, losing "one's spiritual equilibrium."[5]   This realization has led many intellectuals to a rediscovery of spiritual values, and even to religious belief.[6] Such new-found humility is not absent from Gorbachev's own candid approach to past inadequacies in the construction of socialism. These are hopeful signs of a healthy reflection on the lessons of the Soviet past, and for the eventual re-integration of the Soviet Union into the community of nations.

The Center for Contemporary Russian Studies (CCRS) is grateful to the Earhart Foundation and to the United States Information Agency for providing support without which the conference, and this volume, would not have been possible. My thanks also to the administration of the Monterey Institute, and to the dedicated student staff of the CCRS. Thanks to Cambridge University Press for permission to reprint a section from Dmitry Obolensky's *The Bogomils* (1948).   My special appreciation to Andrea Medacco, Barbara Poston and Christina Sever for translating the remarks of our Soviet participants, to Steven Green for helping to correct the manuscripts, and to Christina Sever for her selfless work in producing the final manuscript. Special thanks to Rebecca Ritke for her careful review and for seeing this book through the final editing process. As always, I am indebted to our editor at Westview, Susan L. McEachern, for her advice throughout this undertaking, and wish her the best of luck with her new "project." The Library of Congress transliteration system was used throughout the manuscript, except for commonly accepted proper names. Finally, I alone am responsible for any errors in the text.

Nicolai N. Petro
Foreign Policy Research Institute

---

1. V.G. Ovchinnikov, in "Pravoslavnaia tserkov' v istorii nashei strany," gives a highly critical evaluation of the "exaggerated appraisal of the role of the Orthodox Church in our nation's history" in the Party's leading theoretical journal <u>Kommunist</u>, No. 5, 1988, p. 121.

2. For Rasputin's speech see <u>FBIS: Daily Reports</u>, <u>Soviet Union</u>, June 7, 1989, pp. 20-23. Averintsev's speech was published as "K sovesti," in <u>Sovetskaia kul'tura</u>, June 15, 1989, p. 2.

3. <u>Literaturnaia gazeta</u>, June 7, 1989, p. 3.

4. "Zemlia i khleb," <u>Nash sovremennik</u>, July 1985, p. 149.

5. Iurii Bondarev at the R.S.F.S.R. Writer's Congress, <u>Literaturnaia gazeta</u>, December 18, 1985, p. 4.

6. R. Balandin, "Veruiushchii intelligent," <u>Sovetskaia kul'tura</u>, Februry 18, 1989, p. 6.

Part 1
Christianity and the Soviet State

RELIGION IN THE SOVIET UNION: SURVIVAL AND REVIVAL

Philip Walters

"All political work with the clergy is carried on in the interest of the state" and is aimed "not only at keeping them within the bounds of law, but at diminishing their activity and limiting their influence with believers." So writes V. Furov, a deputy chairman of the Council for Religious Affairs in the Soviet Union, in a secret report to the Central Committee of the Communist Party of the Soviet Union on the current state of the Russian Orthodox Church, dated 1974. The "law" referred to here is the Law on Religious Associations of 1929, which is still in force today. According to this law, the only permitted activity for believers is to meet in a registered building for an act of worship. Everything else is either illegal or in fact discouraged by the authorities: organizing meetings, libraries, educational activity for young people; evangelizing; unofficially printing and distributing religious literature; and raising money for welfare or charitable activity.

We are all familiar with the fact that the witness of the churches in Soviet society is disastrously truncated as a result of the consistent anti-religious attitude of the authorities. Let us take just two examples. There is a grievous shortage of religious literature. In the thirty years since 1956 the Russian Orthodox Church received permission to print about 450,000 pieces of scripture. Hence the growth of *samizdat*: over a ten-year period in the 1970s and early 1980s, and despite all the difficulties involved in setting up and dismantling secret printing presses and moving them from place to place, the unregistered Baptists have managed to produce a comparable number of pieces of scripture unofficially. There is also a grievous shortage of places of worship;

believers are in fact prevented in many parts of the Soviet Union from exercising the one right they enjoy according to Soviet legislation. Visitors to Moscow will find over forty working churches in that city; but the diocese of Irkutsk, which is roughly the same size as Australia and has a comparable population, has about fifty working churches, while Australia has over 19,000.

The ideal church from the point of view of the Soviet authorities would consist of a docile hierarchy, some church buildings opened for worship in the major cities, especially those visited by foreigners, and a dwindling elderly flock. What the authorities particularly distrust are active clergy or younger believers who attempt in any way to relate their faith to everyday life. As Furov says in his report, "if a priest gives sermons, they must be strictly Orthodox in content, containing expositions of the Gospel or Epistles. . . sermons must contain no political or social issues or examples." The type of bishop of whom the state approves is one who will speak positively of conditions for believers in the Soviet Union while doing the minimum to encourage those believers in their spiritual growth. Furov describes with approval "Bishop Palladi," who "leaves a favorable impression, with his loyal attitude towards the organs of Soviet power. . . as far as religious activities are concerned, the bishop limits himself to periodic services in the Cathedral on religious festivals, and he never travels outside the town;" while Bishop Iona "delivers regular sermons, but they are very short and not very expressive. . . in the seven years he has been head of a diocese he has never visited any of the rural parishes of the region."

Despite the 1929 legislation, the churches in the Soviet Union have in fact been allowed to run very few monasteries and theological educational establishments and to undertake only a small amount of publishing activity since the Second World War. This activity is obviously closely monitored, and the authorities could put a stop to it at any moment. The price church leaders pay for these concessions is that they are expected to promote the Soviet image and Soviet policies abroad, and the main activity here is to speak on the subject of peace. There may seem to be a discontinuity here between what they are expected to do abroad and what they are expected to do here - that is, keep well away from political matters. But if we look more closely at the terms in which their contribution to the international peace debate is couched, we will soon see that this does not represent an occasion for religious leaders to give a specifically religious analysis on questions of peace and war.

A Peace Conference in Budapest in December 1987 brought together peace activists from East and West, from official and unofficial groups. Archbishop Kirill of Smolensk gave one of the three introductory speeches. He argued that world peace can be achieved only on the basis of the widest possible consensus. "Humanity," he said, "should unite. . . *on the basis of common moral principles*. In other words, the world view to unite human spirit in the struggle for survival should be described in moral terms common for all men." What he had to say intrigued many, excited some and left others baffled. Those who were baffled included many who had been looking forward to hearing a particularly Russian Orthodox perspective on the theology of peace. In fact, the Archbishop's words are readily understandable if one bears in mind that the Soviet authorities always appeal on peace questions to as wide a constituency as possible and expect representatives from the religious organizations in the Soviet Union to do likewise.

The appeal is to "all people of goodwill." In 1976 The *Journal of the Moscow Patriarchate*, describing the Helsinki process, recognized the contribution of "all peace-loving forces of our planet, including the religious community, and also including the efforts of all people of goodwill." In 1978 the *Journal* reported the message from Mr. Kosygin to the Prague Peace Conference: "Problems connected with the preservation of peace on earth. . . are important to all people, irrespective of their religious or other convictions. . ." Therefore "all people of goodwill are united." A recent atheist pamphlet quotes the late Metropolitan Nikodim to the effect that a Christian must recognize the ethical superiority of the classless Soviet society over any other social system, and the commentator observes that "in this way, renouncing the role of bystanding spectator and giving approval to the socialist system, religious ideologues come out in defense of spiritual values which belong to the majority of Soviet people regardless of their relation to religion or the Church."

It is actually impossible, as far as the Soviet authorities are concerned, for a churchman to offer a distinctively religious contribution on any social or political matter. If it is a religious view, it is automatically invalid before it is uttered. I have before me a pamphlet from December 1987 which promises to tell us what

"Leninist" principles are in relation to religion. We may remember that Mr. Kharchev, Chairman of the Council for Religious Affairs, said in August 1987 that under conditions of perestroika Soviet church policy would be governed by these Leninist principles. How to explain, asks the author, the fact that while religious beliefs are in themselves reactionary, many believers and even clergy throughout the world are backing the peace struggle? "The point is that we as atheists do not share the theological view that religious belief defines or ought to define all the actions of believers." Amongst other factors which define their actions are "the objective conditions of their existence - their class interest. And the process of involving the members of the working class who are religious believers in the struggle for socialism can precede the creation in them of a scientific materialist and atheist world view." Religious believers who support the Marxist political program "inevitably try to give a religious interpretation to their new progressive political views, and the fact that such an interpretation is scientifically baseless is no reason for Marxists to refuse the cooperation of believers." There is a well known liberal maxim, "I disagree with what you say, but I will defend to the death your right to say it." The attitude of the Soviet authorities towards those who would enter the peace debate from a religious perspective is to some extent the opposite of this: "I may well agree with what you are going to say, but I oppose absolutely *your* right, as a religious believer, to say it."

I have dwelt on this point at some length because it seems to me that it is a point which is often misunderstood, particularly by religious believers in the West who would like to take the involvement of the churches of the Soviet Union in peace discussions as evidence for the fact that they enjoy the freedom to put forward a specifically religious point of view. Nevertheless, I also believe that by and large and to an encouraging extent the leaders of the churches in the Soviet Union are aware of the fact that it remains a vital element in their activity that they should continue to try to preserve an area of spiritual freedom, however small, for their religious community and to try persistently to extend it. Hence, not only the Soviet authorities but also the religious leaders themselves, for different reasons, are anxious that the churches of the Soviet Union should continue to be represented on international religious bodies such as the World Council of Churches. Churchmen from the Soviet Union, by their regular appearances at these gatherings, prevent themselves from sinking into total isolation; and they provide their western counterparts with the opportunity to say things to them about the domestic situation in the USSR which they can then report to the authorities when they return and perhaps use as bargaining chips to gain a few more concessions. Hence, too, we should not be afraid of raising so called "difficult" questions with Soviet churchmen in these international gatherings; they are certainly not going to withdraw from those bodies of their own accord.

The awareness of Soviet church leaders that they have to defend their real spiritual integrity dates to the time of the Renovationist experiment in the 1920s. The Renovationist church split from the Patriarchal church on the platform of total identification with the aims of the new socialist state. When Lenin died in 1924, Patriarch Tikhon of the Patriarchal Orthodox Church declined to attend his funeral, saying that his presence would upset Lenin's adherents and furthermore would not fit in with what Lenin himself would have wished. Not so the Renovationist leaders. A delegation of them accompanied Lenin's coffin and sent a message which included the sentiment,". . . eternal memory and eternal rest be with your hard-tested, kindly and Christian soul."

In the early months of the Renovationists' triumph, when Patriarch Tikhon was already under house arrest, two clergymen, Aleksii Simanskii and Nikolai Iarushevich, who were later to become respectively Patriarch and Head of the Church's Department of External Relations, tried to establish a third approach for the church. A little later came the activity of Archbishop Manuil, who led the Tikhonite counter-reformation in 1923. Exiled religious writer Anatolii Levitin-Krasnov describes his aim as the formation of a "free, pure and independent Russian church in a free socialist Russia."

According to the Furov report, only about a third of the bishops of the Orthodox Church in the mid-1970s could be totally trusted to combine a vigorous loyalty to the state with suitable neglect for the nurture of the faith. Nevertheless, many observers and involved activists both in the West and in the USSR are very frustrated with what they see as the pusillanimity of the leaders of the churches and will even blame them for the fact that the state has managed to exert such complete control over internal church matters in violation of the constitutional guarantee of separation of church and state.

Unfortunately, the Soviet authorities are also interested in driving a wedge between "good" and "bad" believers, between the "loyal" hierarchy and their faithful flock and the "disloyal" lawbreakers, that is, the more articulate believers, including the "dissidents", who are concerned to relate faith to life. It is my belief that we should take every opportunity to insist that we are dealing with *one* church, *one* body of Christ; it is my belief that we should make it clear that the two sides of religious experience in the Soviet Union will need to be complementary rather than antagonistic in the regeneration of religious life in that country.

Having thus surveyed the background to the current religious situation in the Soviet Union, let us look more closely at developments under Gorbachev.

There are a number of problematic issues which are currently inspiring debate in the Soviet Union. Let us take just two examples: the question of the search for moral values and the question of nationalism. There are of course many more; the question of "peace," for example, is one such. On controversial topics such as these, the authorities would of course like to set the agenda for the debate, to control it from above. The topics we have mentioned are controversial, however, in that those involved in discussing them will be drawn to using "spiritual" terms when debating the origins and nature of morality, national feeling or peace. The authorities would like the spiritual element in each debate to be tamed, muted, made unspecific, deprived of any transcendent element, or redefined in less potentially subversive terms: in terms of aspirations common to all humanity (as we have seen in the peace debate), or of mythology (as far as the search for moral standards is concerned), or of culture (as far as the nationalist question is concerned), for example. But the tendency is that the deeper one allows the debate to go in any of these fields, the more the terms of the debate are likely to depart from those the authorities would prefer.

Let us look first, then, at the search for moral values. Under Gorbachev there has been open recognition of the moral collapse and corruption in Soviet society, and there has been widespread discussion of the potential role of religion in keeping a society morally sound. As one psychotherapist said in a recent round table discussion reported in the Soviet press on the rising divorce rate: "traditions have changed, parental authority has collapsed. . . there is no fear of God. . . in other words, the external mechanism for keeping families together has weakened." What we have here is a recognition of the passive role of religion as a sort of social cement. But of course once the debate has begun, it moves on. Since the 1970s more and more writers in the Soviet Union are concerned with religious and moral themes. These preoccupations have been criticized in the Soviet press but also discussed in some detail; there is official recognition that moral problems in society are real and must be solved. Here the dilemma for the authorities presents itself. These themes will be discussed; the question is, in what terms. How far, then, can writers go in their religious quest? Pronouncements from on high continue to indicate that a line will be drawn at some point. In October 1986 Egor Ligachev said, "sometimes when certain people encounter violations of socialist morality they begin to talk about the advisability of showing tolerance for religious ideas and of returning to religious morality. In doing so they forget the Marxist truism that religion is by no means a source of man's moral principles. It was not religion that gave mankind the moral norms that are now shared by mankind."

One response by the authorities to the discussion of morality in religious terms has been to try to redefine religious concepts and give them a Marxist content - to change as it were the meaning of the very terms in which the debate is being conducted. One Vladimir Shinkaruk argued in 1986 in the publication *Argumenty i fakty* that the notions of "faith" and "the sacred" are not exclusively religious, but psychological phenomena independent of religious impulses. Today, he urges, "the sacred" is a term which should be applied to the cultural phenomena of ordinary life and to the new Soviet values. He calls for a form of "unreligious" faith in the inevitability of a communist future, reinforced by a system of symbolic rites which are an integral part of socialist culture.

There was of course a previous attempt earlier this century to reinterpret religious concepts in the context of socialist construction - the "godbuilding" of Gorky and Lunacharsky. As outlined in Gorky's novel *Ispoved'* [Confession], godbuilding is about inspiring man's faith in his own creative potential as an individual, expressed through the collective. It is about promoting creative social energy, which becomes the incarnation of a living deity. In the context of godbuilding, we may look at the novels of the contemporary Soviet writer Chingiz Aitmatov. One commentator on these novels has recently seen a development in Aitmatov's thinking, from a preoccupation with individualism, through a growing concern about collective integration, towards an affirmation of moral and social collectivism as the highest value. In Aitmatov's novel *Plakha*, Christ speaks of "the god of tomorrow," and says of him that "in him is all the essence, the sum total of the activities and aspirations of men, and hence the nature of god tomorrow - whether he is to be good or evil, merciful or vengeful - depends on men themselves." It is arguable, then, that in the novels of Aitmatov we can read a progression from the question of the moral motivation of the individual to the question of the morality of the social collective. Thus defined, the religious terms in which the moral search is carried on may well be more acceptable to the Soviet authorities. It certainly seems that Aitmatov is not at the moment as popular among the reading public in the Soviet Union as he used to be. The novel *Plakha* seems to have been received with a certain amount of skepticism. Readers may well be feeling that the religious search in Aitmatov is running into familiar channels.

At one point in *Plakha*, the hero talks to a priest who tells him that his (the hero's) search for moral values and his desire to inculcate these in others are bound to upset the social status quo. We have only Aitmatov's word for it that this is in fact what a priest would say. This brings us to a fundamental problem regarding the moral search in contemporary Soviet literature, one which is of essential urgent importance: where is the voice of the church to be heard on these issues? Where are the reviews of Aitmatov, Rasputin, Belov or Rybakov in the *Journal of the Moscow Patriarchate*? Where is a critical assessment of contemporary godbuilding from the point of view of Orthodox theology? It would be of vital interest to hear, for example, a criticism of the moral search in contemporary Soviet literature from the point of view of traditional Orthodox teachings on *Sobornost'*, or "individual diversity in free unity," as a reconciling of the principles of the individual and the authentic collective. It would also be vital for the church itself to have this opportunity to define its own stance and attitude and make its own contribution in the current urgent debate about moral motivation; and of course the most profitable state of affairs would be if the church were able to contribute to this debate in the course of making a positive practical contribution by involvement in social and welfare work to help overcome the effects of moral decay in contemporary Soviet society. In other words, the church should be able to press successfully to be allowed to involve itself in work with alcoholics, marriage guidance counselling, and to set up and run old peoples' homes, orphanages and so forth.

Let us now turn to the second theme I noted earlier, that of nationalism.

In Central Asia, the Soviet authorities are trying to work out how to foster genuinely national customs while not at the same time encouraging a growth of religion. They are presented with the same kind of dilemma by Russian nationalism, which since the 1960s has been a manifold and complex phenomenon. At one extreme of the Russian nationalist spectrum are the religiously motivated liberal-minded *vozrozhdentsy* who are inspired by genuinely Christian motives, and at the other extreme are the chauvinist, non-religious National Bolsheviks with their positive attitude towards the authoritarian state and even to the Communist Party itself. Alexander Yanov advances the thesis that it is a delusion to think that the "good" or religiously inspired nationalism can possibly prevail against the "bad" chauvinist nationalism. He says the latter is likely to take power in the Soviet Union, with consequences for the West and for world peace far more serious than are inherent in the present situation. Other observers, including historian Dmitry Pospielovsky, take a different view. Pospielovsky discerns the following tendency: "that wherever national Bolshevism as a calculated policy gives way to genuine spiritual and intellectual searches, its better adherents are attracted by the church and her teachings, and an evolution takes place in the direction of personal conversion and towards a more humane, broader form of nationalism." He speaks of a continually observable phenomenon whereby nationalists encounter the Orthodox Church and become imbued with its teachings.

What is certain is that the situation in the Soviet Union is changing from day to day, and there is certainly widespread dismay among liberal and democratically-minded intellectuals and writers about the current growth of *Pamiat'*, a broadly based nationalist movement which has an increasingly obvious following among blue collar workers. While it does not necessarily have the sympathy of anyone in the Politburo, it is clear that plenty of influential and powerful people in the academic and cultural establishments are in sympathy with its aims, which can be broadly described as anti-western, anti-democratic and pro-religion only inasmuch as religion is a means of preserving social order.

Surely we are presented here, then, with another very obvious area in which the Russian Orthodox Church as such should be mobilized, or mobilize itself, to activity which will benefit those very reformist tendencies in the Soviet Union which Gorbachev has put in train. The church ought to be given every opportunity to encourage those enlightened and truly Christian elements in the Russian nationalist movement. If the church were mobilized in this way, with tactful, intelligent and discriminating support from the West, Gorbachev would find himself with an ally in his struggle against those racially motivated nationalists who are suspicious of any reform and who hanker for a return to Stalinism.

Let us now look at what has happened so far since Gorbachev came to power as far as practical measures affecting the position of believers are concerned.

Most notably from the point of view of the western media, there has been the release of some 200 prominent prisoners of conscience who had been charged with crimes arising out of their religious activities. And there has been considerable discussion in the Soviet press of specific problems experienced by particular religious individuals or communities. Ordinary Soviet citizens who are religious believers, including many who would until very recently have described themselves as "dissidents," have been able to assemble to discuss the implications of their faith and even to hold press conferences for foreign journalists. There has been continuing evidence that certain members of the church leadership are prepared to raise outstanding problems with the authorities, and a number of unprecedentedly frank articles have been published even in the *Journal of the Moscow Patriarchate*.

At the same time, however, there has been little evidence so far of any intention by the authorities to make ideological concessions towards the believing sector of the population. Gorbachev's own pronouncements on religion have contained little that is new. His most publicized remarks in this field were made in November 1986 in

Tashkent when he called for "a decisive and uncompromising struggle" with religion. However, few would have predicted three years ago that things could have moved so far in the Soviet Union in so short a time, and it would be foolish to assert that there could not be before long a more accommodating attitude towards religion on the part of the authorities. As I have shown, there are areas of urgent debate in Soviet society where the specific input of religious believers and the authoritative voices of their churches would benefit the program of reconstruction. The question is when, and indeed whether, those in authority will perceive this fact. Gorbachev has spoken of the fact that he needs to win the cooperation of all sectors of the community in order to bring his perestroika to a successful conclusion. In January 1987 he told the Central Committee that "one important aspect of the democratization of public life is the promotion of non-party comrades to leading work. This is a question of principle." It seems only natural that Gorbachev should take steps to increase the area in which religious believers can be of positive support. After all, they constitute at the very least one fifth of the population and are often the best motivated and hardest workers in any locality as well as being overwhelmingly loyal to their Soviet motherland. Whatever policy Gorbachev develops towards religious believers must take place in cognizance of the fact that interest in religion in the Soviet Union is growing rather than shrinking. Some observers doubt whether the phenomenon can be called a general revival or renaissance, but it is certainly an observable social phenomenon, and it is clear that interest in religion affects people from all parts of the population, educated and uneducated alike.

The churches in the Soviet Union have, then, survived; they are now also undergoing revival. There may be all kinds of new opportunities for them just around the corner. In this present situation, it is clear that we in the West have certain tasks. We must do the best we can to aid this revival and hence benefit the society in which Soviet believers live. So far the western ecumenical movement has failed to work out any coherent policy towards religious bodies in the Soviet Union. Now, with things actually beginning to happen in the Soviet Union, we need as Christians to take urgent action before it is too late.

Among the most urgent tasks are the following.

We should impress upon everyone involved in Soviet studies the uniqueness of the place occupied in that society by the churches in both their official and unofficial manifestations and their unique potential importance in the future development of those societies. After all, it seems that religious organizations are the only legally existing institutions which are not under the direct control of the Communist Party.

We should not be afraid to raise basic questions about church-state relations with representatives of the Soviet churches in international gatherings. They are not going to withdraw voluntarily; on the contrary, our concern helps them in their continual representation of their own case with their own authorities at home and in their continual effort to win more freedom for their churches.

We should continue to press for the abolition of the extremely restrictive legislation on religion in the Soviet Union. The churches should be allowed freedom to witness, to educate, to produce religious literature, to become involved in social and welfare work. In this way the gulf between hierarchs and ordinary believers, a gulf whose widening is encouraged by the authorities, will start to be bridged.

We should impress upon the Soviet authorities that a real debate involving the authentic views of the churches on social and moral problems will only be to the benefit of the whole society, enabling it to reach new solutions to pressing problems - problems which will not solve themselves, but which on the contrary, if neglected, are likely only to become more acute.

We should be prepared to provide all kinds of material aid to the churches of the Soviet Union should the laws be changed in such a way as to make it possible for the churches there to witness properly. We should remember that the western churches were caught unprepared in 1968 when it suddenly became possible to import literature and other materials freely to Czechoslovakia. Stocks of religious literature in the Czech and Slovak languages simply did not exist. The kinds of resources which might be needed are as follows: Christian personnel to advise and train medical and charitable workers and to help set up charitable work; Christian actors, poets and musicians; theological seminary teachers; financial aid for new church building; videos for Christian education; and of course plenty of Bibles and other religious literature.

Let us be ready now to encourage the painful process of reform in the Soviet Union, constantly bearing in mind the key role the churches must play there if social and moral problems are to be solved effectively. As the Russian Orthodox believer Alexander Ogorodnikov writes at the end of his letter to this conference: "we believe that the time has come for a new self-determination by the church. Those spiritual processes which have been growing in peoples' hearts and in grassroots communities have come to fruition. The harvest is ready to be reaped."

2

THE CONTEMPORARY STATUS
OF RELIGION IN THE USSR

*The Archbishop of Ivano-Frankovsk
and Kolymia, Makarii*

What is changing today in the life of the Russian Orthodox Church? If you take, for example, the theological schools in the Russian Orthodox Church, today almost one third of all entering students have received the highest education available in the Soviet Union. It is the students who finish universities in the Soviet Union who are entering our theological schools. This is a new development in the life of the Russian Orthodox Church. Before, the majority of our students who came into the seminary had only a high school education. Today, we are starting to have more and more university graduates enrolled in our theological schools, and I think this is a very important trend in the life of the Church.

Also, I think today the whole attitude of the population towards the life of the Church in our country is changing in a very positive way. We feel the changing situation every day. The people are looking to us in a hopeful way. They are expecting some kind of leadership. They are waiting for some kind of inspiration on the part of the churches, and I think that it is very important that today the leadership of the Soviet Union is allowing more possibilities in the life of the Russian Orthodox Church and the other churches in the Soviet Union.

If you look at the daily press in the Soviet Union, the main newspapers of the Soviet Union, such as *Izvestiia, Literaturnaia Gazeta* or the journal *Ogonek* and so on, you will find in their articles a changing attitude toward the role which the church is playing or which they want the church to start playing in Soviet society. For example, take a field such as *miloserdie* [charity, compassion]. Today we all feel that there is a lack of charity in the Soviet Union, a lack of compassion in the people, and people understand that compassion cannot come to life without the impact which only the churches could have. You are probably familiar with the role which the Sisters of Compassion (*Sestry miloserdiia*) played in the history of Russia. Today people are coming back to this great and important role which the Sisters of Compassion played in our life. They are asking why the churches are not taking this role again in our society.

The American press, for example, recently covered the decision of the Yaroslavl church council. It was decided to give back to the Russian Orthodox Church the famous Tolgskii Monastery near Yaroslavl. It was famous for the image of the Virgin Mary of Tolgsk and was very much venerated - thousands of pilgrims came there to venerate the image of the Virgin Mary of Tolgsk. Now that this monastery has been given back to the Russian Orthodox Church, the government has asked the Russian Orthodox Church to organize on the territory of this monastery the first home for elderly people and to take care of this elderly home. We will fully finance this home, and we will open a convent at this monastery to take care of the elderly. We are returning to the old functions which the church played throughout the history of our country. I think it is a very encouraging sign.

Consider the current attitude of the Soviet leadership particularly toward the Russian Orthodox Church. Early last year, for example, an international peace conference was organized in Moscow, called "For the Survival of Humanity against the Nuclear Catastrophe." What is interesting about this conference was that the largest organized group at the conference was the religious group. It consisted of about 250 people, and the document produced by this religious group was the best. It was the foundation of the main document which was produced by the conference. The conference document was then presented in the Kremlin Palace to Mikhail Gorbachev. It was the first time in the post-revolutionary history of Russia that a metropolitan was given the honor of reading an important document in the Kremlin. The metropolitan of the Mollavar Church in India, Metropolitan Mark Grigorus, read this report in front of Mikhail Gorbachev, and it was broadcast on nationwide television in the Soviet Union. It was the first time that representatives of the Russian Orthodox Church were permitted to appear on Soviet television.

During the break at this meeting in the Kremlin, Mikhail Gorbachev personally approached some of our metropolitans and spoke with them privately. I think that this was a very friendly step toward the church in the Soviet Union. It was especially important that they later appeared on the popular television show, "Do i posle polunochi" [Before and After Midnight] on which very distinguished scientists and famous artists sometimes appear. Now they have started to invite some of the metropolitans of the Russian Orthodox Church to this program. They participate in round table discussions on some burning issues of contemporary life in the Soviet Union.

People in the Soviet Union are paying great attention to this new opportunity which the church is receiving. The church is clearly becoming increasingly popular, especially among the Soviet intelligentsia. For example, during the international film festival which took place in Moscow last year, Metropolitan Pitirim of Volokolamsk was invited for the first time to the discussion club at the festival, and he was seated at the presidium of this discussion club with some of the most famous film stars of the West. When they gave Metropolitan Pitirim the opportunity to address the audience, they greeted him with a standing ovation. It was wonderful that film stars greeted Metropolitan Pitirim of Volokolamsk so warmly. It demonstrates the great sympathy for the Russian Orthodox Church which still lies deeply inside the present Soviet intelligentsia.

The upcoming millennium of receiving Christianity in Russia is like the ringing of a great bell which people are beginning to hear in the Soviet Union. It is calling the people's attention to the great history of Russia in which the church played an extremely important role. The influence of the Russian Orthodox Church upon Russian cultural life, upon spirituality, upon all aspects of life, was enormous. It is felt even today in our literature, in our music, in our paintings, in everything. It is very important today that some people, people of very high standing, are starting to understand that the church could play a very important role in this "new" process of democratization of the Soviet society, in this new process of perestroika. What is most important is that the leadership of the Russian Orthodox Church is not, as some people in the West think, just waiting for some directions from above.

Do not think that the Archbishop of Astrakhan, Feodosius, was the first to address the Soviet government on behalf of the Russian

Orthodox Church in order to open the King of Kings monastery. It was not Archbishop Feodosius who approached the Soviet government on this subject first. It was the Metropolitan Filaret of Kiev and Galitsia who addressed the Soviet government.

And we do believe that the Kiev Monastery of the Caves will be given back to the Russian Orthodox Church. This is still uncertain, but we do believe that this, the most important holy place of the Russian Orthodox Church, will be given back to us because it is not just one bishop or just the bishops of the Russian Orthodox Church. This is deeply desired by all believers of the Russian Orthodox Church.

As you have read in the press, not only has the monastery of Tolgsk been returned to the Russian Orthodox Church. You have heard about the very famous Optina Pustin'(TN) which played a very important role in the history of spirituality in the Russian Orthodox Church. It was a place which many Russian writers, such as Gogol', Dostoevsky and Tolstoy, visited. They were looking for spiritual guidance there. Tolstoy, notably, had not been on especially good terms with the Russian Orthodox Church when he visited Optina Pustin' for the first time. He was so impressed, he said, "Today, I met a holy man. And it became much easier for me. I felt so good."

Today as well, people are looking for this spiritual leadership; they are looking for inspiration because they feel an emptiness in their hearts which they need to fill. The future will depend very much upon the leadership of the Russian Orthodox Church, and upon the clergy of the Russian Orthodox Church. Today we in the Soviet Union are trying to use all opportunities, not just those given to us, but also those which we can take. And we see from the life of the church that in those places where, for example, a priest is active, where he really cares about his flock, the church community is prospering.

I greatly rejoiced this last Christmas when I saw in my cathedral in Ivano-Frankovsk more people than I had seen in previous years, and especially when I saw representatives of the local intelligentsia who came for the service. And when at the Christmas reception I spoke with my clergymen, the majority of them told me that this year in our churches there were more people than ever before.

The celebration of receiving Christianity is today so inspiring to religious people in the Soviet Union that if you consider the life of the church, I think you could call it a kind of renaissance. For example, during the last five years in Ivano-Frankovsk, I think I have visited some 300 churches out of my 351 churches. Outside and inside elderly people told me, "You know, *Vladyko*,(TN) when this land was under the Polish rule we never saw such beautiful churches in our villages." I think it is wonderful that this feeling of optimism is reigning today all over the Soviet Union.

In the last two years, the Russian Orthodox Church opened fifty-two new churches in the Siberian and Far East regions. Most of them were newly built. And I think this trend will increase.

Not long ago the Soviet government addressed the Russian Church, and now we are having talks with the representatives of the Soviet state to re-open the Solovetsk monastery. I think that this is only the beginning.

If you consider the Publishing Department of the Moscow Patriarchate, they have more possibilities today to publish religious literature. For the first time in the post-revolutionary history of the Russian Church, they are going to publish the history of the Russian Orthodox Church in five volumes. Also, they are now publishing the new edition of the Holy Bible. They will print 100,000 copies. Indeed, for the first time, they are publishing the New Testament in the Ukrainian language. They are going to renew the publication of a prayer book in the Ukrainian language in Kiev as well.

I believe that these are just the first signs of healthy development of church life in the Soviet Union. I think you have seen in your newspapers last week that Metropolitan Pitirim of Volokolamsk was elected as a member of the Board of Trustees of the very prestigious Committee for the Survival of Humanity. I think it is very important that people in the Soviet Union see that church representatives are receiving these very important appointments.

TN (p. 20) Optina Pustin' - Famous former monastery, situated in the Kaluga Oblast' of Central Russia, founded in the fifteenth century.

TN (p. 21) Vladyko - A title of respect of the high clergy in the Russian Orthodox Church.

3

THE LEGAL STATUS OF RELIGIOUS ORGANIZATIONS AND THE CLERGY IN THE USSR

Vladimir Al'brekht

To His Grace Khrizost, archbishop of Kursk and Belgorodsk, from the Church Council of the Troitsk parish in the village of Ol'shanka, Cherniansk district, Belgorod oblast.

We hereby inform Your Grace that on September 27 around 17:00, an authorized state agent of religious affairs from the Belgorod Oblast, Mikhail Emel'ianovich Zhdanov, along with his collaborators, visited our church. He tore down a wall painting and said that we should show sketches of any painting to the district Soviet executive committee for approval, and that if the committee does not like the sketch, then it cannot be painted. According to him, we also do not have the right to hire artists from Moscow.

Your Grace, what kind of authority does the district Soviet executive committee have over Church art? Furthermore, sketches are an unnecessary expense. At whose expense should these sketches be done? The painting in our church is only displeasing to an authorized state agent. Visitors praise and like the painting. This is not the first time that an authorized agent has prohibited us from inviting master craftsmen from other oblasts, especially from Moscow. Our collective farm uses machines from Moscow to gather the harvest. Why can we not hire people from Moscow? Is it legal for an authorized agent to interfere in our affairs and intimidate us?

30 September 1983 Church Council /signature/

Let us try to explain the legal status of the clergy and the church.

Presently, only Article 52 of the Soviet Constitution guarantees all citizens "the right to worship." However, Article 39 maintains that the exercise of citizens' rights and freedoms should not harm the interests of society and state. Therefore, we will first try to discern, as completely as possible, exactly what the interests of our society and state are. The preamble to the Constitution states, "The Soviet people, governed by the ideas of scientific communism. . . have the rights, freedoms, and responsibilities of citizens." The highest goal of the Soviet state is to build a "classless communist society," and the main task "is to bring up a person in communist society." According to Article 6, "The Communist Party of the Soviet Union is the guiding force of society, and is the core of. . . state and social organization." And elsewhere, "armed with a Marxist-Leninist opinion, the Communist Party alone determines the general line of domestic and foreign policy of the USSR." Article 25 states, "In the USSR, there is a single system. . . of education for the communist upbringing of youth." Moreover, Article 27 reads, "The state takes care of protecting. . . and extensively using spiritual values for. . . the education of Soviet peoples," of course in agreement with the ideas of scientific communism, which, as was already stated, guide the Soviet people.

It turns out that the right to worship established by Article 52 is incompatible with the atheistic ideas of scientific communism. In strict accordance with Article 39, freedom of religion should not have been allowed because if this right was exercised to its fullest, it could damage the interests of the State and society. Moreover, a believer's right to join religious organizations is also a dubious privilege. Article 51 declares that Soviet citizens have the right to join only those social organizations that function "in accordance with the goals of building communism." However, Soviet citizens also have the right, according to Article 52, "to profess any religion", but only if it is a secret from their own children, because in Article 66 citizens are obliged "to raise their children to be worthy members of the socialist society." Article 25 states that people are to assist "the goals of communist upbringing" and must be directed by those ideas of scientific communism that guide the people. It is in these people's interests, according to Article 50, that citizens have the various rights and freedoms declared in the Constitution. These include the rights and freedoms of speech, the press, gatherings, meetings, street processions and demonstrations. Article 51 asserts the right of citizens to join various social organizations and to participate in their activities. However, the question is really whether a believer can be a member of any social organization. In other words, can a believer materially and morally support atheistic propaganda? This question arises because the CPSU guides all social organizations and propagandizes uncompromising atheism. Of course, no one would have the right to stand in the way of a believer joining, for example, a trade union. However, whenever a believer opens his trade-union card, he reads that his trade union is a school for communism. As a member of a trade union, the believer is obliged to raise his consciousness, i.e., to stop believing in God. Numerous resolutions of the All-Union Central Trade-Union Council demand that atheistic propaganda be conducted using those funds into which the believer pays membership fees. In the USSR, there is not a single trade union which, though led by CPSU members, could allow itself not to support atheistic propaganda. It might be thought that these obscurities and contradictions are insignificant when we recall that Article 52 reads, "The church in the USSR is separated from the state," i.e., the church is outside the jurisdiction of the state. Does this mean that the church is outside the law? Obviously, it should not be. Through an examination of relevant legislation, we can most likely understand the legal status of the church in the USSR, and therefore both of religious organizations and of the clergy in our country. There is a certain difficulty in doing this because too many statutory documents concerning worship are published "for official use only," i.e., the documents are not accessible to everyone.

Usually, the entire body of legislation (various laws, resolutions, enforceable enactments) that have a relation to religious associations' activities is referred to as legislation on religious worship. This type of legislation has gradually accumulated and reflects the historically changing attitude of the authorities to the church. This legislation has not always been this openly hostile to the church. In 1906 Lenin wrote, "The unity. . . of the revolutionary struggle of the oppressed class to create paradise on earth is more important for us than the solidarity of views of the proletariat about paradise in heaven."[1] All fundamental freedoms were adopted in a 1903 Russian Social Democratic Workers' Party program. They included: freedom of conscience, speech, press, and assembly. On January 23, 1918, the interrelations between the state and church were legislatively defined for the first time by a decree of the Council of People's Commissars.[2] The purpose of the decree seemed to be to keep the church from interfering with state affairs. It is almost as if the state interfered in the affairs of the church by accident. Lenin asserted, "the state should not be involved in religious affairs, and the religious society should not associate with state authority."[3] However, in practice, the situation turned out differently. In 1918, for example, the People's Commissariat of Justice explained the attitude toward the church in the following way:

> . . . Arrests and searches of clergymen during a service should only be done when it is urgent. . . . Certain Soviet deputies are absolutely forbidden to use repressive measures against clergymen in churches no matter what purely religious themes were being discussed in the sermon. A measure such as this is extremely illegal and does not achieve its goal. It must be remembered that we must fight against religious prejudices not so much by punishments and repressions as by communist propaganda. . . . . When handing over liturgical belongings to groups of citizens, it is absolutely inexcusable to seize church vestments, robes, and altar cloths and use them for revolutionary purposes (resewing them on flags, etc.). It is also inexcusable to take the silver framework and adornments from icons, crosses, Gospels, and altars. All of these actions are first of all completely illegal since there is no general directive. . . for removing. . . religious objects, and, secondly, they are meaningless since these actions ruin and depreciate the objects, often destroying their artistic value. The use of these objects for revolutionary emblems, banners, flags, and other things showed no common sense. . .

The instructions obviously propagandize not the humane treatment of an indisputed enemy, but institute a reasonable tactic for a successful fight with the enemy to ensure a quick victory. It turns out that during the priests' services, they can be arrested, even though it is better not to do this during the service. Altering church vestments into flags is pointless because religious prejudices can be fought using repressive measures by order. Communist propaganda is also needed to fight prejudices. It must be pointed out that the attitude of communists toward religion was always hostile although this attitude was not always too closely influenced by principles. As is clear from the 1921 Resolution of the Central Committee of the Russian Communist Party (Bolsheviks), believers were permitted, as an exception, to join the Party, if "the believers proved by their struggle or work that they were devoted to communism." After Lenin's death, the situation changed quickly and dramatically. The massive repressions of this time are well-known. They encompassed all levels of society, and fear was each person's constant companion. "Fear," as Lenin wrote, "created the gods. . . fear in the face of a naked force. . . ." Lenin's words,[4] said with the intention of explaining the sources of religious awareness in capitalist society, to a certain extent explain the sources of the mysticism of the newest religion which subsequently came to be called the "cult of personality." This peculiar form of idolatry quickly developed its own "iconography," its "martyrs," heretics, and enemies but most importantly its own fanatical intolerance toward dissidence.

The freedom of religious propagation was soon abolished. It had been guaranteed by the Constitution of the RSFSR in 1918 and then by the Constitution of the USSR in 1924. It was abolished in May 1929 at the Nineteenth Congress of Soviets in order to, as was then stated, "prevent the use of religious observances for political aims." Actually, this measure only limited the preaching activities of the Church. At that time, the Church could not lay claim to any political role. Only the new communist cult had the right to use propaganda for the only true doctrine, and it had the right to an exclusive political role both in society and in the world. With the Orthodox Church in mind, Lenin wrote, "state churches should not receive any payments from the state."[5] However, we will never know what Lenin would have said had he known about the huge price the state paid for Stalin's personality cult propaganda (Stalin being a "living God"). In comparison the freedom of several thousand people was at the time almost officially regarded as worthless.

In 1934, while the USSR Supreme Soviet was discussing a draft of a new law concerning All-Union military service, one important point was clarified. The number of individuals exempt from military service for religious reasons, based on the decree passed on January 23, 1918, proved to be very small. Based on this fact, the Statute on Exemption from Military Service for Religious Reasons, adopted in 1918, was not included in this new law. Military service became universal. Under these conditions, when the Soviet regime no longer had any more obvious enemies, and hidden enemies had disappeared, the need faded for discriminatory measures that deprived the clergy of the right to vote. The 1936 Constitution of the USSR, established during Stalin's rule, granted all citizens equal suffrage as well as the right to profess any religion. This latter right still remains. However, at that time it was not easy to profess one's religion. The fundamental piece of legislation on worship was the resolution published on April 8, 1929, by the All-Russian Central Executive Committee and the RSFSR Council of People's Commissars.   This resolution was edited and changed a few times and was published in its final version in the June 23, 1975, Decree of the RFSFR Supreme Soviet Presidium.   This document contains a number of important provisions.

Article 4 states, "A religious society or group of believers can begin its activities only after registering. . . with the Executive Committee of the Working People's Deputies." Articles 3 through 7 define this registration system. It is interesting that this law does not list the reasons for which registration can be refused. This is done, of course, to maintain the state's arbitrary discretion. According to Article 12, before believers can conduct a meeting, they must obtain authorization from the executive committee of the local soviet. Article 14 gives the registering organ the right to reject any person who has been selected at a meeting in the executive organ, or in an auditing commission for a religious society or group of believers. There is also nothing stated about the reasons for such a rejection or the option to appeal it, about the reasons for being denied authorization to attend a meeting of believers, or about the role which is given at such a meeting to the representative from a registering department. And this, of course, is also a basis for arbitrariness since it turns out that the registering department has the option to assign any leader to a believer.

It is also not quite clear what constitutes a meeting of believers. For example, Professor Gidulianov believes that a meeting of parishioners of any parish should be considered a "general meeting" of believers.[6] Another author, N. Orleanskii, regards a "general meeting" as a gathering of only those people who have signed an agreement for the use of a house of worship.[7] However, if we were to add to this that the law does not provide a time frame in which the executive organ and the revisionary commission are chosen, or periods for their accountability, and that there are no rules for new members joining a religious society, then it turns out that the members and founders of the so-called *Dvadtsatka* [the Twenty],(TN) executive organ members, and members of a revisionary commission are "chosen" virtually for life. According to Article 31, new members of the Dvadtsatka can be brought in only to replace those who have left. This can be done after an agreement has been signed concerning the use of a building and properties. The situation is completely hopeless when a religious society never received any property from the State, that is, there is no agreement on the transfer of property. Because of the stipulation in Article 3, a religious society could simply disappear, and it would be because the number of people who have signed a registration agreement was less than 20 (believers are often elderly and there is a relatively high death rate among them).

Legislation on worship contains (as does legislation on any other subject) a certain list of prohibitions and authorizations. However, in this branch of law it is not always clear where the prohibition ends and where the authorization begins and what the aims are. There are many examples of this, and some must be cited.

The law, for example, prohibits any religious propagation. However, any liturgy, rite, or ritual is in itself religious propagation. So, since it is forbidden to directly write what has been banned, it is also impossible to ascertain if the members of the executive organ of a parish are violating the legislation on worship (Article 43 of the Resolution). However, such a decision is neither fair nor sensible since the legislation does not provide believers with either the possibility of knowing about this earlier or the possibility of re-electing members of the parish's leadership. Yet, Article 14 of the Resolution states that the registering department has the right to reject any member of that leadership who was chosen earlier. It turns out that the law is designed so as to allow the registering organization to set up the kind of parish leadership which could close the parish down at any time.

The law prohibits churches from engaging in charitable activities, prohibits the use of church funds and properties for other than non-confessional purposes. However, the legislation does not define where these unused funds should go. Of course the high taxes placed on church revenue and the clergy were intentionally established to use a part of the believers' money for atheistic purposes, but even so, there will still be some money that is not spent. In any case, it is not clear what is and what is not considered charity. For example, how should we view the church's monetary contributions to the Soviet Peace Fund?

Article 142 of the Criminal Code of the RSFSR stipulates punishment "for teaching religion to minors in contradiction to established regulations."[8]   Even though Article 17 of the Resolution states that there are no rules against teaching religion, any organized religious instruction is prohibited. However, this contradicts Article 5, ratified by the USSR Supreme Soviet Presidium, about the "Convention for the Campaign against Discrimination in Education."[9]

According to the January 23, 1918, Decree, "No religious societies have the right to own property. They do not have juridical status."[10] This condition of the decree has still not been officially changed even though, in fact, religious societies both acquire ownership and, in some ways, do currently possess juridical status. For example, they can purchase transportation, lease, build, and buy building materials and buildings. At the same time, transactions dealing with the maintenance or repair of these structures, oddly enough, must be concluded only by a member of the executive organ, on his own behalf - this is stipulated in Article 11 of the Resolution. However, almost all religious property is already owned by the state and is in fact used only with the knowledge and authorization of a government official appointed by the State. This official then has economic control over religious societies to such an extent that he has the right to transfer to the state all the church's property or to revoke the religious society's registration. This being the case, the official should probably be considered to embody the juridical status of the religious society. Still, a religious society cannot be considered to have real juridical status if only because it never completely owns its own property. For example, let us say that as the owner of church property a group of believers pays the fee for fire insurance on this property. According to Article 35 of the Resolution, the believers would have to take into consideration that in case of a fire, the insurance settlement could be seized by the district executive committee and used for completely unrelated needs in the district.

Generally, an organization that has juridical status has its own publications, letterhead, and seals. However, according to Article 23 of the Resolution, these cannot be used for anything except "strictly church business." In other words, the legal force of a document certified by a certain print or signed on a certain letterhead is far from indisputable.

It must also be added that in most branches of Soviet law, religious organizations are almost never mentioned as a subject of law.

There is yet another important condition that cannot be overlooked. Article 34 of the USSR Constitution declares all citizens equal under the law irrespective of "religion, sex, occupation, residence, and other conditions." Unfortunately, this does not seem to apply to those who are directly involved in religious activities. This is why in Resolution No. 686 on May 23, 1956, the USSR Council of Ministers established a system by which the labor legislation for workers and employees of religious organizations applies only when a labor agreement with the religious organizations was concluded in the presence of trade union organs. The Presidium of the Central Committee of the Worker's Trade Union for Local Industry and Municipal Services (which controls those who work in religious organizations) issued a decree (August 21, 1962) including the following "list of workers' jobs in religious institutions" for which the labor legislation applies: 1. cleaners; 2. watchmen; 3. caretakers; 4. stokers; a total of four positions. And if these people work for church elders or members of the executive organ, or participate in worship services, then the labor legislation does not apply to them, and the trade union organization will not participate with these workers in concluding agreements on hiring. This is exactly what is written.

The result is that the law as established by the USSR Supreme Soviet and the Soviet Constitution is limited by the USSR Council of Ministers and the lower-level governmental organs through the application of membership conditions in organizations which are officially outside the jurisdiction of the government. Meanwhile, these organizations themselves promote conditions discriminating against anyone who has a direct relationship to religious activities. Labor legislation, therefore, does not apply to the clergy, and obviously the system of State insurance also does not apply.

A certain legislative peculiarity must also be noted. By decree of the USSR Council of Ministers (May 10, 1966, No. 301), an enactment of the Council on Religious Affairs of the USSR Council of Ministers was issued. According to this document, the Council on Religious Affairs supervises the adherence of religious organizations to the Constitution of the USSR, the correct execution of Soviet laws and decrees of the Presidium of the USSR Supreme Soviet, etc.   The Council is thus involved in all dealings with the activities of religious organizations by both the administrative and procuratory organs and even by the interpretation of the laws. The result is an already familiar picture: the prerogatives of the USSR Public Prosecutor's Office (responsible for the correct interpretation of laws) are transferred to an organ subordinate to it. In this absurd situation, the executive organ of power becomes the legislative authority.

Article 17 of the Resolution contains a number of prohibitions. In particular, religious associations are forbidden to offer their members material support, organize special handwork, literary, or labor meetings, groups, or circles, set up trips, open libraries, or give medical aid. Most members of a religious association (or at least many of them) are often well acquainted with each other, and it would be natural for them to go somewhere, work together, or argue about a theological issue. It would also be natural for them to join together to help a colleague. How can these completely natural actions possibly cause unpleasantness, accusations, and violations of the law? It is obvious that the restrictions in Article 17 (just as in Article 19 where the necessity of limiting a clergyman's activity to a certain geographical territory is discussed) came about from that extreme intolerance towards religious ideology which arose with the emergence of the "cult of personality". And of course the government official, whose duty it is to carry out these restrictions, needs a very large staff to persuade clergymen to help him, that is, to inform on law violations by his colleagues. It is understandable that this official shows kindness towards these clergymen, that is, he gave them incentives, and he had both the opportunity and the motives for implementing his policy. After all, a religious organization is the only public, non-socialist organization covering both the spiritual and the social sphere. Therefore, to a certain degree the function of ideological control over religious activity by party organs might appear necessary. The Party certainly cannot be indifferent to who is in the highest position in the church hierarchy, or who will manage church affairs abroad, or who will appoint priests, bishops, etc. After all, without the consent of the Party, regardless of what they want, no manager of an enterprise, public prosecutor or collective farm chairman can be elected. It is clear that when bishops of the church are appointed, so the argument goes, the practice should be the same. It is possible that with time this practice will be liberalized. Even now we see directors of enterprises occasionally elected. However, we will probably not know for quite a long time how metropolitans are selected. The church is by its very nature hostile to the ideas of scientific communism. According to the Constitution, the Soviet people are guided by these ideas, so it turns out that the church is hostile to Soviet society. How then should people act who are called upon to be the leading and guiding force of society?

This is an extremely important question.

We often see in the movies how during World War II, a Soviet (naturally, communist) agent, pretends to be a fascist in order to penetrate the enemy's camp and paralyze the system. The agent used this hostile system to his own advantage. A similar scenario is used at times against religion. When we examine the legal status of the clergy and the church, we keep running up against the extreme vagueness and deficiencies of the legislation, and are forced to wonder: do these deficiencies exist for a reason? To a certain degree, they probably do. The legislation on worship is like an old fence with many gaps through which it is easy, when necessary, for an agent to penetrate. The agent can then not only ascertain the plans of the ideological enemy, but also, importantly, he can correct these plans. A similar situation probably exists in other socialist countries. In any case, a well-known occurrence provides the basis for such a deduction. A very unfriendly clash took place between representatives of the Russian and Chinese clergy at one theological conference. This occurred exactly at the time when the CPSU and the Chinese Communist Party were experiencing sharp disagreements.

Imagine the following situation. A state, ideologically hostile towards the church, separates the church from itself, hoping that the church will soon wither away, and the state will in the end also just wither away and die. However, it turned out differently. Separated from the state, the church was separated from society, yet it did not separate from the entire society. Priests and the parishioners separated along with the church. Of course, many of them remained Soviet citizens and patriots, but at times they were treated like emigres from and traitors to their homeland (in the ideological sense). Then the state decides that it needs to "return" them. And they were "returned." Even in Stalin's time, some churches were opened, and clergymen were freed from the camps. But it was not these people that needed to be returned, but the state itself. After all, those who separated the church from the state were themselves alienated by their privileges, *nomenklatura*,(TN) special distribution networks, etc. However, some of them even vanished without a trace.

Did the state die off as a result? Hardly. Maybe morality died, but the state and the separated church existed. That is why a kind of legal mechanism was needed to manage this separate part. You see, there is no better law than when it is your own. The state simply broke a piece off its legal system and separated it along with the church for the state's own convenience. The Council on Religious Affairs was thus also separated from the State. There are other examples of this practice. The nomenklatura was also separated from the state, by having privileges that the rest of society did not have. These privileges were provided by legal mechanisms as distant from the state as the heavens are from the earth.[11]

Incidentally, something similar occurred with the international and legal obligations of the Soviet Union, and this has a direct bearing on our topic. On March 23, 1976, the International Pact on Civil and Political Rights went into effect. Article 18 of this Pact affirms freedom of conscience and religion along with freedom of thought. Article 19 asserts every person's equal "right to the free expression of one's opinion." And this right is known to include the right to search for, receive and disseminate any type of information and ideas regardless of State borders." However, this approach, which equates the right to disseminate the ideas of scientific communism with the right to disseminate any ideas and beliefs is contradicted by both the spirit and letter of the Soviet Constitution passed in 1977, one year after the Pact entered into force. This, despite the fact that in Article 2 of the Pact, the Soviet Union pledges itself to: a) bring its internal legislation into accordance with the obligations concluded in the Pact; and b) not tolerate, with regard to the Pact, any discrimination on the basis of religious, political and other convictions.[12]

As we have already noted, the Constitution of the USSR establishes the freedom of anti-religious, but not religious, propaganda, and therefore, does not make provisions for discrimination against and restrictions of religious propagation since any propagation of religion is prohibited. One might be surprised at how blatantly Article 19 of the Pact contradicts Article 52 of the Constitution of the USSR; or one could simply appreciate that different texts have two different functions: one has domestic policy tasks and the other quite separate "foreign policy" task. There is no use searching for legal snags here because there are none. Frankly speaking, the state is teaching us how to deceive. However, as intelligent people, we should understand that if this continues, then the government will simply be snatched away from us entirely. This is why it makes sense to discuss the legal status of the church only in the expectation of future changes.

Generally speaking, I think that there are three stages in the church's development. The first stage will end when it is recognized that the Church will not wither away, and the number of believers will never become so small that all parishes can be closed "at the request of the workers." The second stage is marked by the State attempting to penetrate, control, and manage all areas of economic and public existence. The church is no exception. The state tried to integrate the church into the system of state management and create a legal mechanism for serving the Church's needs. It appears that this stage is now ending. There is much talk of so-called "brigade contracts," i.e., initiatives which, while separate from the state, will still be tied to the state by agreements. Most likely, this idea will apply to the church as well. If conditions are good, the church can expect a degree of independence, become a kind of autonomous social organism with the freedom to exercise internal and contractual agreements with the state and other public agencies. This would probably permit the church to fulfill the Will of its Founder.

Thy kingdom come. Thy will be done.

---

1. V. I. Lenin, Polnoe sobranie sochinenii, XII, p. 146.

2. The separation of church and state is not obligatory for a country which is building socialism. For example, in Czechoslovakia, the church is not separated from the state.

3. Lenin, Polnoe sobranie sochinenii, XII, p. 143.

4. Lenin, Polnoe sobranie sochinenii, XVII, p. 419.

5. Ibid., XII, pp. 143-144.

6. P. V. Gidulianov, Otdelenie tserkvi ot gosudarstva [Separation of Church and State], Moscow, 1926, p. 130.

7. N. Orleanskii, Zakon o religioznykh ob'edineniiakh [The Law on Religious Associations], Moscow, 1930, p. 10.

TN (p. 28) Dvadtsatka is a term that refers to the original group of twenty people who sign their names as official members in order to register a church in the Soviet Union and agree to be responsible for that church organization.

8. RSFSR Supreme Soviet Presidium Resolution of March 18, 1966.

9. According to Resolution #18, Article 5 of this Convention, parents should have the opportunity to send their children to private, that is, to non-state institutions and raise their children in a religious manner.

10. According to Article 24 of the Resolution, property necessary for a worship service that has been both repurchased or donated and has been transferred according to agreements is nationalized. According to Article 31, authorities at their own will have the right to seize a house of worship from a religious society.

TN (p. 34) The term nomenklatura refers to lists drawn up by higher Communist Party authorities, containing names of individuals deemed eligible for important party and state posts. They are eligible as well for actual though unofficial privileges which are unavailable to the general population.

11. As we have clarified, Article 34 of the USSR Constitution declares the equality of all citizens before the law regardless of their attitudes toward religion and their occupation choice. However, the article does not deal with people pursuing religious activities. It must be noted that the legislation on worship is different for different republics (for example in the Ukraine and in the RSFSR). And that is why it turns out that the laws are very important for believers and somehow influence these believers' choices of where they will live; that is, in Article 34 of the USSR Constitution and in this part there is a certain strange exception, especially for believers.

12. For example, it could be only the restrictions necessary for respecting the rights and reputation of other people, for maintaining state security, social order, well-being and the morality of the population.

4

FREEDOM OF RELIGION: MOVING AWAY FROM THE STALINIST LEGAL CODE

A. Bessmertnyi-Anzimirov

Freedom of thought, conscience and religion not only immediately follow from the natural human freedoms (the right to life, the inviolability of person and property, and the right to family), but they are also the foundation of all other rights and of the human rights movement itself as a whole. The Church of Christ trod a long and difficult road before the ideas of tolerance and fairness became the property not only of church consciousness, but of all mankind. The church has struggled for these rights from the time of Saint Paul the Apostle, who called for the observance of civic freedoms, to Saint Justin the Martyr, who, as far back as the second century A.D., petitioned the Roman Emperor "for people of all nations, unfairly accused and persecuted," through the blood of such confessors and martyrs for religious freedom as Saint and Metropolitan Filipp Kolychev in Russia and Saint Thomas More in the West, until the great Dutch theologian and writer Hugo Grotius founded the discipline of international law and formed the principles on which the contemporary Human Rights Charter is based.

It was in the struggle for religious tolerance, for the rights of religious minorities and rejection of all forms of discrimination against the human spirit and conscience, that the idea of a social contract came into being that would assure mutual security and peaceful coexistence as well as the idea of the inviolability of the person and of universal international law.

Before we examine the degree of correlation of the Soviet legislation on cults with the main international documents which regulate cooperation of nations in the area of human rights, including those documents ratified by our country, we must take note of the fact that besides legislative restriction, there can exist at least two other forms of discrimination against believers - ideological and propagandistic.

In comparison with the period of genocide of believers carried out by Ezhov and Beria, the current status of religious organizations in the USSR is much more satisfactory. However, the end of open persecution does not mean that there is no discrimination.

What are the basic criteria of religious freedom and religious discrimination? Although in this case we are concerned with the situation of Christians in the USSR in general and the Russian Orthodox Church in particular, these criteria to a greater or lesser degree will apply equally to Islam, Judaism and Buddhism.

According to church teaching, drawn from Jesus Christ, the church is founded, so to speak, on three hypotheses.

First, the church is a gathering of the faithful, a community involved in ongoing brotherly contact and mutual aid among its members, as well as group bible study.

Second, the church is a religious institution unified by mysteries and holy beginnings; in its churches and prayer houses ("little churches"), public service, i.e., the liturgy, is conducted, the nucleus and center of which is the Eucharist.

Third, the church is the Apostolate, that is, the constant witness in the world about Christ through the clergy and active service to neighbors.

Not one and not two, but only all three of these points together comprise the essence of the church and the meaning of life of the people forming it. Even if only one of these aspects of church life is forbidden by legislation, there is discrimination or "nonovert persecution" against the church.

The later the inescapable process of secularization occurs in society, the more painful and severe it is. It is enough to recall Bismarck's *kulturkampf* in Germany and the year 1905 in France. Therefore, it is not surprising that this process in Russia was even more severe although the decree of the Council of People's Commissars in 1918 "On the Separation of Church from the State and Schools from the Church" basically copied the action of the French authorities at the beginning of the century. This decree can be considered acceptable for the church with the exception of the unfair and discriminatory Article 12: "No church or religious society has the right to own property. They do not have the right of juridical status." This completely explainable maximalism would be corrected over time by the course of history itself. But in 1929, when Stalin declared war on all of Russian society, including the Leninist wing of his own party, the resolution of the All-Union Central Executive Committee and the Council of People's Commissars of the RFSFR "On Religious Associations" was approved. The severe consequences of this action will be felt in our society until this odious document is repealed.

The Stalinist legislation about cults, in force even today, absolutely contradicts the International Charter on Human Rights. Inasmuch as the juridical force of the documents comprising the Charter varies (the U.N. Declaration of Human Rights only states recommended standards), the Soviet religious legislation must be judged against the United Nations Pact on Civil and Political Rights, which contains obligatory norms of behavior.

Article 18 (Paragraphs 1-2) of the Pact states:

> Each person has the right to freedom of thought, conscience and religion. This right includes the freedom to have or adopt a religion or conviction by one's own choice and the freedom to profess one's religion or conviction both privately and meeting with others in public or private circumstances, for the exercise of religion or performance of religious and ritual ceremonies and instructions.
>
> No one may be subjected to coercion which lessens his freedom to have or adopt a religion or conviction by his own choice.

Article 19 of the Pact also directly relates to this article:

> 1. Each person has the right to freely hold his own opinions. 2. Each person has the right to freely express his opinion; this right includes the freedom to seek, receive and disseminate any type of information or ideas, independent of state limitations. These ideas and information may be oral, written or published or creative forms of expression or by other means according to his own choice.

Despite the norms provided by international law, Article 11 of the Stalinist legislation on cults prohibits religious communities from renting a printing press for printing books on religion and morality, and

Article 17c prohibits: "the organizing of common religious study of the Bible or literature in meetings, groups, circles or departments or the opening of libraries and reading rooms; only books necessary for the liturgy of a given cult can be stored in prayer houses and rooms."

Article 18 of the 1929 Resolution goes even further: "The teaching of religious dogma can be allowed exclusively in religious educational institutions opened according to an established procedure."

It is easy to see that these articles do not allow the seeking, receiving or disseminating of religious views, or the acceptance of religion according to one's own choice. These articles would not have been so discriminatory if the Russian Orthodox Church and other religions in our country would have had within their jurisdiction a network of libraries and Sunday or catechism schools for teaching basic religion to children of believers' families and in general to all those wishing to receive baptism (or to join Islam, etc.). There is nothing like this in the USSR. The spiritual academies, which the official bureaucrats and church officials so often pointed to during the recent decades of silence, provided a restricted liturgical education which cannot be considered appropriate for the general population who wanted instruction in dogma and religious practice, because they are for the purpose of preparing professional priests and theologians. The libraries of academies and seminaries are closed to laymen and not accessible to the majority of priests whose dioceses are located far from Moscow, Leningrad and Odessa.

In our country in general there is no possibility of freely acquiring even a Bible, the Gospels, prayer books or a liturgical text; no private person can buy or subscribe to the few periodical publications of the Moscow Patriarchate or other religious centers. There are no catechism centers in churches, and if in the Baltic republics priests and pastors have official hours to receive the population, the Russian Orthodox Church in general has no such privileges. In those instances where priests receive seekers or begin to teach religion at their own risk, they are subjected to heavy pressure from representatives of the local authorities and to persecution in the press.[1] Meanwhile, the *Journal of the Moscow Patriarchate*, available in the USSR only to an extremely narrow circle of people, is published in English so that foreigners may have access to it, but this free access is not permitted to the population of our own country. The Patriarchate publishes neither catechisms nor bible commentaries, neither handbooks nor guides, and does not publish books about the teachers and fathers of the church, Orthodox and non-Orthodox theologians or church writers.

To profess one's faith in Russian, as in any other language, means to "openly follow some kind of religion, teaching or conviction" and presupposes both the right to hear sermons and the right, stipulated by international agreement, to receive and distribute information by means of the press and other media, unfettered by state limits. Despite the right stipulated in Article 52 of the Constitution of the USSR that citizens may profess any religion, any form of public worship, except simple participation in the liturgy in a limited number of churches, is quickly classified as "religious propaganda" and even as "extremism" even though not one legislative document contains a word of direct prohibition of "religious propaganda." And this is odd because the right to profession of faith includes the right to propagation of that faith. As a result, a vicious practice emerged in our country in which believing theologians, publicists, and novelists over the course of many decades were forced by the state to publish in the foreign church press, which then gave the same state the chance to accuse the authors of cooperation with emigre anti-Soviet publications. Meanwhile all these writers would be glad if only they could publish their writings in their native land, but where?

The foregoing applies equally to the problem of receiving religious information. Where there was a complete absence of religious literature in the USSR (limited editions of journals and other literature or none at all), it is only natural that Christians obtained foreign publications in Russian and in foreign languages by any means possible. Soviet bureaucrats and propagandists called all this literature either "religious pulp," which is an anti-constitutional insult of believers' feelings, or "products of clerical anticommunist centers whose purpose is to establish and support religion in the USSR." Unfortunately this illegal discriminatory attitude has not changed one iota even today.

On November 17, 1987, on the Soviet television program "Religion and Politics," A. Belov, an official anti-religionist, declared that sending religious literature to the USSR from abroad is an "ideological diversion and the action of militant anti-communists in league with militant clerics."

As examples of "anti-Soviet" literature they showed on the screen close-ups of publications not only of an exclusively religious nature such as the journal *Bulletin of the Russian Christian Movement*, the newspaper *Orthodox Russia* or the book *Christ is Coming*, but even the Bible! The very Holy Scripture which Soviet Baptists can officially receive in limited quantities from abroad.

As a result of searches of believers formally carried out according to the "anti-Soviet" articles of the penal code, literature of a purely religious nature is withdrawn from circulation and even confiscated. Even today absolute illegality and arbitrariness reigns in this area.

For example, at the time of a search in the apartment of well-known Orthodox writers, Felix Svetov and Zoia Krakhmal'nikov, several dozen purely religious books were seized along with works of Boris Pasternak, *Suicide* by N. Erdman, and *Dog's Heart* by Mikhail Bulgakov. In response to inquiries, the office of the public prosecutor has declared that not only all these books, but also most of Svetov and Krakhmal'nikov's literary archives and even the letters of Svetov's deceased mother, "have been destroyed as not subject to distribution in the USSR." However, not one of these books was even presented to the court.

There is no sense looking further for examples although there are very many of them. On January 28, 1984, a search was carried out at my apartment by Prosecutor Zhdanovskii's investigator from the Moscow region. He sought "slanderous" literature, but finding none, seized virtually all my books and brochures of church liturgy or of religious or philosophical content, commentaries on the Holy Scripture and bible studies in English and French, as well as publications of the New Testament in Russian, French, English and German.

In response to my recent inquiry to the Prosecutor's Office, I received from I. A. Kudriavtsev, the Deputy Regional Prosecutor, a report from October 22, 1987, that stated that the "literature taken from you during the search was destroyed, based on expert evaluation that this literature is forbidden to be distributed in the territory of the USSR." I must especially emphasize that despite the absence in our society of official lists of forbidden literature, *both the prosecutor and*

Soviet television officially declare that the Bible and the New Testament are prohibited from distribution in our country.

These declarations do not leave any illusions about freedom of religion in the USSR. There are no areas of free choice nor acceptance of religion, nor even of distribution of Bibles and Gospels here.

The Stalinist legislation of 1929 also violates all standards of international law relating to the children of believers. In Article 29 of the U.N. Pact on Civil and Political Rights, the family is acknowledged as "the only fundamental unit of society." In Article 24 the primacy of the family before society and the state is asserted in the matter of child rearing, and Article 18 (paragraph 4) states: The states participating in the Pact are obliged to respect the freedom of parents as well as legal guardians to provide the religious and moral upbringing of their children in accordance with their own convictions.

However, in our country, any organized form of religious instruction for children (instruction must be carried out by professional catechists, not by individual parents) is not only prohibited, but is punished by a special article of the Penal Code. Article 142 of the Penal Code of the RSFSR (and corresponding articles in other republics) warns that the "organization and systematic administration of religious instruction of minors is punishable by corrective labor for a term of up to one year or a fine up to fifty rubles." Second offenses "and also organized activities directed toward these same acts are punishable by imprisonment for a term of up to three years" (Resolution of the Presidium of the Supreme Soviet of the RSFSR of March 18, 1966).

In addition, the above mentioned Article 17 of the Stalinist legislation of 1929 states: Religious associations are prohibited from organizing special childrens' and youths' prayer and other types of meetings, groups for studying religion, or planning excursions and childrens' playgrounds.

Any one of these decrees would suffice to prove discrimination against believers and the violation of childrens' rights in the USSR; however, the most discriminatory articles are contained in the 1969 RSFSR Code concerning marriage and family (Article 52) and the Resolutions of the Supreme Soviet of the USSR in 1973 "concerning education" (Article 57), where it is emphasized that parents and guardians *must actually raise the children in a spirit of atheism*. We believers consider ourselves obligated to raise our children in a spirit of patriotism, respect for the state and loyalty to the ruling ideology, but we cannot accept atheistic values, morals and principles of explaining the world, and consequently we will be considered violators of the law.

Moreover, Article 18 of the U.N. Pact on Civil and Political Rights describes the right of an individual to publicly profess his or her religion; Article 21 of the Pact acknowledges the right to peaceful assembly; and Article 22 of the Pact states that "each person has the right to freedom of association with others for protection of his interests. Enjoyment of this right is not subject to any limitation, except those which are necessary in a democratic society."

In contradiction to this article, the same Stalinist Article 17 prohibits religious associations from holding all types of meetings, groups, circles and sections, including those for prayer, bible study, study of literature, needlework, or any work groups for religious instruction. This same article prohibits believers ". . . from creating mutual aid funds, cooperatives or production associations; from financially supporting their members; or from organizing sanitoriums and medical care."

In other articles of this still operative religious legislation, discrimination against believers in the USSR is reinforced by the principles of total state control over believers as if they were criminals or mental patients. For example, "meetings of religious societies and groups of believers (besides prayer meetings) function only with the permission of the local executive committee [*ispolkom*]." (Article 12) "In particularly unsuitable locations, believers' prayer meetings take place only upon notification by the executive committee." (Article 57) "Religious processions, performance of religious rites and ceremonies out in the open, as well as in apartments and believers' homes are permitted only with the special permission which must be granted each time by the executive committee." (Article 59) All these articles are intended for the general meetings of active official members of the religious community.

This last point in Article 59 directly violates Article 17 of the U.N. Pact, which emphasizes that "no one may be subjected to arbitrary or illegal interference in their personal or family life by arbitrary and illegal encroachment on the inviolability of their residence."

All types of groups, meetings, cooperatives and associations of believers are prohibited in the USSR. The very idea of such associations seemed so unacceptable and forbidden to the state bureaucrats that V. A. Kuroedov, the former president of the USSR Council on Religious Affairs, writes in his book *Religion and the Church in Soviet Society* (Moscow, 1984, p. 157): "Recently the Baptists even raised for discussion the possibility of establishing a Baptist youth alliance, a so-called Bapsomol."[2](TN)

In general nothing belongs to religious communities in the USSR. For example, Article 25 of the Stalinist legislation of 1929 asserts that all cult property of religious societies, including that voluntarily given up, is nationalized; and Article 36 states that the state can arbitrarily take cult buildings from believers for other purposes, about which the religious organization need only be peremptorily informed.

Returning to the issue of basic criteria for religious freedom and religious discrimination with respect to existing legislation in the USSR, it is not difficult to reach the following conclusions.

1) All organized forms of interaction and mutual aid among believers are prohibited in the USSR, as well as all forms of group study of the Holy Scripture and sacred literature, and all forms of religious associations except the primary "parish community" without which the church simply would not exist.

2) The cult buildings and property in the USSR are not the property of the religious communities and can be taken away by the state, based only on its needs and not considering the needs of the believers. Believers have no way of obtaining liturgical texts with commentary.

3) In the USSR organized church charity is prohibited by legislative decree. This charity is an integral part of the social life of the church. It arises out of its very heart and was the source of the basic concept of social security for people. Also prohibited are all forms of private and public expression of one's faith through literature or mass media. Teaching religion to children or adults is likewise prohibited.

In other words, out of all the elements which are necessary for normal religious activity, on the part of both the church and the separate individuals which comprise it, the believers have left only the liturgy, in itself the most important aspect. But without the liturgy we would only be left with the alternative of an underground church (as it was during Stalin's era), and this element cannot substitute for the two other fundamental aspects of church life - parish life and apostleship.

Believers in the USSR not only live in a situation of total discrimination, but this discrimination is upheld by legislation which is contrary to the basic standards of international law.

So far we have been discussing legislation, the most scandalous level of discrimination against believers in our country. On the level of propaganda this discrimination is carried out by strictly professional anti-religionists and takes the following forms:

1) The banning of equal time for religious sermons or, expressed in non-church language, "religious propaganda"; the inability of believers to protect themselves against accusations and lies leveled against them in the press.

2) Misinforming the populace by the deliberate misrepresentation of religion and the church for atheistic propaganda purposes. For example, the book *100 Responses to Believers* (Moscow, 1974), states that Christians canonized the goddess Aphrodite and "the gods Hermes and Mercury," that the majority of saints are "people who are not fondly remembered," and that the concept of God arose out of worship of unclean spirits. In A. Grigorenko's book *The Many Faces of Magic* (Moscow, 1987), Christian mysteries are equated not only with certain acts of witchcraft, fortune telling and other occult practices, but also with the rituals of the "Church of Satan."

3) Slander and defamation as a method of harassing believers who protest against discrimination. For example, in O. Vakulovskii's book, *The Double Bottom of Amnesty International*, Father Gleb Yakunin is accused of having "systematically monopolized and resold religious objects, antiques, books, industrial goods, precious gems and metals and silver coins which were minted before the revolution."[3]

4) The use of quasi-mythological propagandistic stereotypes appropriate for especially harsh pressure tactics against extremely active believers. Without these stereotypes atheistic propaganda could not exist, but we nevertheless hope that these propagandists will find the self-respect and the ability to reject those stereotypes which are neither serious nor deserved.

There is no sense in recounting these propagandistic slogans and stereotypes; it is enough only to say a few words to refute them.

The majority of clergy in pre-revolutionary Russia were very poor, with limited rights, and in no way belonged to the "richest ruling classes" (a substantial number of Russian revolutionaries came from this estate). The church had been the leading cultural force in society since the Petrine reforms, and in no way "contributed to the cultural backwardness of the country."

The Russian Orthodox Church has not been wholly counterrevolutionary in opposition to Soviet power; a broad spectrum of groups has existed within it, including completely pro-Soviet. The supporters of Bolshevism have come from absolutely every layer of society, including peasants and workers.

In the USSR there are no "religious extremists who demand unlimited freedom of action for themselves," since everyone who speaks out for freedom of religion recognizes from the outset the limitations which are necessary in any democratic society. The believers are only petitioning for review of discriminatory legislation and for permission for them to live in accordance with the requirements of faith.

Foreign institutes for the study of religion in the USSR are not anti-communist centers. They attempt to reflect the situation objectively. Their information is distorted as a result of the previous lack of openness brought about by the "period of stagnation."

Two television programs in 1987, one on October 10 ("Under the Mask") and another on November 17, dedicated to Keston College and to the Institute "Faith in the Second World", could not produce even one argument proving the anti-communism of these organizations which are belittled by unsubstantiated slogans.

The third level of discrimination against believers in our country is ideological. This discrimination occurs because the prevailing world view cannot abide theism in general and objective idealism in the particular philosophy. This is a question of diametrical difference in convictions; therefore, arguments and discussions are senseless here, except for mutual well-wishing. Nevertheless, discrimination on this level is still discrimination since the prevailing ideology until quite recently has made the following two mistakes.

1) Interpretation of laws which regulate relationships between the state and the church have undergone "ideologization" as a result of the mixing of the concepts of ideology and state. The result has been the discriminatory Stalinist legislation of 1929 and the anti-religion articles of the Penal Code of the RSFSR (Articles 142 and 227).

2) In the ideology itself the impression prevailed that "religion in communist society is completely dead." This is now officially acknowledged as a mistake by the President of the Council on Religious Affairs. This idea generated crude and at times openly hostile and aggressive actions against believers, both on the part of bureaucrats and of atheistic propaganda. These have taken place in the past and unfortunately are still apparent at times even today.

Such practices, not established by law, have for several decades violated two more articles of the Pact on Civil and Political Rights. "Any action in support of religious hatred which incites discrimination, hostility or violence, must be prohibited by law." (Article 207) "The right to life is an inalienable right of each person. . ." (Article 6) The commentary of the Soviet legal expert L. I. Shestakov concerning this article in the foreword of the collection *The Rights of People* (Moscow, 1986, p. 12) is apropos here: "Genocide does not consist only of murder. The crime can be completely different and not associated with killing. For example, the transferring of children from one human group to another is genocide if this transfer has the objective of ending the existence of a specific human group."[4]

The current status of believers in the USSR is that while the Soviet state has formally signed all international legal documents, in practice, discrimination against believers continues, especially if you take into account the presence of Stalinist laws which put all religious organizations into their own type of "invisible ghetto". The USSR has even signed the Helsinki Accords, which states:

> Participant states will respect human rights and basic freedoms, including freedom of thought, conscience, religion and beliefs for all, without respect to race, sex, language or religion. . . . The participant states will acknowledge and respect the freedom of an individual to profess religion or faith alone or with others according to the dictates of his or her own conscience."[5]

Despite the fact that the USSR has acknowledged and signed all the aforementioned documents, the ideological pressure, propaganda and the very existence of anti-religious legislation of such unprecedented discriminatory scope, violates in various ways the basic principles of freedom of conscience in the USSR. It reduces the official hierarchy to being a passive appendage of the state and severely limits the sphere of life and activity of individual believers and loyal independent religious groups.

The processes of glasnost and perestroika now developing in our country, which are associated with the furthering of democratization and humanization of our society, make it possible for believers to hope for state review of the obsolete and archaic Stalinist dogmas concerning religion. It leads us to hope for the elimination of juridically formulated discrimination and the creation of fundamentally new interrelationships with the state, based on mutual free agreement in common interests, in mutual respect and *real* separation of church and state. Any violation of the principle of freedom of religion inflicts damage not only to the dignity of a person, but also undermines the foundations of freedom, fairness and universal peace. It is necessary, once and for all, to end all forms of intolerance in the area of the human spirit, all forms of religious hatred and one-sided unscrupulous propaganda.

An effective means to this end would be an international conference of experts on the question of freedom of religion and the creation of an authoritative control commission with the participation of both the official hierarchy and lay people. To this end we appeal to all countries and all religions.

---

1. See, for example, Literaturnaia gazeta, October 21, 1987, p. 12.

2. V. A. Kuroedov, Religion and the Church in Soviet Society, Moscow, 1984, p. 157.

TN (p. 45) A play on the word Komsomol, which is an acronym for Communist Youth League.

3. O. Vakulovskii, The Double Bottom of Amnesty International, Moscow, 1987, p. 60.

4. L. I. Shestakov, The Rights of People, Moscow, 1986, p. 12.

5. The Final Act of the Conference on Security and Cooperation in Europe, Helsinki, July 30 to August 1, 1975, Moscow, 1987, p. 7.

5

THE SOVIET STATE
AND RUSSIAN PROTESTANTS

Douglas Durasoff

Under the banner of perestroika, accompanied by pennants of glasnost' and "democratization," Soviet society and the communist party-state system have entered a significant new era, an era of change and of conflicts over the nature of change. As must always be the case, legacies of past eras accompany and interpenetrate these changes, providing both continuities with and significant barriers against reform. General Secretary Gorbachev, in his drive to overcome those barriers which derive from Stalinism and Brezhnevite bureaucratism, has specifically and regularly appealed to continuity with Lenin, especially to "Lenin's works in the last years of his life," the years occupied with operation and management of a real system.[1] During that period Lenin derived, from necessity and from his views on Hegelian-Marxist dialectics, a significant willingness to tolerate, absorb and utilize "non-communist" people and practices so long as they were not actively pitted against him. He also criticized fellow Bolsheviks when they pursued overly radical agendas or "futuristic" reforms divorced from historical legacies and relationships. By stressing his continuity with this Lenin, Gorbachev positions himself towards pragmatism, or in terms perhaps more satisfactory to dialecticians, to "complex relationships conducive to progress." Thus the drive for perestroika, in nearly open combat with vested interests, represents a period combining major possibilities for positive change with significant sources of tension and possible conflict within state and society.

The role of religion within this fluid and dynamic period appears neither settled nor accorded a particularly high or visible priority in regime policy, yet significant events have occurred. On the one hand, major speeches and policy statements make no specific mention of religion; apparently striking concern with society's "spiritual development" is set in the context of modern culture and Communist morality.[2] On the other hand, many imprisoned believers have been released before expiry of their terms; the millennium celebration is accorded comparatively positive treatment; and at least one sharp, strikingly visible debate on the relationship of religion to morality has occurred in the party-run press.[3] A key, even decisive factor in the position of religion under perestroika may well be the relationship between the major appeals of Gorbachev for new legal codes (and "increase of Soviet legality" generally) and the eventual treatment of the infamous 1929 legislation on cults (and its amendments).

Within this dynamic context, the place and role of Russian Protestants is also unsettled. As might be expected for a group of "religionists" not linked to major nationality groupings or to pre-revolutionary state institutionalization, Protestants have a somewhat lower profile in Party-state concerns than do the Russian Orthodox or Central Asian Moslems. Nevertheless, their role is neither trivial nor irrelevant to the present era. Indeed, it may be argued that Protestant believers in Russia represent a special challenge and opportunity to the Soviet state in the era of perestroika, and that state policy toward the Protestants will be one indicator of the success or failure of the current (to use the most ironic translation) "reformation."

PROTESTANT MINORITIES IN RUSSIAN AND SOVIET SOCIETY

Our very word "Protestant" derives primarily from religious protest in the context of Western European history and Roman Catholicism, and is in that sense not part of the mainstream of Russian history. Although there have been "protestants" of Russian Orthodox origin, the groups we generally refer to today as "Russian Protestants" are primarily Baptists, Evangelicals, Pentecostals, et al., in other words, denominations with origins outside Russia. Interestingly, however, and importantly, these groups today are not generally lineal descendants of those Protestants who were first in Russia, such as the "foreigners" of the time of Peter the Great, and the "Germans" of the Volga and elsewhere. Rather, they primarily result from evangelization contacts of the nineteenth and early twentieth century, contacts which long ago lost any immediate relationship to their converts. Thus today the Russian, Ukrainian and other Protestant groups are true "indigenous churches" in the USSR, not under any external hierarchy, and also cutting across ethnic and traditional national lines.

In several ways this history has created a unique branch of Christendom. Churches of foreign initiation yet now fully indigenous, active evangelical Christians in a Communist society, they are living out an apparent oxymoron: "Soviet evangelicals." In addition, since 1945 the major public institutionalization of these groups has been the only formal union in the world integrating Pentecostals with Baptists, the All-Union Council of Evangelical Christians-Baptists (AUCECB). These Protestants, along with several varieties of "unregistered" brethren, most notably the *Initsiativniki*, are now found in all Soviet republics, with membership from several national groups. (For example, the one registered Protestant church allowed in Tbilisi has four services each Sunday, one each in the Georgian, Russian, Azeri and Ossetian languages.) They thus represent a "different" church for the Soviet regime, not a "remnant of pre-revolutionary times" and not a national church potentially linked to ethnic manifestations in the USSR or abroad. Add to this the exemplary lifestyle and work ethic of these groups and their primarily working-class membership, and they are altogether not easily labeled nor very well understood in Marxist-Leninist terms.

CYCLES AND SOURCES OF FREEDOM AND PERSECUTION

From the nineteenth century to the present, the Russian, then the Soviet, state has not administered a consistent program or policy approach vis-a-vis the Protestants. Rather, relative freedom (or "mostly benign neglect") has alternated with vigorous suppression in an irregular cycle. The challenge is to analyze the sources of these irregularities and to apply the lessons gained to present and future relationships. This "application" has at least three referents, namely the Soviet state, the Soviet evangelicals, and those outside the USSR who are interested in their plight.

Roughly, the history of state-Protestant relations falls into eight phases, although of course there are subdivisions and even other possible divisions. My purpose is not to present a refined historical analysis, but to provide a basis for current analysis with a brief review of historical variation. Others have presented the history quite carefully.[4]

The first period might be called "origins." Today's "indigenous evangelicals" can be traced to the 1867 baptism of Nikita Voronin near Tbilisi, an event cited by the leadership of the primary group of registered Protestants in the USSR today, the All-Union Council of Evangelical Christians-Baptists (AUCECB), as their point of origin.[5] Early evangelical growth after this event, followed by its eventual visibility as distinct from expatriate or non-Russian Protestants, quickly led to the second period, a time of severe persecutions under "the Russian Saul," Pobedonostsev, tutor of tsars and "Over-Procurator of the Holy Synod." A decree of 1893 and law of 1894 under the Ministry of Interior Affairs removed the right of assembly of most Russian evangelicals, with ensuing persecution for their activities. One might label the period "imperial state religious policy ascendant".

The events and climate of 1905 ushered in liberalization and signficant freedom of assembly, with concomitant expansion of evangelical congregations. This third period reverted towards the policy of the second, however, with another Ministry decree in 1910 which regulated "sectarian meetings," a policy which began to lead to harassment, arrests and accusations of foreign sympathies during World War I. Interestingly, persecution in period two focused on the "Russian-ness" of evangelicals as an affront to the state church, yet persecutions after 1914 focused on a purported link to German and other external denominational groups. This ominous willingness to define a problem from regime fears or convenience rather than from reality has been one persistent theme of the cycles of repression.

The fourth period is in several ways especially interesting in relation to the perestroika of seventy years later. After the 1917 revolutions and in the early Soviet state, Protestant evangelicals flourished. Both the separation of church and state in the Bolshevik decree of 1918 and the "complex Leninism" of the early operation of a

Soviet state created space within which growth of the indigenous Protestant sects was significant. Sawatski, citing a Soviet source, suggests a quintupling of evangelicals by 1924, from a 1917 base of 150,000. A 1928 article in Pravda complained that there were more new youth members in the Baptist youth organization than in the party Komsomol.

Although Lenin's positions against religion were clearly stated, so were his positions about the dangers of "inventing one's own culture," bureaucratism, and radical "sweeping away" of difficulties. His positions on dialectics were compatible with his practiced willingness to expect "contradictions," and so to accept many manifestations of religion, especially those which seemed potentially useful in his key struggles. Thus the evangelicals might have been seen by Lenin as a counterforce to the prior state church, made up primarily of useful workers and peasants, and only troublesome when some of them advocated refusal of military service. Had he written a treatise on them, I suspect he would have seen them as somehow misguided but useful, displaying the "contradictory tendencies in all phenomena," not to be applauded but to be tolerated as playing their part in the processes of development of society which, of course, would ultimately result in socialism and communism.

Stalin did not see the world this way. After his consolidation of leadership, the fifth period, "crushing persecution," was signaled by the infamous 1929 law on religious cults. Stringent and restrictive at face value, its "application" went beyond formal legalities to overt persecution. Six of seven Baptist churches in Leningrad and five of six in Moscow were closed and confiscated; pastors, presbyters and lay believers were arrested, and executions sometimes followed. Evangelicals were by no means solely targeted; Orthodox faithful, Moslems, Jews and others were also attacked.

The clear exigencies of war brought a sixth period, a rapid shift in regime policy toward Russian Orthodoxy and also toward the Russian evangelicals. Atheist publications were stopped; successful patriotic appeals were made in the churches; and evangelicals prayed, fought and raised money for the war effort. An institutionalization of unity among "Evangelical Christians" and Baptists was suggested in 1942 and consummated in 1944 (the AUCECB). Pentecostal evangelicals were added in 1945, and the union has persisted to the present.   In a pattern common to communist regimes, a "parallel control mechanism" was created, the Council for the Affairs of Religious Cults (CARC), a state organ under the Council of Ministers. It was later combined with its counterpart, which monitored the Orthodox church, to form the Council of Religious Affairs (CRA), which remains to date as state overseer. While this institutionalization eased the position of the AUCECB after the war compared to prewar oppression, it also created a pattern of close state supervision, stiffening prosecution of unregistered churches, and a susceptibility to episodes of renewed pressure as the regime saw appropriate.

Stalin's death in 1953 and the emergence of a reformist era after Khrushchev's consolidation of power in 1957 would seem likely to have led to further liberalization, but instead another major wave of persecution was launched, similar to the period after 1929. (Sawatsky reports that by 1964 more than half of the Orthodox and Baptist churches were closed and the Orthodox clergy cut by two thirds.) Although some condemnations of this appeared in official statements after Khrushchev's ouster in 1964, the Brezhnev group resumed oppressions by 1966, including a general stiffening of both policy and criminal codes on registration, rules of assembly, youth policy, printed matter, education and family policies.   With the emergence of a significant "dissident" evangelical movement, the Initsiativniki, and formation by them of the Council of Churches of Evangelical Christians-Baptists (CCECB), an unregistered counterpart to the AUCECB, state policy focused perhaps even more strongly on its "catch-22" registration policy, wherein it was illegal not to register but virtually impossible to do so.   Arrests of pastors of such groups increased and remained a regular feature of regime behavior.

Although there have been obvious variations and occasional temporary easings of pressure, the era from 1959 into the 1980s has been rather consistently an era of heavy state pressure, ranging from oversight and restraint of the few permitted registered churches to heavy suppression and persecution of unregistered congregations and especially of their leaders. By its style and duration it paralleled the tsarist suppression of the Protestants under Pobedonostsev although its breadth increased to include Russian Orthodoxy and religion generally. The parallels are even more striking if one considers the oft-noted symbology of Communist "regime religion," including its "saints," "iconography," rites and rituals. Thus the regime could be accused of the development of a new state church, a sort of "nondialectic, bureaucratic, secular religion of Party-state communism" which suppressed contenders or pretenders to the "state faith."   In this perspective, it must now be asked whether perestroika is a temporary breather like 1905, a more sweeping revolution like 1917, or merely a prelude to a "new 1929". More directly to the point, the question is, how will religion come to be treated under perestroika if perestroika is successful? Will it receive Lenin's treatment or Khrushchev's?

SOURCES OF CONTINUITY AND CHANGE
FOR 1988-2000

There is a pitched battle underway in the Soviet Union under the banner of perestroika. The front lines are not fully clear, but reform vs. vested interest is a fair generalization. Within this, of course, are variations. Although much of the older, Brezhnevite generation has been removed from official state and party leadership positions, their replacements are clearly not all ardent Gorbachev clients, and the ruling Politburo itself reflects significant tensions, as surfaced notably in the El'tsin affair. Perhaps the front is more precisely between those who, like Gorbachev, see major reform as necessary to save the regime from loss of power caused by economic and social decay versus those who see major reform as itself a threat to power. Ligachev appears to head the Politburo group restraining Gorbachev, perhaps ready to attempt to remove him if he blunders.[6]

The primary arena for policy initiatives is the economy, but the struggle for perestroika is also appearing in cultural affairs, lifestyle matters, public health policy, women's rights, and so on. Religious policy has not been untouched, but it has not been a focus of policy, and it appears that major resolution of state policy on religion and religious freedom awaits further developments. The issues raised by such policy are very germane to perestroika, however, and should play a large part in our attempts in the West to comprehend the eventual real meanings of perestroika, glasnost' and the Soviet definition of "democracy". Monitoring the position of the Protestants within this policy should have specific utility for our understanding of the sophistication, scope and complexity of the regime's views.

FACTORS FOR ANALYSIS: STATE AND PROTESTANTS UNDER PERESTROIKA

General Secretary Gorbachev is not simply directing a regime policy of perestroika but is in a battle for its implementation and effectiveness. If major fiasco results, or if too many years pass without visible success in the economy, it is not impossible that he will be removed, like Khrushchev in 1964. Understanding this context, Gorbachev has at times been almost strident in his appeals for perestroika and specifically cites "the later Lenin" as a practical leader with whom he identifies (and wishes to be identified for obvious reasons of legitimation). He does not focus on religion in major addresses, but does use analogical concepts and an almost puritan approach to work and lifestyle issues (so much so that Russian street wags refer to him as a "secret Baptist"). It is unlikely that he has any "soft spot" for religion, but pragmatic factors and his campaigns for "morality" and responsible work make it possible that he may accept evangelical Protestants as a pragmatically useful component within the overall struggle for perestroika.

One interesting point, generally overlooked, is that in the 1986 Communist Party Program, the section on atheist propaganda was "softened" between the draft and final versions, deleting several harsh phrasings and inserting the phrase "preventing insults to the feelings of believers." Whether this was a Gorbachev influence or the result of other factors is not visible, but it does demonstrate the presence of some element of "Leninist pragmatism" in the current setting.

The counterproductivity of past regime suppression of religion has been documented by many analysts.[7] This too may be a factor in the current setting although a lesson scorned under previous leaders.

An analysis of "Gorbachev's Lenin" on dialectics and practice might, to the extent Gorbachev himself internalizes this material, suggest current policy applications for the Soviet state.

Tough, pragmatic applications of dialectics to "real life and work," in an analysis by this Lenin might go as follows:

1) If religion is either a) the residue of specific pre-Soviet class relations or b) the manifestation of class (bourgeois) propaganda, then the CPSU must rigorously oppose it in practice.

2) However, if it is primarily some expression of "over 2000 years of human culture," even if an expression contrary to "enlightened materialism," then it must be seen as an aspect of social dialectics, part of complex social reality which moves towards new syntheses and new dialectical expressions "at a higher level" in the future. As such, it can (and should) fit within the overall development of Soviet society.

3) Explorations of its role should then focus on two considerations: a) Which manifestations of religious belief are inimical to Soviet state interests? These are to be suppressed (classism, national separatism, etc.). b) How may its *other* manifestations be appropriated as part of positive dialectical progress in Soviet socialism (work ethic, family life, honesty, etc.)? This appropriation will be useful to perestroika.

4) A "checklist" or "balance sheet" of positive and negative features of Protestant religion in Soviet society, as seen by an official under regime-led perestroika, might look like this (with apologies for the imagined colloquial tone):

"Con": They see God as higher than the state and are willing to "dissent" when their beliefs are threatened.

"Pro": They accept normal state authority as part of their theological beliefs and are known as "law abiding citizens" to a degree unusual in our society. They don't even steal from the factories!

"Con": They are proselytizers and influence youth with religious ideas.

"Pro": They have good effects on the shiftless members of our younger generation. Perhaps Baptist kids are better than gangsters. . .

"Con": They are irrationally stubborn about their beliefs in the face of the progress of socialist materialism.

"Pro": They are hard workers, always honest and sober: real "perestroika types."

"Con": Might they have links to foreign denominational agitators?

"Pro": If we allow them to "be religious" it will probably be good for our foreign image of democratization. The bourgeois democracies seem to place great stock in such manifestations of our tolerance.

"Con":   Could they be an obstacle in the more important relations between the Soviet state and the Orthodox Church?

"Pro": Certainly not a large one. . . It's interesting that their churches are transnational; might it be possible that they could, even in a small way, help moderate ethnic separatism?

On balance, their negatives seem relatively minor at this stage in our social development, and their positives could be useful. Lenin would understand.

5) "If perestroika succeeds," and includes religious toleration, several new questions would be raised. How will Russian Protestants move from a practical "behavioral theology of persecution" to some (which?) sort of "theology of belief within a socialist polity"? Russian Protestants have been especially handicapped in the formation of applied theology by lack of seminaries and study literature. While their harsh experiences have been an effective schooling in the theology of persecution, a rather rapid change to a more benign state would introduce new elements of cultural adaptation, especially to the more fundamentalist groups whose members have been most opposed to any cooperation with the state. Will Protestants succumb to divisiveness over adaptation to ameliorated conditions? And finally, might coming to grips with "the church within socialism" be in some ways even more difficult for the West than for the Soviets? The "salt" of believers within Soviet perestroika may well help to "restructure" socialism in beneficial ways, but these might not all fit western preconceptions.

However, these are for now "pleasant speculations". Unfortunately, particular religious groups or religion in general could yet be attacked anew as a diversion from other pressing battles or failures of perestroika. There has not yet been any institutionalization (or elimination of past law) to prevent this. One empirical measure of "true perestroika" will be whether current "easing" of pressures against religion will be formalized and systematized, evidencing the development of a rule of law rather than the vagaries of merely expedient current policy.

1. Mikhail Gorbachev, <u>Perestroika</u>: New Thinking for Our Country and the World, New York: Harper & Row, 1987, p. 25. See also speech by Gorbachev, 70th Anniversary of the Great October Revolution, <u>Pravda</u>, Nov. 8, 1987.

2. Gorbachev, <u>Perestroika</u>, pp. 30-31.

3. <u>Komsomol'skaia Pravda</u>, July 30, October 3, and December 10, 1986.

4. See Kolarz, 1961, S. Durasoff, 1969, Steeves, 1976, Sawatsky, 1981.

5. Steve Durasoff, <u>The Russian Protestants: Evangelicals in the Soviet Union: 1944-1964</u>, Rutherford, TN: Fairleigh Dickinson University Press, 1960, p. 37.

6. Peter Reddaway, speech at the University of Washington, Jan. 7, 1988.

7. See for example Frederick C. Barghoorn and Thomas F. Remington, <u>Politics in the USSR</u>, Boston: Little, Brown & Co., 1986 and David E. Powell, <u>Antireligious Propaganda in the Soviet Union: A Study of Mass Persuasion</u>, Cambridge, MA: The MIT Press, 1975.

RUSSIAN ORTHODOXY
UNDER GORBACHEV

Gleb Rahr

According to a study by Vladimir Beliaiev (*Possev*, March, 1982) there were 75,556 Orthodox churches and chapels in the Russian Empire in 1909, 9.9 percent of them newly constructed within the previous five years. According to Konstantin Kharchev (*Nauka i religiia*, November, 1987) there were 6,794 Russian Orthodox congregations in the Soviet Union in 1986 while five years earlier, in 1981, there still were 7,007. During one five year period the number of churches increased by 3,722. In another five year period it decreased by 213. Kharchev asserts that "not any more believers, but people adhering in one form or another to the materialistic world outlook constitute the absolute majority of the population" in the Soviet Union. I think we have to challenge this assertion. It is difficult to establish figures and percentages where conscience and things spiritual are involved. But David Barrett's "*World Christian Encyclopedia*" offers an approach much more suitable for real assessment of the religious stituation when it speaks not only of believers and of non-religious people but of Christians - professing, affiliated, practicing or non-practicing, of religious people of non-Christian denominations, of active and presumably persuaded atheists, and of people whom the Encyclopedia calls "non-religious." The estimate of the World Christian Encyclopedia for the mid-1980s in the Soviet Union is 36 percent Christians, 13 percent adherents of non-Christian religions, 22 percent atheists, and 29 percent non-religious people. If this estimate is correct, atheists and non-religious people do constitute 51 percent of the population, and Kharchev seems to be technically correct when he asserts that the "absolute majority" adheres in one form or another to the materialistic world outlook, 51 percent as opposed to 49.

At the same time we must pay attention to figures given by Soviet sources. For instance, *Argumenty i fakty* (29, 1987) informed us that 30 percent of young people who do not regard themselves as believers participated in baptisms while 40 percent visited "working" churches. *Argumenty i fakty* commented on these figures: "God-seeking tendencies and unhealthy interest in religious literature are frequent especially among young people with a high educational level." Publications like the "Dialogue" between William Fletcher and Hieromonk Innokentii Pavlov in *Sotsiologicheskie Issledovaniia* (November 4, 1987) seem to confirm such tendencies. My point is not to challenge figures or estimates, but merely to state that we should not try to see the Soviet population as divided into two ideological "camps" or blocs - believers in one, non-believers in the other - but rather as a society subject to efforts of two opposing forces to draw as many souls as possible to its respective side. You may call it God or the Devil or just active believers and active militant atheists as rivals in their fight for adherents. Non-religious people might in certain aspects be closer to atheists (for instance in their understanding of contemporary natural sciences); in other respects they would however stand on the side of believers (mainly in questions of morals, ethics, human rights and democracy).

The Soviet state, the Soviet system (*Sovetskii stroi*) is an ideological atheistic system. The Soviet state is an ideologized state. Mikhail Gorbachev, in his speech of January 8, 1987, at the conference of leading mass media personalities at the Party Central Committee headquarters, gave excellent proof of this, saying, "*My za glasnost' bez vsiakikh ogovorok, bez ogranichenii, no za glasnost' v interesakh sotsializma*" [We are for glasnost without preconditions, without limitations, but for glasnost in the interests of socialism.] What Gorbachev means is of course not the political and social doctrine of socialism, as adhered to by British Labour or West German Social Democrats. It is a religion, a dogma, which dominates the legal system, the internal and foreign policies, which is prescribed for every citizen by the Constitution and cannot be abolished or changed because it is the only legitimation of the further existence of the regime. More than that, "socialism" is a quasi-religious belief without which the system would have no right to exist. The only justification of the existing one-party dictatorship is the allegedly sacred task to "construct socialism and communism," to force the nation into an atheistic society.

Those who fight for religious freedom in the Soviet Union usually point to Article 17 of the legislation regulating the activities of religious associations promulgated April 8, 1929. They ask that this paragraph be immediately abolished. Of course, this article is one of the most obviously discriminating. It prohibits any welfare and educational activities by religious associations. But this and other discriminating laws will and can be dropped only in the case of a perestroika much deeper than the one envisaged by Gorbachev at the present time.

An unknown Orthodox priest, Father Gennadii Fast, from the Siberian city of Krasnoiarsk, probably a young man and definitely a wise and intelligent one, wrote to Gorbachev proposing to start improvements in the situation of religious believers, not by changing certain articles of the laws regulating the activities of religious associations in an antireligious state, but rather by changing the fundamental law, the Constitution itself, namely Article 52. This is the article about separation of the church from the state, the article which gives atheists the right to propagate their views, but limits the activities of religious believers to church services only. Father Gennadii proposes to change Article 52 of the Constitution. According to him it should read: "In the USSR both the church and the propaganda of atheism are separated from the state." In other words, Father Gennadii Fast believes in a technical state, not an ideologized one, in a state which is neutral as far as ideology is concerned. Both ideologies - the religious and the atheistic - should have the same right to exist, but they must stand on their own feet and not claim any support from the state. If the general idea of an ideologically neutral state would be accepted, this would also mean that the state-supported schools of all ranks and levels would also have to become ideologically neutral. Both teachers of religion and teachers of atheism should be allowed to teach in extra-curricular classes in which students would participate on a voluntary basis. It is my personal opinion that Father Fast's letter to Mikhail Sergeevich Gorbachev should not just be filed. It should stay on our desks.

We do not know whether the Soviet leadership intends to extend its perestroika policies to the field of religious life and relations between church and state. But should they ever come to the conclusion that the time has come, and perestroika in this field becomes unavoidable, the way pointed out by Father Gennadii Fast appears to be the most logical and practical one: an ideologically neutral state, ideologically neutral schools, and both religious and atheistic propaganda allowed, but not as a matter of governmental policy.

Part 2
Christianity and Soviet Russian Culture

7

MAKSIM GORKY AND THE
DECLINE OF BOLSHEVIK THEOMACHY

Mikhail Agursky

INTRODUCTION

An outstanding place in modern Russian history belongs to Gorky. Actually, he was the most charismatic of the Russian revolutionaries and a founding father of Soviet society. To regard him as mainly a literary phenomenon would be to distort history.

Neither Marxist nor materialist, Gorky exercised an extraordinary impact on Soviet society. In his excellent book, Emanuel Sarkisyanz exposes the religious roots of Bolshevism, arguing that they proceed from total rejection of the world as one of non-truth and from the attempt to build a new world, a "New Man," purely by human efforts.[1]

Throughout the history of Bolshevism, Gorky was the only Russian revolutionary thinker to express to such a degree the religious roots of early Bolshevism, the "Promethean Theomachy," as some authors have termed the spiritual background of Bolshevism.[2]

Erich Voegelin regards as an expression of gnosticism any millenarian movement in history that tries to achieve a perfect world. For him gnosticism is rooted in the human rebellion against a transcendent God. Voegelin suggests the six main features of gnosticism as a spiritual-social phenomenon:

> 1. It must first be pointed out that the gnostic is dissatisfied with his situation. This, in itself, is not especially surprising. We all have cause to be not satisfied with one aspect or another of the situation in which we find ourselves.

2. Not quite so understandable is the second aspect of the gnostic attitude: the belief that the drawbacks of the situation can be attributed to the fact that the world is intrinsically poorly organized. For it is likewise possible to assume that the order of being as it is given to us men (wherever its origin is to be sought) is good and that it is we human beings who are inadequate. But gnostics are not inclined to discover that human beings in general and they themselves in particular are inadequate. If in a given situation something is not as it should be, then the fault is to be found in the wickedness of the world.

3. The third characteristic is the belief that salvation from the evil of the world is possible.

4. From this follows the belief that the order of being will have to be changed in an historical process. From a wretched world a good one must evolve historically. This assumption is not altogether self-evident because the Christian solution might also be considered: namely, that the world throughout history will remain as it is and that man's salvational fulfillment is brought about through grace in death.

5. With this fifth point we come to the gnostic trait in the narrower sense - the belief that a change in the order of being lies in the realm of human action, that this salvational act is possible through man's own effort.

6. If it is possible, however, so to work a structural change in the given order of being that we can be satisfied with it as a perfect one, then it becomes the task of the gnostic to seek out the prescription for such a change. Knowledge - gnosis - of the method of altering being is the central concern of the gnostic. As the sixth feature of the gnostic attitude, therefore, we recognize the construction of a formula for self and world salvation, as well as the gnostic's readiness to come forward as a prophet who will proclaim his knowledge about the salvation of mankind.[3]

Gorky fulfills all these conditions, but he was not an unwitting gnostic. He was well acquainted with gnostic history and ideas, and for him it was not only an intellectual idea. Gorky's Promethean Theomachy was his response to the problem of world evil which he saw as life's main existential challenge.

From his early years Gorky lived under extraordinarily harsh conditions. He witnessed outright violence in his own family and in the world around him; he witnessed unbridled cruelty, enmity, treachery, ignorance and poverty. Gorky could easily have rejected the existing world, even emotionally, but he also absorbed many ideas which brought him to the belief that nature per se is the origin of world evil and must undergo a total change. Humanity must make its own efforts to create a new nature and a new man.

Gorky's outlook was developing on two levels: philosophical-scientific and religious. Elements of both levels influenced one another, and as a result Gorky came to a unique synthesis although this was accomplished only by the beginning of the 1920s. Gorky was a self-didact: some inconsistencies can be found in his statements, but mostly in the secondary aspects of his synthesis.

NATURE AS BLIND CHAOS

Gorky's world outlook was strongly influenced by nineteenth century German philosophy, by its view of the world and nature. Schopenhauer, von Hartmann and Nietzsche were Gorky's main philosophy teachers although he did not share their pessimism or ethics. Gorky, however, never truly identified with any philosopher. His views were eclectic and sprang from many sources, but Schopenhauer was his first philosophical inspiration. Gorky purchased a popular edition of his works at the end of the 1880s,[4] and by the middle of the 1890s he had already read all the works of Schopenhauer that had been translated into Russian.[5] During this period he also read Hartmann and Nietzsche.[6] In 1927 Gorky confessed in a letter that Schopenhauer had remained his favorite,[7] and in 1931, when he was already censored in the Soviet Union, he said that he had read Schopenhauer in his youth without harming himself[8] - a formulation open to various interpretations.

It is Schopenhauer who first supplied Gorky with the theoretical legitimacy for his emotional negation of nature as blind and hostile chaos. In December 1930, Gorky wrote: "I find it [nature] stupid as Arthur Schopenhauer claimed."[9]

However, the negation of nature was also rooted in Russian tradition, and especially in Dostoevsky, about whom Gorky was very ambivalent. Nikolai Alekseev stressed Dostoevsky's "acosmism", which was primarily manifested in the total absence of nature in Dostoevsky's world and more explicitly in the direct negation of nature by Ivan Karamazov. Alekseev noticed that, according to Dostoevsky, the "human world was not only excluded from nature, but nature was declared the main enemy of man."[10]

The negation of nature as a crucial point of Gorky's outlook is usually ignored, but it could not be said that no one has ever paid attention to it. A leading party literary critic of the 1920s, Alexander Voronsky, pointed out at that time that Gorky regarded nature as "an unreliable and treacherous chaos." According to Voronsky, the world for Gorky was "unfaithful, unreliable, shaky. The Universe lacks harmony and order. Blind elements dominate the world, there is a preponderance of the unexpected and sudden." Voronsky also noted that Gorky did not believe in the stability of the world.[11]

Gorky pretended to contest Voronsky's claims, but in such a way as to give the impression that he countered only some of the latter's formulations. He contested, for example, Voronsky's claim that he saw no harmony in the cosmos simply because he cared nothing for the cosmos, thus leaving all Voronsky's criticism in force. With regard to another of Voronsky's claims that Gorky did not believe in the stability of the world, Gorky claimed that the world was stable enough in order not to perish, but it was nothing more than raw material for man to work on.[12]

In September 1928, Gorky said:

> You assigned to me the view of nature and cosmos as chaos; this is not entirely true. I am not ashamed to confess that I don't care too much for the cosmos. When I read the works of cosmologists, astrophysicists and astronomers, I sincerely admire their imagination, intuition, the power of logic. However, the cosmos still remains to me a field of multi-ciphered numbers. I agree that it is majestic; however, it would be very boring if man had not populated this field in ancient times with fears and horrors, later by gods and eventually by "conformity with law." The conformity of cosmic phenomena with law I assign entirely to the powerful efforts of mind and imagination to see existence as harmony; and since our science established this harmony, I am interested in the cosmos only from the point of view of its influence on literature as a good topic for poets. Worlds emerge and perish; comets run homelessly "around numberless luminaries" and everything goes on as predicted by astronomers - all this is wonderful! Let us deal with our earthly business, which is no less wonderful.
>
> You also said that I "don't believe in the stability of the universe." I don't see any reason for this claim. No, I am confident that the universe is stable enough that one can work without being

confused by speculations about its death. About nature, however, it is my opinion that it is raw material which is being processed more and more actively by our will, intuition, imagination, mind, in the interests of our enrichment by its "gifts" - its energies. . .

Nature is a chaos of disorganized, elementary forces which award men with earthquakes, floods, tornadoes, droughts, intolerable heat and the equivalent cold. . . Nature senselessly wastes its forces to create pathogenic micro-organisms - bacillae; to create the most harmful insects - mosquitoes, flies, lice, which transfer the poisons of typhus, fever, and so on into human blood. Nature creates numberless harmful or useless plants and grasses, draining healthy juices which are needed for the growth of cereals and fruits which feed man - for the propagation of parasites.[13]

But if Voronsky somehow reproached Gorky for such a view of nature, ten years later another leading party literary critic, Isai Lezhnev (Voronsky was already on the way to being purged), then head of *Pravda's* cultural department, praised Gorky for this very attitude. Lezhnev showed a correct grasp of Gorky's views when he said: "The chaos of the non-organized forces of Stepmother Nature, the blind destructiveness of its elemental disasters, its senseless lavishness, the harmfulness of the countless hordes of its parasitic trash, evoked contempt and hatred in Gorky."[14] He also remarked: "Gorky's pathos is revealed in the simple words: 'To create a new world.'"

Gorky's view of nature was widely shared at that time by many Bolsheviks. Senior party official and ideologist Ivan Skvortsov-Stepanov (who was also a friend of Gorky) wrote in a textbook in the middle of the 1920s: "One cannot help recognizing the natural processes as rude, barbaric, destructive, lavish. . . Where is there even a hint at so-called 'predestination,' 'harmony,' 'expediency?' There are only the blind actions of blind processes of blind nature. Man is incomparably more reasonable, more expedient, more economical, when he interrupts natural processes and controls, regulates, and directs them."[15]

Anthropocentrism

It is natural that such a view would have as a corollary extreme anthropocentrism which became a real cult of man as absolute perfection versus nature. It was taken by Gorky from the German philosophical tradition and from the Russian spiritual tradition as manifested, for example, in Dostoevsky.[16] Anthropocentrism became Gorky's guiding light. Indeed, it was not man whom he saw as absolute perfection so much as man's mind. Here one comes across a striking inconsistency. How is it possible for blind, senseless chaos to create a miracle of perfection such as man and his mind?

In contradiction to the monistic philosophy of Ernst Haeckel,[17] whom he greatly admired, Gorky not only did not consider man as part of nature, but held that the emergence of man had overcome nature, partly through human efforts and partly through some mysterious force. In March 1920 Gorky approached this subject:

> That which we call Nature created man as its organ, the organ for self-recognition. Insofar as our highest quality, our highest virtue is the brain, the most delicate matter in all the human organism, it might be that man serves as nature's brain, created by some mysterious force unknown to us.[18]

Gorky tried early to formulate his anthropocentrism. In 1896 he wrote:

> Man... he is the holy of holies. He is the whole world - complicated, interesting, deep, wild... Will people ever learn, if not to understand, at least to respect each other silently? Will they ever realize that apart from man there is nothing interesting in the world and that man alone is the judge and the creator of life?[19]

In a letter in 1899 he wrote:

> I know nothing better, more complex, more interesting than man. He is everything. Even God was created by him... I am convinced that man is capable of infinite self-improvement and everything he does will also develop with him through the ages. I believe in the infinity of life and I understand life to be movement towards spiritual improvement.[20]

Again, in 1901 in another letter:

> There is only man, everything else is an opinion. You say that a 'conscious creature is a misunderstanding of nature.' Let it be - but it exists, therefore it is a real fact and it alone is conscious - therefore it is free to create life according to its wish.[21]

In 1903 Gorky made a full-fledged declaration of his anthropocentrism.

> Majestic, proud, and free, he valiantly looks into the eyes of truth, and speaks to his doubts: 'You lie about my impotence, and the limitations of my consciousness! It is growing! I know this, I see and feel that it is growing within me! I perceive the growth of my consciousness by the measure of my suffering, for I know: if it did not grow, I should not suffer more than I did before. 'But with every step I desire more, I feel more, I see more and deeper, and this swift growth of my wants is the mighty growth of my consciousness. For the present it is like a spark in me - what of it? Are not sparks mothers of conflagrations? I am, in the future, a conflagration in the darkness of the universe! I am summoned to illumine the world, to melt the darkness of its secret riddles, to find harmony between me and the world, in myself to create harmony, and after having exposed to light the whole gloomy chaos of life on this much suffering earth, covered as with a skin disease by a crust of unhappiness, sorrow, misery, and malice, to sweep away all its ugly filth into the grave of the past!
>
> I am summoned to untie the knots of all errors and misconceptions, which have tangled up cowed men into a bloody and repellant bundle of beasts devouring one another.
>
> I have been created by Thought for the purpose of overthrowing, destroying, trampling down all that is old, all that is narrow and filthy, all that is malicious, and with the aim of building a new life on the unshakable foundations, forged by Thought, of freedom, beauty, and respect for men.
>
> Implacable foe of the disgraceful niggardliness of human desires, I want every one of our men to be a Man.[22]

Annihilation of Matter and Collective Immortality

One can understand Gorky's rejection of materialism. If the material component of nature were indeed only an inert, senseless, hostile chaos which could not give birth to anything purposeful (let alone man, who, according to Gorky, emerged from nature), how can one consider materialism as the foundation of a correct philosophical outlook?

Gorky could have extracted scientific arguments against materialism from the monistic philosophy of nature of the famous German chemist Wilhelm Ostwald[23] and also from the French philosopher and physicist Gustave Le Bon.[24] Actually, they all argued that it was not matter which was the origin of all world phenomena, but energy, which was regarded as an indestructible substance capable of endless transformations, rather than an attribute of matter.

Ostwald extended the notion of energy to all mental and social phenomena and measured human progress by the extent of energy accumulated in human society. According to Ostwald, the notion of energy removes the conflict between matter and spirit. All mental activity, Ostwald claimed, was a process of pure energy.

However, Gorky discovered energetism not from Ostwald, but from his friend, the outstanding Bolshevik left-wing philosopher Aleksandr Bogdanov, a rival of Lenin.[25] Bogdanov stressed that energetism also removes the conflict between materialism and idealism. For him, concepts of matter and spirit are only confusing. The only difference for Bogdanov is that between mental and physical experience. The first represents a higher level of human organization since it is collective, while the second is individual and precedes the collective.[26]

Gorky's remarks on energy are derived from Ostwald, Le Bon and Bogdanov. For example, in a public lecture delivered in 1920, Gorky said: "Matter is identical with energy."[27]

In the middle of the 1920s he noted:

> Extend materialism to the idea: matter equals energy, and the highest quality of energy - thought and human will. All natural processes can be reduced to this, to the extraction of this energy.[28]

His most comprehensive statement on this issue was made in 1928 in his answer to Voronsky:

> I am not hostile to materialism, though certainly I am in the position of an heretic towards it. My attitude here is not that according to many great scientists materialism does not fit the theory of atoms. A famous physicist, our contemporary, formulates the very notion of matter in the following way: "Matter is the spot of space where we objectify our impressions." I don't care for this, since I am not a philosopher.
>
> However, I think that materialism is also a "temporary" truth, while it often seems to me that some interpreters of materialism raise it to the level of an absolute or eternal truth. And since all such absolutes remind me inevitably of divine features -

omnipotence, omniscience, etc., and since every religion is in essence inhuman, I am afraid: has a very old and harmful message passed into new words?[29]

Gorky followed Bogdanov's line in opposing the conflict between materialism and idealism. Nevertheless, Gorky made one strange remark which cannot be found in Bogdanov: materialism is only a temporary truth. To Gorky, the central place in the historical process belonged to the transformation of matter into energy through the release of nuclear energy, as a result both of its natural disintegration and the conscious and purposeful release of energy due to human activity.

It therefore follows that if inert, chaotic nature is the origin of world evil, then the release of energy from the captivity of matter is the only legitimate way to eradicate it. In the end, all matter must be annihilated. Gorky was certainly aware of Le Bon's theory of the inevitable annihilation of matter, which the latter claimed had emerged as the result of some cosmic disaster and was doomed to return to its original state - energy.[30]

On the other hand, this view exactly coincides with von Hartmann's idea that eventually humanity should coordinate its efforts and annihilate this world, which brings only suffering and cannot be improved in principle.[31]

This is the explanation of Gorky's remark that materialism is a temporary truth. If matter is evil, and energy is identified with its opposite - the mind - then humanity's objective should be the transformation of matter into energy. If there is no matter, there is no materialism.

Gorky first hinted at his project to annihilate matter in his public lecture in 1920:

Matter is the same as energy. It is the same force, but in a stable equilibrium. If man, the human mind, will discover how to transform every single piece of matter into energy, we will have the following picture: we will not have to descend into mines to look for coal, we will not have to be buried in peat bogs extracting peat in cold seasons, since we will be able to do it much more comfortably, we will not need this hard labour, which is essentially stupid. It is necessary, we cannot avoid it, but it is a stupid labour.[32]

But his most comprehensive statement on this subject was made quite publicly in his "Fragments from my Diary" which was strangely ignored by critics. In it he describes his project in a conversation with Alexander Blok:

> "Personally, I prefer to imagine man as a machine, which transmutes in itself the so-called 'dead matter' into a psychical energy and will, in some faraway future, transform the whole world into a purely psychical one."
>
> "I do not understand - this is pan-psychism, isn't it?"
>
> "No. For at that time, nothing will exist except thought. Everything will disappear, being transmuted into pure thought, which alone will exist, incarnating the entire mind of humanity from the first flashes of it until the moment of its last explosion."
>
> "I do not understand," Blok repeated, shaking his head.
>
> I proposed that he should picture to himself the world in an uninterrupted process of dissociation of matter. Matter, dissolving, continually gives off such species of energy as light, electricity, electro-magnetic waves, Hertzian waves, etc. To these are added, of course, all signs of radioactivity. Thought is the result of the dissociation of the atoms of the brain; the brain is composed of the elements of "dead" unorganic matter. In the brain-substance of man this matter is uninterruptedly transformed into psychical matter. I myself believe that at some future time all matter absorbed by man shall be transmuted by him and by his brain into a sole energy - a psychical one. This energy shall discover harmony in itself and shall sink into self-contemplation - in a meditation over all the infinitely varied creative possibilities concealed in it.
>
> "What a dismal phantasy!" said Blok, smiling sarcastically. 'It is pleasant to know that the law of preservation of matter contradicts it.'
>
> "As for me, I am pleased to remember that the laws issuing from laboratories do not always coincide with the laws of the universe, unknown to us. I am convinced that if we could weigh our planet from time to time, we should see that its weight was gradually diminishing."[33]

It is clear that the creation of such an immortal energetic brain was regarded by Gorky as the achievement of human collective immortality. In fact, he referred many times to this issue. In 1912 in his *Tales of Italy* he claimed: "Christ is arisen. . . And we shall all rise from the dead, invoking death upon death."[34]

In March 1920 he approached this subject once again:

The human mind declares war on death as a natural phenomenon. On death itself. My personal belief is that sooner or later, probably in two hundred years or possibly one hundred years, man will indeed achieve immortality.[35]

In 1933 he suggested a specific project to overcome the elemental forces of nature, illness and death.

> Two Natures
> Part One:
>   Nature's power over Man.   Man's enemies: wind, thunderstorms, bogs, cold, intense heat, river rapids, deserts, beasts of prey, poisonous plants, etc.
> Part Two:
>   Man's war against hostile Nature and the creation of a new nature. Subjugation of the wind and water, electricity. Marshlands provide fuel, peat and fertilizer. Animals and plants in Man's service, etc.
> Part Three:
>   Man's power over Nature. Planned and organized labour in socialist society. Victory over the elements, sickness and death.[36]

In fact, the annihilation of matter and the achievement of collective immortality is a full-scale theurgical project which not only does not need the intervention of God, but is even directed against him. In this respect it is totally different from other theurgical projects suggested by Russian Orthodox mystics such as Andrei Bely,[37] Pavel Florensky[38] and Nikolai Fedorov.[39] Christian theurgy was regarded by its protagonists as a duty to be performed only in cooperation with God; it was personalist, anticipating the resurrection of the dead whereas Gorky's project was totally impersonal.

Gorky was well acquainted with such writings. He could not sympathize with Christian theurgy since it looked to the enlightenment of matter by spirit, while Gorky dreamed of the total annihilation of matter. Still he was very fond of Christian theurgists because of their active attitude to life. For example, Gorky expressed a limited sympathy with Fedorov in a letter he wrote in 1926: "A most interesting old man. His sermon about the 'active' attitude to life is of great value and close to my heart."[40]

In 1928, he remarked of Fedorov in *Pravda*:

> We had a very fine thinker - not very famous because he was original
> - N. F. Fedorov. Among his many original theories and aphorisms
> there is the following: "Freedom without the conquest of nature is
> just like the liberation of the peasants without giving them land."
> This, I think is irrefutable.[41]

There is another interesting link. As is known, in the 1920s the outstanding Russian geochemist Vladimir Vernadsky suggested that living nature was developing as a whole in the direction of a planetary impersonal brain. The idea influenced Pierre Teilhard de Chardin who gave this brain the name of "Noosphere," and Vernadsky accepted the term. It is difficult now to establish who influenced whom - Gorky-Vernadsky or vice versa. They had been acquainted since at least 1917. Gorky repeatedly praised him for his book *Geochemistry* at least since 1926.

It is more interesting to compare Gorky and Teilhard de Chardin. They certainly had a common denominator, but they also differed radically. Teilhard's vision is not theurgical, but the result of the immanent development of the universe. Moreover, it is personalistic.[42]

GORKY AS A RELIGIOUS THINKER

Gorky repeatedly referred to himself as an atheist, and there is an abundance of evidence that he was indeed a militant enemy of institutionalized religion. However, this is not enough to qualify him as an atheist. An analysis of his works, including his letters, leads to the conclusion that his militant "atheism" was no more and no less than theomachy. God was always a focal point in Gorky's thinking. In an early story (1896) about a hermit, Gorky confessed:

> I am always closer to heaven than he (the hermit); however, why is my
> soul farther from the Lord than the soul of an old man whose body is
> buried in the earth?[43]

But it would be a mistake to think that this focal point faded towards the end of his life. In the middle of the 1920s, for example, he wrote in his notebook:

> Black dust fills my head and every speck has a marvellous capacity. . .
>
> There is in each speck an [endlessly] insoluble, intricate, enormous bale of thoughts of God (soul), or some creator of the universe with some other name - even a mechanical jolt born from chaos itself.
>
> God and jolt are totally indifferent and equally incomprehensible. However, if (God) existed, I would not envy him (since the duty to understand this world is too heavy) - I see nothing wise (what is) wise if he replaced cosmic chaos with human chaos, and chaos in my head. But God doesn't exist, and the cursed necessity of understanding this world lies on man, only on man.[44]

Only a few months before his death, Gorky published in *Pravda* an article in memory of the Russian physiologist Ivan Pavlov, who was, as is well known, a committed Orthodox Christian. Gorky quoted the following words of Pavlov without any criticism:

> I can believe in God, but certainly I prefer to know. Belief is also something which needs investigation. It develops from abstract notions, i.e., from the activity we still don't yet know how it works. Will we know? This is the question.[45]

Gorky's gnostic religious oulook was built on two main foundations: modern theosophy and Gorky's own reconstruction of the old Slavic gnosticism - Bogomilism.

Theosophy

Gorky was introduced to theosophy quite early; his interest in occult phenomena and in theurgy formed only part of his theosophical views. He had evidently read Blavatsky at least as early as 1899 because he criticized her.[46] But later his attitude changed, and in 1912, for example, he requested all her writings published in Russian.[47] Taking into consideration that theosophy never claimed it was a religion but only knowledge, one can understand how Gorky could reconcile with it.

Actually, theosophy categorically denies the existence of a personal, transcendental, anthropomorphous God, whom it regards as only a giant shadow of man.[48] This was repeated often by Gorky.

Theosophy denies categorically the physical resurrection of the dead and - even more important for our purposes - it identifies matter and energy.

Blavatsky set the following three main objectives for theosophy: 1. The creation of a universal human community with no racial and religious discrimination; 2. The study of esoteric traditions; 3. The study of nature's secrets (an alias for occult phenomena).[49] These were all shared by Gorky.

Gorky was also introduced to ancient gnosticism which was part and parcel of modern theosophy. This was also early on, some time between 1893 and 1895, and was carried out by the prominent mystic Anna Schmidt, who worked in Nizhnii-Novgorod as a journalist on the same paper where Gorky began his literary career. Schmidt decided to convert the young Gorky to her esoteric creed and took several hours to explain her credo:

> But it was a stranger who sat facing me, talking in a strictly professional way, ornamenting the speech with quotations from the Fathers of the Church, mentioning gnostics, Vassilides and Aennoia. The voice sounded dictatorial and powerful, the blue pupils of the eyes had widened and gleamed at me in the same new way as did the words and thoughts. Gradually everything commonplace and comical in this stranger disappeared, became invisible, and I well remember the glad and proud amazement with which I observed how the flame of thoughts on the evil of life, on the contradiction between flesh and spirit, were born and burst out from under the grey outward shell, with what firm assurance resounded the ancient words of the searchers of perfect wisdom, of implacable truth.[50]

She did not succeed in making Gorky her personal disciple, but she had a lasting influence.

Gorky's first reference to gnosticism can be found in 1910. In his book *The Life of Matvei Kozhemiakin*, a pilgrim preacher expresses a central point of gnosticism:

> The first and bitterest enemy of the soul is the flesh, the soul in the flesh is like a prisoner in jail, a man has two natures, and therein lies his eternal suffering. The flesh is of the devil, the soul is of God, the devil wants the soul to be part and parcel of all man's sins of the flesh, but a man ought not to allow this.[51]

A local priest immediately identifies the source:

That old man's thoughts jumped back one thousand seven hundred years: in the second century after the birth of Christ certain people maintained, as he does, that one must give full rein to the flesh and this will do no harm to the spirit. They even affirmed that the more licence the flesh is given, the most pure the spirit will be. Such people called themselves Gnostics.[52]

A most important exposition of gnosticism can be found in *The Life of Klim Samgin*, written in 1930. The protagonist of gnosticism is Marina Zotova, the spiritual leader of a Russian gnostic sect, who was presented by Gorky with great sympathy. She asks Samgin:

> "You want to know if I believe in God. I do. But in the god who in ancient times was called Propator, Proarch, Aeon - are you acquainted with the Gnostics?"
> "No. That is - "
> "You are not. Well, now - they taught that Aeon had no beginning, but some saw the beginning in the community of thought about it, in the urge to understand it, and out of that urge sprang up the thought Aennoia, coinherent with Aeon. That was not reason, but the reason-impelling force springing from the depths of the parent spirit divorced from the earth and flesh ..."
> "You are a most interesting character," exclaimed Samgin with genuine surprise. "How can you combine mysticism with. . ."
> "In the first place gnosticism is not mysticism, and in the second place, there is a saying: 'A big bag is not a hard clay pot; what's put in with care will stay safely there; now around you can take it - all right, but don't shake it.'"
> "I loathe priestly Christianity. My mind is working for the fusion of all our communes, and such as are kindred to them, in one union. I don't like Christianity - that's all! - If the people of your - caste, if I may say so, could understand what Christianity is, how it affects the will power. . ."[53]

It is very interesting that probably the first to discover Gorky as a gnostic was the German historian of religion, Adolf von Harnack. In a book on ancient gnosticism, he points to Gorky's *The Lower Depths* as an expression of rebellion against the creator:

> Gorkis ergreifendes Stueck "Das Nachtasyl" aber kann einfach als ein Marcionitisches Schauspiel bezeichnet werden; denn "der Fremde," die hier auftritt, ist der Marcionitische Christus, und sein "Nachtasyl" ist die Welt.[54]

Later, Semen Frank, a prominent Russian religious philosopher, pointed out that Gorky's outlook is a mutation of gnosticism.[55]

Gorky had a very keen interest in medieval theosophy, alchemy and all kinds of secret doctrines. His favorites were Paracelsus and Swedenborg, from whom he took, for example, his view of man as a microcosm - a typical theosophic doctrine.[56] Gorky liked Paracelsus so much that he succeeded in including his biography in the prestigious Soviet biography series, and it was published in the USSR in 1935.[57] He also liked the theosophic works of Fabre d'Olivet and Eduard Schure, and their influence on him can be clearly seen. For example, Gorky subscribed to d'Olivet's harsh criticism of the idea that there had ever been a golden age in the history of humanity.[58]

A look at Schure will help us understand why Gorky tried so hard to conceal his real views, which we are now trying to reconstruct. It is a matter of principle for Schure that profound truths may not be disclosed to those who are unprepared for them. The revelation of Truth is only a process, which starts from Rama and ends in Schure's book on Christ. "Philosopher-initiates," Schure claimed, "never wished to reveal these profound ideas to the people, for the latter would have understood them only imperfectly and would abuse them."[59]

Let us also look at Schure's interpretation of the Last Judgment. According to him:

> The Last Judgment. . . means the end of the cosmic evolution of humanity or its entry into a definitive spiritual condition. This is what Persian esotericism called the victory of Ormuzd over Ahriman, or spirit over matter. Hindu esotericism called it the complete reabsorption of matter by the Spirit, or the end of a Day of Brahma.[60]

In the light of Gorky's theosophy one can better understand his famous involvement in the so-called God-Building trend among left-wing Bolsheviks. However, Gorky's commitment to God-Building differs greatly from that of his contemporary allies, Lunacharsky or Basarov.[61] For Gorky, it is first of all a theurgical action, the theurgical creation of the new Nature and the annihilation of the old, and therefore God-Building coincides fully with the Kingdom of the Spirit. God is for Gorky a theurgical outcome of a collective work, the outcome of human unity and the negation of the human ego. God can become a reality as a result of occult concentration. This idea of the creation of God was expressed by Gorky for the first time in 1901:

> Now, God is slipping away from the shopkeepers, and the sons of bitches are left without a shelter. That's how it must be! Let them jump about in life naked with their empty little souls and moan like cracked bells. And when they die from cold and spiritual salvation we'll create a God for ourselves who will be great, splendid, joyous, the protector of life who loves everyone and everything. So be it![62]

Certainly Gorky was here also influenced by the religion of humanity which he inherited from Vasily Bervi-Flerovsky whom he knew personally, and which the latter took in his turn from Auguste Comte.[63] For Comte it was, however, a philosophical concept; for Gorky it became theurgy.

The main exposition of Gorky's God-Building is to be found in his novel "The Confession," written in 1908. For Gorky, the real theurgists are people, and the most important manifestation of popular theurgy is early Christianity before it was distorted by the church. "Christ was the first true people's God, born from the soul of the people like the phoenix from the flames."[64]

However, when popular occult energy had weakened, Christ died; but the people-theurgists can resurrect him:

> The time will come when the will of the people will again converge to one point, and then, again, the unconquerable and miraculous power will arise and the resurrection of God will take place.[65]

Gorky's God-Building was not a passing attraction. In 1927 he published, for example, an article in *Pravda* in which he once again subscribed to his earlier idea, though in veiled form:

> There was a time, during the gloomy years of reaction, 1907-1910, when I called him a "god-builder," meaning by this that both within himself and on earth a man creates and embodies the capacity to perform miracles of justice and beauty, and all the other miracles which idealists attribute to a power that supposedly exists outside of man. Man's labour tends to convince him that, except for his reason and will, there is no miraculous power apart from the forces of nature, and that these he must master so that they may serve his

reason and will, and thus lighten his labor and life. He believes that "only man exists - all else is thought and deed."[66]

Bogomilism

It is difficult to say where Gorky came across the Bogomils for the first time. In his memoirs he claimed that when he was an apprentice in his teens he met an Old Believer who mentioned the Bogomils as the main source of Russian religious nihilism [*netovshchina*]:

> The mind of man wanders in the forest of its own thoughts. Like a fierce wolf it wanders, the devil's assistant, putting the soul of man, the gift of God, on the rack! What have they imagined, these servants of the devil? The Bogomili, through whom netovshchina came, taught thus: Satan, they say, is the son of God, the elder brother of Jesus Christ. That is what they have come to! They taught people also not to obey their superiors, not to work, to abandon wife and children; a man needs nothing, no property whatsoever in his life; let him live as he chooses, and the devil shows him how.[67]

It seems that there is an anachronism here. Indeed, Russian ancient literature is full of Bogomil influence, but the word itself is absent, and the Old Believer whom Gorky quotes could not have known it unless he had read contemporary Russian academic theological literature, which is impossible.

Gorky also mentions the Bogomils implicitly in *The Life of Klim Samgin*. A character in that novel, Kumov, says:

> Body. Flesh. Has soul, but not spirit. Know the teaching of the Bogomil sect? God gave the form, Satan the soul. . . Awfully true. That's why the masses have no spirit. Spirit is created by the elect.[68]

According to Dmitry Obolensky, who studied Bogomilism,

> Behind the numerous discrepancies in the teachings of the different Gnostic sects there lies the basic idea that matter, which is essentially evil, cannot be the creation of God. The Gnostics explained the origin of matter either by regarding it as eternally evil in itself or by positing an intermediary between God and matter, the Demiurge, one of the emanations (aeons) of God, whose nature had been

basically corrupted by a transgression which caused his expulsion from the divine pleroma; this Demiurge created the material world, which consequently shares in his essentially evil nature. Man himself, in Gnosticism and in every truly dualistic theory, mirrors this fundamental dualism: his soul is of divine origin, his body ineradicably evil. . .

From all eternity there exist two opposite and mutually independent principles, God and matter, represented respectively on the physical plane by two "natures," Light and Darkness. Our present world appeared as a result of an invasion of the realm of Light by Darkness, or Matter, and is a "mixture" of both natures, an amalgam of divine particles of Light imprisoned in a material envelope. The future, or final, state of all things will come about as the result of the complete restoration of the original dualism by the absolute separation of both principles, which will render Darkness forever incapable of further aggression. The present, in so far as it is a preparation for the future, consists in a gradual liberation of the particles of Light, consubstantial with God, which are the souls of men, from the prison of Matter, of the body. The separation of Light from Darkness is the work of God Himself, who desires that those elements which He lost when they became "mixed" with Matter should return to their true abode, and is furthered by a series of "evocations" (hypostatized divine attributes) which God sends into the world. One of these "evocations," the Demiurge, created our visible world from materials belonging to the realm of Darkness; the purpose of this world is to be a prison for the powers of Darkness and a place of purification for the souls of men, a kind of machine for the distillation of Light. . .

The Byzantine Bogomils taught that the Devil, or Satan, is the first-born son of god the Father and the elder brother of the 'Son and Logos.' His original name was Satanael. Like the Bulgarian Bogomils of the tenth century, they held him to be the 'unjust steward' of the parable in St. Luke. Second to the Father in dignity, Satanael was clad in the "same form and garments" as He, and sat on a throne at His right hand. Stricken with pride, he decided to rebel against his Father. . .

Assisted by his fallen companions, Satanael crested the visible world, with its firmament, its earth and its products. This, according to the Bogomils, was the creation of the world, described in the first chapter of the Book of Genesis and falsely attributed by the Christians to God Himself. The motive of Satanael's creation of the world was to imitate his Father, and the world he created is in fact an imitation of the celestial world over which God reigns. Satanael next created Adam's body out of earth and water. But when he set the body upright, the water flowed out of the big toe of the right foot and assumed the shape of a serpent, Satanael then tried to animate the body by breathing into it, but his breath went out by the same channel as the water and entered into the body of the serpent, which thus became a minister of the Devil. Seeing his failure to give life to Adam's body, Satanael begged his Father to send down His Spirit on Adam and promised that man, a mixture of good and evil, should belong to both of them. To this God agreed, and Adam came to life, a compound of a divine soul and a body created by Satanael. . .

The Bogomils considered the greater part of the Old Testament to be the revelation of Satanael. Moses, according to them, was led astray by him and in his turn deceived the Jewish people through the power given him by the Demiurge. The Law given to Moses on Mount Sinai came from Satanael.[69]

The God mentioned above is a rather helpless God if he could permit such abuse. Indeed, the God of the Gnostics is actually an alien God, a nonexistent God, or a God whom it is impossible to know.

The Bogomils denied the resurrection of the dead. Their soteriology only looked for the liberation of the spirit from the captivity of matter. It is also important to note that like any other millenarian movement, the Bogomils were socially very radical. They negated the social system, let alone the church, which they simply hated because they saw it as a creation of the Devil. As is known, the Bogomils were the matrix from which the gnostic millenarian movements of the Middle Ages, the Albigensians, Cathars, Taborites and others emerged.

Bogomilism had a very strong impact on Russia. According to Ivan Porfiriev, who published many ancient Russian apocrypha:

Apocryphal elements were spread so strong in ancient Russian literature that there is almost no manuscript in which we do not see, if not an apocrypha, at least some apocryphal detail. . .[70]

He also said that these apocrypha came to Russia from Byzantium via Bulgaria and Serbia, where they were not only translated but also edited under the influence of the Bogomil heresy.

A prominent Russian Orthodox Church official, Ivan Aivazov, recognized in 1906 that

already at the beginning of the eleventh century Bogomil ideas had penetrated Russia from Southern Slav areas with their strong denial of the Church in all her historical development, with their dreams to establish the Apostolic Church on the grounds of quotations taken willfully and tendentiously from apostolic writings, which allegedly justified their extreme democratic views and finally with their rude cynicism under the disguise of monastic asceticism.[71]

According to Aivazov, the seed of religious skepticism sown by Bogomilism in the soul of Russia did not wither. He regarded, for example, the most widespread Russian gnostic sect, the Khlysty, as rooted in Bogomilism.

Gorky took up Bogomilism and studied it very carefully. (By the way, he included the story of Satanael in the biography of Chaliapin, writing it as if Chaliapin had heard the story from his mother.)

> My mother could tell quite terrifying stories, one of which I vividly remember. It was the story of Satanael. The Lord had an archangel in heaven, whose name was Satanael, and he was head of the Heavenly hosts. He became proud and persuaded the other angels and Heavenly officials to rise up in revolt against God. God discovered this and threw him down, after which he sought out the one who must replace him. There was a creature there, Mikh by name, shaggy and hairy, the hairs growing out of head, ears, and nose. The Mikh was kind, and also guileless, for once he had stolen a piece of land from God. God admonished him and demanded its return, upon which Mikh began taking the land from his ears and nose, but refusing to reveal what lay in his mouth. Whereupon God issued the command "Spit," and Mikh spat, and mountains rose up. God sent for him and said: "Although you are not clever, I will take you as head of the Heavenly forces and as arch-strategist. You will start no trouble here, and henceforth you will be called, not Mikh, but Satan."[72]

Gorky hated the demiurge who created this evil world and as an agnostic he distinguished two gods, whom he speaks of in his memoirs as if he had known them in his childhood.

> My grandfather took me to church, on Saturdays to vespers, on Sundays to late mass. Even at church I would tell which god people prayed to. The priest and the deacon prayed to grandfather's god, but the choir always sang to grandmother's.
>
> To be sure, I have given a crude picture of the childish distinction I drew between the two gods, a distinction which I remember having caused me much spiritual conflict. I feared and disliked grandfather's god, who loved no one and kept a stern eye on everyone. He was primarily interested in unearthing something wicked and vicious in man. It was clear that he did not trust people,

was ever waiting for them to repent, and took pleasure in meting out punishment.

During those days my mind dwelled primarily on God, the only beauty I found in life. All other impressions repulsed and saddened me with their filth and cruelty. God, my grandmother's god, friend to all living things, was the brightest and best of all that surrounded me. And naturally I could not understand why grandfather was blind to God's goodness. [73]

Gorky evidently identified the evil god with the god of the Old Testament. His favorite of the books of the Bible was that of Job, who represented for him the archetype of man unafraid to rebel against God. In a letter to Vasily Rozanov, Gorky wrote:

My favorite book is the Book of Job. . . . I always read it with the greatest emotion and especially chapter 40, where God teaches man that he should be equal to God, and how peaceful it is near to God. And always while I am reading this chapter, I shout in my mind to myself, to Russians: Stop being slaves of God at last! [74]

Gorky appealed to Rozanov to overcome his slavery to God. "Your slavery before God, and Dostoevsky's, Tolstoy's, Soloviev's, will be defeated. Either we will defeat it or we will perish 'jako obri.'"[75]

To Gorky, God is an indifferent, capricious and weak Demiurge. In 1923 he wrote of God as he had seen him in his youth:

I have seen God: he is Sabbaoth, exactly as he is presented in icons and pictures: comely, whitebearded, with indifferent eyes. Sitting alone on the great heavy throne, he is sewing a horribly long white shirt with a golden needle and blue thread. The shirt hangs down to the earth like a transparent cloud. There is emptiness around God and it is impossible to look at him without horror. [76]

But this was exactly the alien god of Gnosticism. He assigned the following words to his teacher of philosophy:

Up to its very last days, humanity will recite facts and base more or less unsuccessful guesses about the essence of truth or, if they do not take facts into account, will create phantasies. Above, below, surrounding, is God. But God is unacceptable to me. Probably he does exist, but I don't want him. [77]

Gorky modified Nietzsche's idea of the death of God. He sometimes said that it was the good god who had died. In Gorky's novel *Summer* (1909), a wanderer says:

The world is ruled by Satan! The Lord was thrown out of heaven, deprived of immortality, and crucified under the name of Jesus Christ. It was not devils. . . expelled from heaven by the Lord, but people, together with the Lord, who were expelled by Satan. And God died after he touched earth.[78]

In his story "Hermit," written in 1922, the hero said:

God is not a fiend; He is a dear friend to people; but this is what has happened, owing to His kindness: he's meted in our tearful life like sugar in water, and the water is filthy and full of dregs, so that we do not feel Him any more; we do not get the taste of Him in our lives. Nevertheless, He is spread over the whole world and lives in every soul as the purest spark; we should seek Him in man, collect Him into a single ball, and when the divine spark of all these living souls is gathered into this powerful whole - the Devil will come and say to the Lord: "Thou art great, my God, and Thy might is measureless - I didn't know this before, so pray forgive me. I won't struggle with Thee any more now - please take me into Thy service."[79]

PROMETHEAN THEOMACHY

Theomachy holds a central place in Gorky's writings. The Soviet literary critic Henrich Lenoble has written that

Gorky's heroes are characteristic for their attitude to God, who they think organized the world very badly, who is not so clever, and who is not at all just. In other cases. . . he is said to have created Hell on earth and therefore he doesn't deserve to be glorified. . . In the quarrel between Man and God (this latter is often an alias for nature or external necessity), Gorky is not simply on the side of man. He insistently stresses and poeticizes the superiority of Man over all forces which oppose him.[80]

In Gorky's creative work there are two images of fighters against God that are especially remarkable. One is the ancient epic Russian hero Vasilii Buslaev, to whom Gorky gave a new interpretation. At the end of the 1890s he wrote an unpublished poem on Buslaev's challenge of the God-creator.

Vas'ka boasted before God, hurling him a mocking challenge: God gave people the earth in the form of a plain stone, and the people transformed it into a jewel. "Thou hast thrown it into the heavens like a stone, and I made it into a costly emerald!"

Look, O Lord, see what the earth looks like
How Vas'ka has decorated it![81]

The Soviet literary critic Iosif Yuzovskii correctly noted: "there is a motif of theomachy rare in literature, in which man contests God not for domination over the world but for its creation, to contest Him as a creator putting himself in God's place."[82]

But the most interesting theomachian in Gorky's works is the deacon Egor Ipatievsky in *The Life of Klim Samgin*. Like Ivan Karamazov, the deacon believes in God but challenges Him.

"Don't you believe in God?" asked Varvara, pleased for some reason.

"In a god who demands a theodicy, I cannot believe. I prefer to believe in Nature, which requires no justification, as Darwin has proved. As for Mr. Leibnitz, who attempted to prove the existence of evil to be entirely compatible with the existence of God, and this compatibility to be demonstrated, completely and incontrovertibly by the Book of Job, this Mr. Leibnitz is nothing but a German freak. The truth is not with him, but with Heinrich Heine, who called the Book of Job "the song of songs of scepticism."[83]

"Cruel, satanic words did the prophet Nahum utter. There, you youngsters, wherever you look, punishments and vengeance are excellently worked out for us. But what of rewards? Of rewards we know naught. The Dantes, the Miltons and others, right down to our people themselves, have limned hell unto the smallest detail, and most awesomely. But what of paradise? Of paradise naught is told us; we know but one thing; there angels sing hosanna unto Sabbaoth."

He struck the table suddenly with his fist, rattling the dishes. His eyes glowered; he began to shout in a drunken voice:

"But wherefore the hosanna? Wherefore, now the hosanna, I ask? There, youngsters, is a question for you: Wherefore the hosanna? And for whom, for whom, then, is the anathema, if voices be uplifted in a hosanna to the architect of hell - eh?"[84]

Gorky assigns to the deacon his own theomachian poem:

Sleep would not come to the Lord Jesus,
And over the stars went the Lord a-strollin'

Over the heavenly, the golden road,
From one star to another little star a-steppin'
And as company for our Lord Jesus
There were Nikolai, the holy Bishop of Myra,
And Thomas the Apostle - just those two, no others.

And the Lord he thinketh great thoughts,
He looks down below - there the earth's a-twirlin'
There's a little black ball, a-spinnin' like a whippin'-top;
'Tis the devil with an iron chain that whips it.[85]

God and the Devil cooperate in their abuse of the world.

Satan's playing cards with God Almighty!
Kings and queens - those are we;
God in his hands low cards only;
All trumps in Satan's paws you see.[86]

Not only God but the Devil, too, is frightened:

The devil at our life looked most intently,
Shuddered at the sight, and shrieked with terror:
"Lord - what is it I have done so madly?
I conquered thee, O Lord - thou seest that truly?
I crushed thy laws and rules completely.
O, my friend and unsuccessful brother,
Thou, my Abel. . ."
Embraced and bitterly both started crying. . .[87]

The deacon openly rebels against Christ:

The Deacon struck the table with his palm.
"And what good are God's and the Devil's tears about their impotence? What the people are asking for is not tears, but a Gideon, Macabees. . ."
He struck the table again, and this time the blow assisted him. He rose, lean and lank, and in loud coarse voice rattled forth: "We need a Joshua! It isn't I who say this. It's the sigh of the people. I heard it myself: We haven't a man; if we could only get a man! Yes!"
A shiver undulated over his long body from shoulder to knee.
"There used to be a preacher here, who lived in a cellar, selling rubbish in the Sukharevka market. He used to teach: stone is fool and God is fool! I kept still then. 'You lie,' I said to myself, 'Christ is clever!' And now I know - all this is only for comfort. It's all words. Christ, too, is a dead word. The truth is with those who

deny, not those who affirm. What can be affirmed against horror?
Falsehood. Falsehood is affirmed. There is nothing except the great
human sorrow. The rest - the houses, the beliefs, luxuries of every
kind, humility - is all falsehood". . . .

"And about slaves, too, it is not true. It is falsehood," the
deacon was saying, fastening his coat with hands that trembled.
"Before Christ there were no slaves - merely prisoners. The slavery
was that of the body. But since Christ, the slavery of the soul has
begun. There!"[88]

Neither Christ nor Abel is needed for poor mortals. Mortals
stand in need of Prometheus - Antichrist.[89]

But all this passionate controversial rebellion does not exclude
love for God. The deacon also says:

> "Christ! Be thou not angry at us poor folk,
> Ne'er are we forgetful of thy sweet self, Jesus,
> Even when we hate thee, still we do but love thee;
> Even in our hatred we are but thy servants."
> The deacon heaved a noisy sigh and said:
> "That's the end."
> "No one can understand this!" Liutov shouted. "No one! All
> these cold-blooded European outlanders will never understand the
> Russian deacon Egor Ipatievskii, who has been on trial for scoffing
> and blasphemy because of his love for God! They could never
> understand!"
> "That's true. I loved God very much," the deacon said simply
> and assuredly. "Only my demands towards him are strict. He's not
> man; there's nothing to pity him for."
> "Hold on! But what if he - does not exist?"
> "They that do affirm this err."[90]

A month before his death Gorky referred to the biblical god in
such a personal way that it cannot fail to strike the observer. He
recommended a publication which he supported to "mention the
biblical god, who advised - even demanded - the rooting out of aliens;
and turning from biblical times to our days, to mention that this
frightening and villainous god still lives, as is claimed by Hitler,
Mussolini and other restorers of agonizing capitalism."[91]

We have seen that the deacon in *Klim Samgin* longed for
Prometheus, whom he identified with Antichrist. Gorky's attraction to
Promethean Theomachy was always very strong, but his interpretation
of this varied from time to time. Already after the publication of the

volume of *Klim Samgin* containing the deacon's poem, he suggested another interpretation of Prometheus. Now for Gorky, Christ was a reincarnation of Prometheus, and Gorky reinterpreted Christ as "the rebellion of the son against the reality created by the father."[92]

One must stress that theosophic Promethean Theomachy was very widespread in the Russian culture of that time. It is interesting to put Gorky's Prometheanism into the context of the Russian composer Skriabin, who wrote a symphony entitled "Prometheus." For Skriabin, "Prometheus is a symbol of the active energy of the Universe, the original creative principle which creates the world by its own power."[93] Skriabin goes much farther. For him Prometheus is equivalent to the Devil. The Soviet philsopher Aleksei Losev, commenting on Skriabin's views,[94] said that "the human self-divinization in the concept of the Devil is here stretched to its utter limit. . ."

Gorky's imagination was long attracted by the Devil. In 1905 Gorky wrote: "Outside the window of my room a blizzard proudly sings the cold song of loneliness, coals smoulder in the stove in front of me, and the wise face of the Devil glitters in a red flame among them."[95]

A year later he remarked in his notebook that the Devil was the human instinct, and he reinterpreted Tolstoy's appeal not to resist evil as not to resist instinct.[96] In 1911, while reading Rozanov's book *The Dark Face*, Gorky stressed the following passage in the margin: "The Devil is life, God is death."[97]

Later the Devil became more and more positive in Gorky's eyes. In 1933 he said that the church generalized Theomachy in the image of the Devil.[98] In 1934, he claimed that the Devil was an alias for the human mind. For Gorky, it was the Devil who was behind the social protest of the Middle Ages, and it was he who inspired the medieval millenarian belief that private property was evil.[99]

Somewhat earlier Gorky had made a most significant remark about his personal attitude to the Devil. In an interview with a French magazine in 1928, he commented on the accusations waged against him in the emigre press:

> I don't see anything insulting for me in the article of Mr. Levinson. He only repeats the opinion, which is often verbalized in the emigre press, that I allegedly "sold myself to the Devil." On this occasion I have only one thing to say: if the Devil exists and leads me into temptation, he is by no means a little imp, but Abaddon, who

rebelled against the creator who lacks talent and is indifferent to human beings.[100]

This is the most compact formulation of early Bolshevik Promethean Theomachy, which never again reached such a passionate and tragic level of expression in the USSR after Gorky.

1. Emanuel Sarkisyanz, Russland und der Messianismus des Orients [Russia and the Messianism of the East], Tubingen: Mohr, 1955.

2. George Kline, Religious and Anti-Religious Thought in Russia, Chicago: The University of Chicago Press, 1968, p. 165.

3. Eric Voegelin, Science, Politics and Gnosticism, Chicago: Regnery, 1968, pp. 86-88.

4. Maxim Gorky, My Universities, Moscow: Foreign Languages Publishing House, n.d., p. 58.

5. Gorky v vospominaniiakh sovremennikov [Gorky in Recollections of Contemporaries], Vol. 1, Moscow: Khudozhestvennaia literatura, 1981, pp. 97-98.

6. Gorky v Nizhnem Novgorode [Gorky in Nizhnii Novgorod], Nizhny Novgorod: Nizhgubkom, 1928, p. 58.

7. Letter to Lutokhin, Arkhiv Gorkogo, Vol. 14, 1976, p. 430

8. "Besedy o remesle," Sobranie sochinenii, Vol. 25, Moscow: 1953, p. 306.

9. Letter to Forsh, Literaturnoe nasledstvo, Vol. 70, Moscow: 1963, p. 610.

10. Nikolai Alekseev, "Priroda i chelovek v filosofskikh vozzreniakh russkoi literatury" [Nature and Man in the Philosophical Views of Russian Literature], Grani, No. 42, Frankfurt: 1959, pp. 197-198.

11. Alexander Voronsky, "O Gorkom" [About Gorky], Pravda, April 7 and 8, 1926.

12. "Reply to Anisimov (Voronsky)," Arkhiv Gorkogo, t. 10/2, Moscow: 1965, pp. 64-65.

13. "O kul'ture" [About Culture], Sobranie sochinenii, tome 24, Moscow: 1953, p. 405.

14. Isai Lezhnev, "Velikii master kul'tury" [The Great Master of Culture], Pravda, June 21, 1936.

15. Evan Skvortsov-Stepanov, Istoricheskii materializm i sovremennoe estestvoznanie [Historical Materialism and Contemporary Natural Science], Moscow: GIZ, 1926, pp. 72-73.

16. Alekseev, "Priroda i chelovek" [Nature and Man]; Czeslaw Milosz, "Dostoevsky and Swedenborg," Slavic Review, 34, June 1975.

17. Daniel Gasman, The Scientific Origin of National Socialism: Social Darwinism in Ernst Haeckel and the German Monist League, London: MacDonald, 1971.

18. "O znanii" [About Knowledge], Arkhiv Gorkogo, Vol. 12, p. 106.

19. "Za bortom" [Overboard], Sobranie sochinenii, Vol. 2, Moscow: 1949, p. 362.

20. Maxim Gorky, Letter to Repin, Letters, Moscow: Progress, 1966, p. 32.

21. Gorky, Letter to Posse, p. 170.

22. Gorky, "Man," American Review, 3:6, 1925, pp. 650-651.

23. Wilhelm Ostwald, Grundriss der Naturphilosophie, Leipzig: Reclam, 1908.

24. Gustave Le Bon, Evolution de la matiere [Evolution of Matter], Paris: Flammarion, 1914.

25. See, for example, Sergei Utechin, "Lenin and Bogdanov" in Leopold Labedz (Ed.), Revisionism, London: G. Allen and Unwin, 1962; Alexander Vucinic, Social Thought in Tsarist Russia, Chicago: The University of Chicago Press, 1976.

26. Aleksandr Bogdanov, Empiriomonism, Vol. III, S. Petersburg: S. Dorovatovsky, 1906, pp. 146-148.

27. "O znanii" [About Knowledge], Arkhiv Gorkogo, Vol. 12, 1970, p. 108.

28. "Ispytatel'" [Experimenter], Arkhiv Gorkogo, Vol. 12, p. 34.

29. "Reply to Anisimov," Sobranie sochinenii, pp. 63-64.

30. Gustave Le Bon, Evolution.

31. Eduard von Hartmann, Philosophy of the Unconscious, Vol. III, London: Kegan Paul, 1890, p. 135.

32. "O znanii," Arkhiv Gorkogo.

33. Gorky, Fragments from My Diary, London: Penguin Books, 1972, pp. 145-148.

34. Gorky, "Tales of Italy," Moscow: Foreign Languages Publishing House, n.d., p. 294.

35. "O znanii," p. 107.

36. Gorky, On Literature, Foreign Language Publishing House, n. d., p. 22.

37. See, for example, Andrei Bely, "O teurgii" [About Theurgy], Novy Put' [The New Way], S. Petersburg, 1903, N 9.

38. See, for example, Pavel Florensky, "Obshchechelovecheskie korni idealizma," Bogoslovskii vestnik, Moscow, 1909, February-March.

39. See, for example, Young George Jr., N. Fedorov, Belmont, Mass.: Nordland, 1979.

40. Letter to Prishvin, Literaturnoe nasledstvo, Vol. 70, Moscow, p. 335.

41. Gorky, On Guard, London: M. Lawrence, 1933, p. 76.

42. See, for example, Inar Mochalov, V. Vernadsky, Moscow: Nauka, 1908; Pierre Teilhard de Chardin, The Phenomenon of Man, London: Fontana, 1959; Pierre Teilhard de Chardin, Human Energy, London: Collins, 1969.

43. "U skhimnika," Polnoe sobranie sochinenii, Vol. 2, Moscow, p. 409.

44. "Zapiski iz dnevnika" [Fragments from My Diary], Polnoe sobranie sochinenii, Vol 5, Moscow, 1977, p. 657.

45. "Iz vospominanii o I. Pavlove" [From Recollections of I. Pavlov], Sobranie sochinenii, Vol. 17, Moscow, 1952, p. 469.

46. "Van'kina literatura," Sobranie sochinenii, Vol. 23, Moscow, 1960, p. 292.

47. Cf. letter to Rumiantsev, Sobranie sochinenii, Vol. 29, Moscow, 1955, p. 259.

48. Helene Blavatsky, Isis Unveiled, Los Angeles: The Theosophy Society, 1931.

49. Blavatsky, The Key to Theosophy, Los Angeles: The Theosophy Society, 1930, p. 39.

50. Gorky, Fragments from My Diary, pp. 222-223.

51. Gorky, The Life of Matvei Kozhemyakin, Moscow: Foreign Languages Publishing House, n/d, p. 320.

52. Ibid., p. 330.

53. Gorky, Other Fires, New York: D. Appleton, 1933, pp. 245, 249, 428.

54. Adolf von Harnack, Marcion, Leipzig: Hinrichs, 1924, p. 232.

55. For example, Semen Frank, "Maxim Gorki," Hochland, Bd. XXXIII, 1936, Bd. 2, pp. 566-569.

56. Cf. Paracelsus, Selected Writings, New York: Panteon Books, 1951. See the introduction by Jolande Jacobi; George Trobridge, Swedenborg, New York: Swedenborg Foundation, 1938.

57. Cf. letter to Wolfson (1926), Arkhiv Gorkogo, Vol. 10/1, 1965, p. 28.

58. Fabre D'Olivet, Hermeneutic Interpretation of the Origin of the Social State of Man, New York: Putnam Books, 1915, pp. 31-32.

59. Eduard Schure, The Great Initiates, West Nyack, NY: St. George Books, 1961, p. 349.

60. Ibid., p. 482.

61. Cf. Raimond Sesterhehn, Das Bogostroitelstvo bei Gorky und Lunacarskij bis 1909 [The Godbuilding of Gorky and Lunacharsky in 1909], Munchen: Verlag Otto Sagner, 1982.

62. Letter to Andreev, in Letters of Gorky and Andreev, Peter Yershov (Ed.), New York: Columbia University Press, 1958, pp. 39-40.

63. Sesterhehn, Das Bogostroitelstvo, p. 307.

64. Gorky, The Confession, p. 219.

65. Ibid., p. 245.

66. Gorky, Culture and the People, New York: International Publishers, 1939, p. 20.

67. Gorky, In the World, New York: The Century Co., 1917, pp. 331-332.

68. Gorky, Magnet, London: Jonathan Cape, 1931, p. 460.

69. Dmitry Obolensky, The Bogomils, Cambridge: Cambridge University Press, 1948, pp. 4-6, 207-208.

70. Ivan Porfiriev, "Apokrificheskie skazania o vetkhozavetnykh litsakh" [Apocryphal Tales of Old Testament Figures], Sbornik otdelenia russkogo iazyka i slovesnosti imperatorskoi Akademii Nauk [Collection of Part of the Russian Language and Literature of the Imperial Academy of Sciences], Vol. XVII, n I, 1877, pp. 3, 7.

71. Ivan Aivazov, "Russkoe sektantsvo," <u>Vera i razum</u>, Kharkov, 1906, N. 17, p. 219.

72. Fedor Chaliapin, <u>An Autobiography as Told to Maxim Gorky</u>, New York: Stein and Day, 1967, pp. 37-38.

73. Gorky, <u>Childhood</u>, Moscow: Foreign Languages Publishing House, 1950, p. 195.

74. Letter to Rozanov, <u>Kontekst</u> [Context], Moscow, 1978, p. 306.

75. <u>Ibid.</u>, p. 307.

76. "O vrede filosofii" [The Danger of Philosophy], p. 61.

77. <u>Ibid.</u>, p. 56.

78. "Leto" [Summer], <u>Sobranie sochinenii</u>, Vol. 8, 1950, p. 465.

79. Gorky, <u>Best Short Stories</u>, New York: Grayson, 1947, p. 342.

80. Henrich Lenoble, <u>O M. Gorkom - khudozhnike slova</u> [About Maxim Gorky - Artist of the Word], Moscow: Sovetskii Pisatel', 1957, pp. 270-271.

81. Quoted from Iosif Yuzovskii, <u>M. Gorky i ego dramaturgiia</u> [Maxim Gorky and His Drama], Moscow: Iskusstvo, 1959, p. 14.

82. <u>Ibid.</u>

83. Gorky, <u>Magnet</u>, p. 115.

84. Gorky, <u>Bystander</u>, New York: The Literary Guild, 1930, p. 608.

85. <u>Ibid.</u>, p. 563.

86. Gorky, <u>Magnet</u>, p. 673.

87. <u>Ibid.</u>, p. 527.

88. <u>Ibid.</u>, pp. 527-528.

89. Gorky, <u>Bystander</u>, p. 571.

90. <u>Ibid.</u>, p. 568.

91. Letter to Proskuriakov, <u>Arkhiv Gorkogo</u>, Vol. 10/2, p. 441.

92. "Eshche raz ob 'Istorii molodogo cheloveka XIX stoletia'" [More of the History of the Young Man of the Nineteenth Century], Sobranie sochinenii, Vol. 26, 1953, p. 312.

93. Leonid Sabaneev, Skriabin, Moscow: Skorpion, 1916. Quoted from Alexei Losev, Problema simvola i realisticheskoe iskusstvo [The Problem of the Symbol and Realistic Art], Moscow: Iskusstvo, 1976, p. 296.

94. Losev, Problema simvola, p. 297.

95. "Publika," Sobranie sochinenii, Vol. 5, 1950, p. 305.

96. "Zapisnaia knizhka" [Notebook], Polnoe sobranie sochinenii, Moscow, Vol. 6, p. 416.

97. "Pomety Gorkogo na knigakh Rozanova [Gorky's Notes in Rozanov's Books], Kontekst, 1978, p. 309.

98. Gorky, On Literature.

99. "O zhenshchine" [About Women], Sobranie sochinenii, Vol. 27, 1953, pp. 193, 200.

100. "Otvet redaktoru frantsuzskogo zhurnala Evropa" [Response to the Editor of the French Magazine L'Europe], Sobranie sochinenii, Vol. 24, p. 403.

8

SOVIET MAN AS BELIEVER AND ATHEIST: ALEXANDER ZINOVIEV'S SPIRITUAL STRATUM

Libor Brom

This paper attempts to trace the remnants of religion in Soviet Man by examining the spiritual stratum in the work of Alexander Zinoviev, former Chairman of the Logic Department at Moscow University, an avowed dialectical materialist and self-professed *homo sovieticus*, who since his exile (1979) has produced numerous uninhibited expository and literary works that deal with Soviet reality.

EXISTENCE SUB SPECIE VANITATIS

In general, the *homines sovietici* in Zinoviev's works do not exhibit any interest in matters influenced or controlled by the "divine spirit." Deity as an invisible and life-giving inspiring power seems absent in their consciousness. Zinoviev's characters are too preoccupied with the daily struggle for survival and have no time to be concerned with any principle that might be considered a gift from God or might provide creative responses to the demands encountered in life. The personages in Zinoviev's *Svetloe budushchee* [The Radiant Future], members of the Theoretical Problems of Scientific Communism Department, have been too thoroughly screened and ideologically molded during their school years and military service to be sidetracked, either at their academic conferences or in private encounters, to reflect on the infinite and the spiritual Word of the Bible as Creator, Sustainer, Judge, Righteous Sovereign and Redeemer. The Bible, or any pantheist or deist philosophy, seems to have been totally eliminated from their consciousness and has been substituted by the allegedly scientific achievements of Marxism-Leninism. Scientific workers submit fully to the guidance provided by the Party as the one ultimate and absolute reality. Doom dominates the novel. At the end, its protagonist fails to reach his secular goals; he is denied the hope for promotion and new privileges. As a result, his wife asks for a divorce and his daughter commits suicide.

Another one of Zinoviev's semi-fictions, *Zheltyi dom* [The Yellow House], continues the depiction of the discontented, demoralized and hopeless existence of the scientific workers. There is, however, one noticeable difference: the narrator engages in thoughts about his past by recalling his optimistic student years when one dared to complain about the morbid Soviet life, how once during "voluntary" field work a peasant woman complained about the people's and her own son's indifference. She had said about him: "I do not believe any more that he is a great scholar. A real learned man would not behave like this."[1] The narrator is faced with the flaws existing in Marxism-Leninism (which he calls "Idiotology"). He is overwhelmed by the thought that life is only vanity. He searches for answers to the fundamental questions about life and death and, finding no satisfaction in his ideologized consciousness, he simply concludes that such questions are not valid. He realizes that something very grave is happening to him as he toys with the idea of ending his life. As he is preparing to terminate his life, other thoughts come to him. Why can't he take advantage of the present situation in a worthwhile way? For instance, why not run away and see the world? Why couldn't he protest the denial of human rights? Or better yet, why couldn't he break into the Mausoleum and put himself on fire on Red Square as a symbol of protest. Or why couldn't he beat up a party officer, the Secretary General himself?[2] The narrator is becoming aware of his need to fill his life with meaning.

The protagonist in another semifictional book, *Homo Sovieticus* (an exiled Soviet intellectual residing in a small West German inn), despises those who voluntarily genuflect. He has never knelt before anyone; this is just not for him - a Soviet man, a product of the revolution. He proudly acknowledges that he is forever and foremost, even in western exile, an ASS (*Agent Sovetskogo Soiuza* [an agent of the Soviet Union]) and willy nilly does his duty as an observer for the

Soviet authorities who are preparing a Great Attack on the West. Later on he is struck with the realization that most individuals live neither for the present nor for any moment in the future, but for eternity, and he asks: "What is the nature of this mania?"[3] While conversing with the Cynic (another emigre who in the Soviet Union was a great anti-religious lecturer for the Council of Knowledge and had everything, then moves to the West and dreams of a house, a couple of cars, a harem of black and yellow-skinned mistresses and of his own yacht docked in warm waters), the protagonist suddenly understands materialist dialectics as "a way of moving blindfolded in an unknown empty space filled with imaginary obstacles."[4] He is dissatisfied with the hypocrisy and the attitude that nothing is good or bad. Ultimately his vision rests upon an edifice being built nearby and yearns for a metaphysical existence:

> There is only one bright spot on the dark horizon of my life. (I am beginning to express myself really beautifully; this is symptomatic.) It is my Edifice. It is especially beautiful in the morning when the sun comes up. It becomes so radiantly joyful that I want to weep from ecstasy. It will, of course, be the Temple of a new and clean Religion. Within its portals a young and triumphant God will dwell.[5]

He follows the construction of his heavenly edifice with anxiety. The building is complete. Now I can see with my own eyes what absolute Perfection is. But what will be housed in this Enchanter's Castle, this Temple, this dwelling of God, this Space-Ship, this Palace of Beauty and Happiness?[6]

His vision ends in a nightmare when he realizes that the building outside his window is meant to be a bank. The narrator in *Homo Sovieticus* feels betrayed.

Zinoviev's lyric sight always seems alienated. In his book of poems entitled *Moi dom - moia chuzhbina* [My Home is My Foreign Land], Zinoviev laments: "I have left my home and now carry on a conversation with myself. What are my impressions of this sodomy? I have left my home and now I live here as at home. Once and for all, get it through your head, blockhead, your home is everywhere, but everywhere is a foreign land."[7]

Toward the end of this well versed book Zinoviev's pride breaks down. He openly confesses that he has lied about being a Soviet agent;

he only wanted to acquire some respect by this claim.   Like
Dostoevsky's man from the underground, he refuses to be a non-entity
and exclaims in despair: "I am not at all a worm; I'm not at all a
depraved creature. In spite of all, I am a Man, I am a God. . . . "[8]

MAN-GOD MADE ABSURD

Zinoviev's book *Idi na Golgofu* [Go to Golgotha] makes an
attempt to depict the life and work of a Soviet Man turned God. The
protagonist's name is Ivan Laptev. He resides in the Russian town of
Ensk - a sponger, drunkard, poet and preacher. The book's narrator is
also a character *sui generis*. The author describes him in the following
way:

> . . . he is sincere and openhearted in a Russian way. And, we
> Russians have lost the criteria for distinguishing between truth and
> invention. We ecstatically believe in lying and frenziedly refute
> obvious truths. And this is why my narrator's words undoubtedly
> deserve questioning.[9]

Marxism has three sources, the narrator insists; so does Ivan
Laptev's new religion called Ivanism (or Ivanianstvo, or Laptism). The
first source of Ivanism is the Russian national religion - hard drinking,
claims Laptev. Hence, Laptev is surrounded by numerous drinking
companions as Christ was by his apostles and followers. But Russian
drinking is not just alcoholism, it is a true religion, "the basis of all other
things like company, friendship, love, spiritual closeness."[10] True, this
hard drinking problem often turns into piggish behavior.   But
swinishness is a Russian national trait, asserts the narrator. "Hard
drinking without pig behavior is not hard drinking at all, but social
drinking western style."[11]

The second source of Ivanism is ideology. As Hitlerism and
Stalinism became similar to each other, even though they were bitter
enemies, so it is with Ivanism and the ideology. While Ivanism is an
enemy of ideology, it is involuntarily similar to it, "if only in that it
includes ideological problems and offers its own solutions."[12]

The third source of Ivanism is Christianity.[13] Christ's teaching
was recorded by his followers while Ivanism is recorded by Laptev

himself. Its traits are the following. 1) Ivanism gives its followers a certain worldview from which they themselves (depending on their individual circumstances and characteristics) establish the rules for their own practical behavior. 2) Ivanism is meant for those who live ordinary lives in the Soviet society, i.e., they go to work, use public transportation, stand in lines, attend meetings, take care of their families, "are submerged fully and wholly in the quagmire of life," and want to be "saints without breaking away from the sinful production."[14] 3) Ivanism in a way creates a paradise for oneself. 4) Ivanism can be studied, interpreted and followed under any circumstances because it is basically without a system. Its objective is to offer man a defense against the negative influence in Soviet society - to protect him from the anger, cruelty, indifference, cynicism and banality. It had its birth at the very depth of human society, in the "everday dirt and rubbish heap. As a matter of fact, it drapes into a poetic literary form all that people themselves have known and done without it."[15] In other words, Ivanism satisfies the basic needs of the Soviet people who have accepted the fact that man is primarily a villainous creature and that religion is the opium of mankind.

In the course of his life, Laptev gathers the missing elements lacking in the Soviet Man and becomes an expert on them: the Soul, Eternity, God. He comes to the following conclusions:

> For me there was no problem whether He exists or not. For a certain time I have lived with a passionate wish that He be. I have understood this very simple truth: if many people want Him to be, then He will come. The point is not in Him, but in us. He is us. All the rest is vanity and vanity of vanities. I tell you this as a Teacher of Truthfulness. . .[16]

Laptev claims to teach people how to live for themselves and to be attractive, healthy, intelligent, successful, young and happy. He gives private lessons and consultations. He takes this stand to balance the irreversible fact that the Soviet people exist in a Communist society without a chance to change it, nor to substitute for it, nor to run away from it. There is no Kingdom of God to wait for, because this Kingdom has arrived in the presence of the Soviet society.

There is a problem, however: how to dwell in the present "Kingdom of God" and yet survive in it as human beings. The rise of this new religion is necessary, says Laptev, because people's inclination to corrupt themselves and others is irrevocable. Laptev believes that nothing but religion can restrain this inclination. God is needed not for life beyond the grave (this life does not exist and never will), but for man's earthly existence so that he may gain dignity while living and dying. If God would exist, He would not be needed; this is the main paradox of reality, Laptev claims. And if He is needed, He will come anyway although He does not exist. As a matter of fact, Laptev says, He is already on His way, and Laptev cries out in ecstasy: "People, I am coming! I will be soon among you and within you!" Laptev then loses consciousness when he discovers that in his new religion he himself is God.[17] He gradually notices his resemblance to Christ and begins his own road to Golgotha.[18] Although God acts as a General Physician, He is not able to cure himself, says Laptev. God is in absolute solitude and helplessness. To be God means to take upon oneself the suffering of others. God must go to Golgotha.

Important for Laptev is the difference between him and Christ, so he develops his own Decalogue:

> Bow only to your God, Christ says.
> Do not bow to anyone, because you yourself are God, I say.
>
> Do not swear, He says.
> Having sworn, keep your word, I say.
>
> Do not resist the evil, He says.
> Resist, I say.
>
> Forgive others their sins, He says.
> No sin can be forgiven, I say.
>
> Do not gather treasures on this earth, gather them in heaven, He says.
> Gather your treasures in the very heaven, I say.
>
> Ask, He says.
> Don't ask, I say.
>
> In everything, do unto others as you want them to do unto you, He says.
> Do with people according to your principles and do not expect from them to do the same, i.e., that they would do according to your principles, I say.

Enter the narrow gate, He says.
Enter any gate, I say, because the person who enters is not depending on the gate.

The healthy do not need the Physician, but the sick, He says.
The healthy need the physician in the first place, I say.

He who is not with Me is against Me, He says.
Don't force anyone to follow you, I say.

Good comes from good, and bad comes from bad, He says.
The evaluation of good and bad does not depend on its causes and sources, I say.

The reward for each one will come after death, when one will understand my ideas, He says.
The reward for life is life itself, I say.

The Kingdom of God is the reward for truthfulness, He says.
A forthright life is the reward for your forthright life, I say.

God is your highest judge, this is the meaning of His ideas.
You yourself are the highest judge of your deeds, I say.

He called us to follow Him, while I say: let everyone go his own way, let our ways coincide and I will be with you. I will not ascend to heaven.
I will stay with you until the end, an unknown and pitiful preacher teaching happiness while being unhappy.[19]

Having established a successful practice teaching, preaching, advising and healing in the community of Novye Lipki, Laptev's reputation becomes known to the Party's hierarchy. Comrade Grobyko asks Laptev to tutor his son Balbes and prepare him for the diplomatic service. Laptev accepts the challenge. In Ivanism, Laptev's first task calls for Balbes' initiation into the complex science of drinking in the Russian style to the extent that he manages to stay sober and never deviates from the straight line of the Party. After two weeks of theory and practice, Balbes consumes two half-liters of vodka and six bottles of beer and then walks a straight line from one end of his study to the other. In his second task Laptev initiates Balbes into the virtue every Soviet diplomat aspires to - the skill of dealing with women.

Laptev explains that the Soviet maxim in this area, is based on the Marxist-Leninist principles which embrace the following fundamental postulates: there is no woman who cannot be corrupted, and there are no conditions under which it is impossible to copulate with a woman. After a month of ideological preparation and intensive practice with old Dus'ka (the Muse of the Soviet creative intelligentsia), which included a sexual experience in front of the monument of the Unknown Soldier as a new wreath is laid by a young wife, Balbes succeeds in corrupting the pedagogic staff of his school and the girls' senior classes.

Laptev's third task requires changing Balbes' appearance to represent the will, tenacity, decisiveness, secrecy and other qualities of a proud king who temporarily fulfills the duties of a minor officer at the Soviet Ministry of Foreign Affairs. Balbes wears glasses because they cover the soul's emptiness, raises his eyebrows because this creates an expressive frown, avoids opening his mouth in laughter to model his face after an historical figure (but not, God save us, after Napoleon, Lenin, Hitler, Stalin and the like because people would laugh). Balbes soon surpasses everyone's expectations; his idiotic, repulsive, pimpled and porous ugly face vanishes and in its place appears the physiognomy of an important personality possessing state secrets and holding the history of the world.

Laptev's fourth task involves teaching Balbes how to handle his boss (the other workers do not deserve any attention). The subordinate workers present no problem, says Laptev, but the boss must learn to fear Balbes. And Balbes must pretend that his position was obtained for him by a higher authority and that his assignment is to watch his boss or to carry out an important state task over which his superior has no control. Balbes must learn to create the impression that he is connected with the higher power. He learns quickly. In a short time the teachers themselves tremble in his presence, and his own father stands up looking like a guilty youngster when Balbes enters his office without knocking. As a fifth task, Balbes must throw away all textbooks and absorb quickly the quintessence of culture which mankind has accumulated through the centuries. To complete the education of a contemporary, talented diplomat, the following elements must be included, says Laptev: 1) anecdotes; 2) sayings of distinguished personalities, catch-words and proverbs; 3) a brief review of significant historical events and personalities, especially those which are anecdotal and entertaining; 4) a survey of cultural creations which every intellectual is expected to be familiar with (Balbes is required to master one hundred from every category). As a final task, Balbes must not only adopt the appearance of an intelligent man, but must also believe that he is more intelligent than any other mortal.

Seryi, an enterprising character, later encourages Laptev to establish a school in the capital. Laptev compares his entrance into Moscow with that of Christ into Jerusalem. He also has a staff of twelve. In his introductory classroom lecture he promises to teach the students how to "be happy in a society of poverty, banality, baseness, dirt, violence, envy, money-grubbing, boredom, anger, greyness and wretchedness."[20]   When the class ends, Seryi treats Laptev as a celebrity and invites him to a luxurious restaurant. However, Laptev is full of frustrations and asks to be left alone. His school is not destined to endure. His "apostles" are greedy and take bribes. His students cheat and take his ideas to establish their own schools and prosper. Laptev cannot hire supervisors to check on the ongoing corruption since they would act in the same corrupt way "in conformity with the general laws of the Soviet society." Moreover, party workers, scholars, physicians, philosophers and priests, all feel threatened by his claim of the human soul and plot against him. Laptev can see that they do not want the coming of God. God carries with himself burdensome duties and limitations. Eventually, the KGB closes his school. Laptev feels betrayed, as Christ was by Judas, when one of his students hands him over to the militia.

Before the court of Soviet law Laptev decides to remain silent as Christ did. He believes himself to be as innocent as Christ. Several witnesses accuse him of having accepted high fees and falsely promising improvement in their lives (by lessening their weight, removing their impotence, curing their stuttering, etc.). Toward the end of the trial, however, Laptev does address the court. He states that he is divesting himself of his Godly powers. If anyone would like to become God, he says, let it be: "It is very simple to become God: go to Golgotha! But it is very difficult to be God; one must keep returning to Golgotha!"[21] Like Christ, Laptev expects death. His is a sample trial that intimidates other self-proclaimed gods and healers that have risen around the country. He urges everyone to drop his fear of Nothingness and treat it as the partner of Being. Nothingness does not have any special dimensions; it is everywhere, limitless and eternal. It knows neither joy nor suffering. To return to Nothingness is only to return as a part to its whole.

In the resulting agony, Laptev reverses himself and turns to God: O God, take from me this moment. Actually I haven't lived yet. Let suffering be! Let depression be! Let fear be! Let disappoinment be! But not Nothingness! All I have talked about, is a lie![22]

ZINOVIEV'S RELIGION

Zinoviev lays down the groundwork for his own personal religion in *V predverii raia* [On the Threshhold of Paradise]. He justifies its rise by the fact that the Orthodox Church in the Soviet Union today collaborates with the Soviet organs of power, and it is this mighty Soviet instrument which prevents the existence of genuine religious experiences in people. Zinoviev's intellectual reasoning for his own personal religion is the cognition that the Soviet society is basically unjust; it is unjustifiably generous to some who do not deserve any generosity, and it is cruel to others who do not deserve any cruelty. Zinoviev claims that when a man realizes this fact, he has only three choices: 1) fight for his place among the privileged; 2) be indifferent and follow his personal wishes; or 3) become compassionate toward society's victims and serve them. However, only the third choice can help man experience Illumination - the birth of the Soul. He is convinced that the rise of a new religion in Soviet society is unavoidable if it is "to make the powerseekers' spectacle look ridiculous, idiotic and worthy of contempt and to perceive life with religious consciousness and behavior as beautiful and worthy of admiration."[23]

Zinoviev's religion is based upon the undeniable existence of an immortal soul which he perceives as an illumination, the realization of a higher mode of existence. Being aware of his own soul gives meaning to Zinoviev's life, something he would not give up. The existence of the soul cannot be explained to anyone who has not yet been exposed to God, claims Zinoviev, as it is also impossible to explain the perception of light to a blind man or the sound of music to a deaf man. God is the abstraction in the human soul - the ideal Soul. In Zinoviev's conception, man is given the freedom to accept or not to accept God. The thirst for God, however, remains "the primary and spontaneous state of the Soul."

If a man experiences within himself the existence of the Soul, he has been given by destiny the greatest of all imaginable gifts; everything else is dust, vanity of vanities. This extraordinary gift has led Zinoviev to formulate his own fundamental religious principles which he calls the "Rules of Self-Denial."

Regarding himself, man must be conscious of the duty he has toward his body. The body, being the servant of the Soul and not vice-versa, must necessarily be cared for so that it is free to serve the Soul, i.e., it must remain clean, fit, strong, subjected to a reasonable diet and regular exercise. Man must not struggle for material goods and social honors. If they are made available, they should be accepted and used to benefit others. Life's goal is determined by its means: if the means are noble, then the goal is noble; if man commits an infamous act to reach a noble goal, then his goal is a fraud.

Regarding one's relationship to his fellow men, man must, above all, maintain his dignity. Zinoviev says: keep your distance; be free in your behavior; be respectful and tolerant; don't commit violence and don't allow violence to touch you; resist violence; don't look down at others, even when they are unworthy and deserving contempt; help those who deserve it; dissociate yourself from evil ones (careerists, plotters, informers, gossippers, cowards, etc.); discuss things, but don't argue; explain, but don't agitate; if it is not necessary to speak, be quiet; when not asked a question, don't answer; don't draw attention to yourself; don't begin intimate relationships with anyone; don't open your soul to others; address others politely, and act as if you were both independent, equal and friendly sovereign states. In other words, develop within yourself the ability to resist pressure and preserve your own identity.

Concerning one's labor, man must be conscientious. However, avoid extracurricular duties; don't join any party, sect, society, nor any collective action; if your participation is inevitable, act as an autonomous unit; do not surrender to the crowd's mood and ideology.

Regarding the Soviet organs of power, man must be opposed to their violence. This may be, Zinoviev says, the crucial task in man's religious ascent. Man must not participate in the Soviet organs of power, nor cooperate with them in any way. Such refusal is entirely possible within the framework of Soviet law, he emphasizes. It is an uncompromising stand working for the rights of human dignity and spiritual independence from the organs of power, which gives society the assurance of freedom from subjugation into an ant-like soulless mechanism. Zinoviev encourages going beyond the Communist ideology, by obtaining a "real, honest, wide and deep education" which will give one mastery over disciplined knowledge and will open the doors to a scientific worldview.

Regarding death, man must live *sub specie mortis*. He must prepare for death by honoring life. The religious man should be aware that life is brief and that a pious life brings satisfaction. The religious man must turn to God - the ideal Soul - directly or through intermediaries, by way of penance, repentance, thanksgiving and prayer. "Tell Him," says Zinoviev, "that you are prepared to undergo difficult trials and are ready to meet death in peace. Beg for strength to do good."[24]

CONCLUSION

Alexander Zinoviev, a highly sophisticated Soviet man, admits that he is a duplex man - an atheist by his education and worldview, and a believer by his upbringing and experience. In his sociological essays and semifictional works (like *The Radiant Future* and *Zheltyi dom*), which depict the milieu of the learned men associated with the Academy of Sciences in Moscow, Zinoviev consistently probes the theoretical validity and practical viability of the Communist tenets. As a trained logician he exposes many flaws in Marxism-Leninism and is virtually overwhelmed by its spiritual emptiness. He cannot help but notice that those around him - walking cadavers doomed to a self-indulgent *carpe diem* and to a nonsensical *bellum omnium contra omnes* - lack hope and meaning in their earthly ephemeral existence and willy nilly live for eternity searching for a higher meaning in life. Ultimately, Zinoviev's protagonist in *Homo Sovieticus* cannot tolerate himself and yearns for a new and pure religion that is not compromised through its collaboration with the Soviet organs of power.

Another fictional protagonist of Zinoviev (the believing atheist Ivan Laptev in the satirical novel *Idi na Golgofu*) - like Dostoyevsky's Man from the Underground - refuses to be a nonentity, a worm, an accidental short-lived accumulation of material destined to vanish into nothingness. He proclaims himself to be God, creates his own religion (Ivanism) in a small Russian community and acquires the reputation of a spiritual teacher and miraculous healer. His teaching - a grotesque mixture of secular materialism, irrationalism, relativism and religious synthesis - promises a happy life in the unchangeable Soviet society stricken by poverty, banality, baseness, dirt, violence, envy, greed, boredom, anger, greyness and wretchedness, but is doomed to perish due to the corruption among his disciples and society as a whole. By Laptev's rise and fall, Zinoviev ridicules the Soviet secular man and shatters the Soviet scientific perspective which aspires to the development of an omnipotent Man-God.

In spite of his secular education and conditional reflexes that stem from the omnipresent Soviet ideological AIDS (Atheism, Imperialism, Dictatorship and Socialism), Zinoviev claims that the Soviet Man has a deep need for religion. While such a modern thinker as Hobbes has admitted the need for religion to maintain morality, and Voltaire regarded religion as a necessity to maintain obedience, Zinoviev claims that religion must bring protection against the abuses of state power. This protection cannot be found, says Zinoviev, in the traditional Orthodox Church which clings to its untenable ancient myths and has already compromised itself by collaborating with the Soviet regime. Zinoviev corroborates his personal stoic ideas in *V predverii raia* and bases his own religious belief upon the undeniable existence of the immortal soul, whose primary state of existence is its thirst for God.

To summarize, Zinoviev's expository and fictional works, both in prose and poetry, constitute the in-depth interior dialogue going on in a highly educated Soviet Man's atheistic/theistic inferno, where Marxist-Leninist theories and practices are successfully challenged, and religious faith remains victorious. Alexander Zinoviev, a Soviet logician par excellence, ultimately concludes that a truly religious soul will assuredly meet with God.

1. Alexander Zinoviev, <u>Zheltyi dom</u> [The Yellow House], Lausanne: L'Age d'Homme, 1980, 2:210.

2. <u>Ibid.</u>, 2:51.

3. Zinoviev, <u>Homo Sovieticus</u>, Trans. Frank Hanson, New York: The Atlantic Monthly, 1985, p. 125.

4. <u>Ibid.</u>, p. 57.

5. <u>Ibid.</u>, p. 161.

6. <u>Ibid.</u>, p. 181.

7. Zinoviev, <u>Moi dom - moia chuzhbina</u> [My Home Is My Foreign Land], Lausanne: L'Age d'Homme, 1982, p. 107.

8. <u>Ibid.</u>, p. 108.

9. Zinoviev, <u>Idi na Golgofu</u> [Go to Golgotha], Lausanne: L'Age d'Homme, 1985, p. 9.

10. <u>Ibid.</u>, p. 12.

11. <u>Ibid.</u>

12. <u>Ibid.</u>, p. 42.

13. <u>Ibid.</u>, p. 59.

14. <u>Ibid.</u>, p. 121.

15. <u>Ibid.</u>, p. 122.

16. <u>Ibid.</u>, p. 18.

17. <u>Ibid.</u>, p. 56.

18. <u>Ibid.</u>, p. 57.

19. <u>Ibid.</u>, p. 84.

20. <u>Ibid.</u>, p. 169.

21. <u>Ibid.</u>, p. 178.

22. <u>Ibid.</u>, p. 182.

23. Zinoviev, V predverii raia [On the Threshhold of Paradise], Lausanne: L'Age d'Homme, 1970, p. 353.

24. Ibid., p. 361.

9

CHRISTIAN PATTERNS IN CONTEMPORARY SOVIET PROSE

Valery Petrochenkov

Russian ethnic and cultural traditions were formed within the mainstream of Eastern Christianity. Orthodoxy in Russia was assimilated into a national form at a comparatively rapid pace. Consequently, Russian Orthodoxy not only united the nation spiritually, but also absorbed into itself and tied together diffuse elements, the totality of which determined the Russian ethos. The Russian national consciousness came into being as a Christian consciousness. Russian Orthodoxy exemplifies the symbiosis of folk culture and Christian doctrine. The christianization of Russian folklore and the folklorization of Christian hagiography proves this point. Everyday life finds its continuation in the *Saint's Life* as the *Saint's Life* finds its continuation in everyday experience.

The daily life of the Russian peasant-Christian is not only evangelically ascetic, but is also oriented toward the Gospel as a guidebook for everyday life. As the church in Russia became a spiritual and architectural center around which people were settled, every hut became a microcosm of the church. In every family the day began and ended in the prayer corner. Life began and ended in the same place. All activity was initiated with a prayer. The prayer and the proverb maintained their generic autonomy and enriched each other. The hagiographic calendar merged with the agricultural calendar. Russian Orthodoxy was rooted in the ethos and therefore maintained its vitality. In the course of time, Russian Christianity was transformed from a borrower into a lender. Centuries of the Tartar Yoke actually strengthened the ethnic and missionary aspect of Russian Orthodoxy.

These terrible centuries also brought about something else: they separated Orthodoxy from the state forever. Thus, Orthodoxy became the nucleus of the folk consciousness. Because of this, the Christian consciousness of the Russian people was not touched in its essence by the period of the Mongol Conquest, the reign of Ivan the Terrible, the Time of Troubles, the Protestantism of Peter the Great and the influence of his German descendants. And so, when describing the development of Christianity in Rus, the question of the separation of church and state is only of secondary importance. This question is important and complicated, but the answer to it does not dramatically impact upon the continuation or non-continuation of Christianity in Russia. Its viability is determined by the vitality of the folk ethos and the culture created from it.

From this point of view, 1917 did not bring anything principally new. The process of the separation of ethnic Christianity and the church was carried out by force, and the Christian ethnic unity began to fracture under the blows of the godless machine. But as in the time of the Tartar Yoke, this comparative fractioning was a source for future unity. The religious ritual was mythologized, and the day-to-day and spiritual asceticism reinforced each other. The believers, divided and suppressed from all sides, focused all their inner strength upon survival. From the spiritual point of view, believers were, to a great extent, not touched by the process of secularization. The spirituality, forcibly debased to a domestic and primitive form, was not touched in its essence and has been waiting for its moment of resurrection. The atheistic propaganda, which operates through a language no less foreign than that of the Mongolian conquerors and which lacks spiritual contact with people, operates only on the superficial shell of life and does not penetrate to a deeper level.

As a contemporary Soviet admits, "From decade to decade, from the Olympus of scientific atheism, lightning bolts struck everyone who dared to express any opinion about atheism, which to one degree or another, exceeded a few iron-clad formulas which were considered sacrosanct by the Olympians."[1]

This phenomenon can be illustrated by the scene from Andrei Platonov's short story "*Vprok*" [For a Rainy Day]. At the end of the 1920s, a local agitator arrives in a village. The goal of his visit is to convince all the peasants who have been forced to gather in the village square that God does not exist. The crowd in the square listens to the agitator in silence. Toward the end of his speech the swaggering agitator addresses the crowd with a question, the answer to which was supposed to be obvious. "Are you now convinced that God does not exist?" An old man from the crowd answered, "How can God be here while you are here. When you are gone, God will come back."

Despite the fact that it developed in the mainstream of world culture, the Russian cultural and, particularly, literary traditions, are at the same time a product of the spiritual issues shared by the Russian national consciousness. Recently, Dmitrii Likhachev reminded us that the church is supposed to be literally, but not formally, separated from the state, which means that the government should not interfere with the day-to-day life of the church and believers.[2]

Even though it might seem a paradox, Soviet Russian (and today, not only Russian) literature has been able to properly evaluate the pretensions of the borrowed and forcefully indoctrinated ideology. The tonality of this evaluation is apocalyptic. It has been done in evangelical terms, and to a great extent relies upon the visions and prophecies of Dostoevsky.

One of the first harbingers of this tradition was A. Blok's poem "The Twelve." The duality of its final stanzas has inspired many controversial interpretations. All of them focus upon the question of who is leading the procession of twelve "without a sacred banner:" Christ, who sympathizes with their disillusionments, or the anti-Christ. It is probable that the image of Christ, as everything in this poem, is dual. An antinomy is established in the narrative structure of the poem. The polyphony of the poem is multi-directional and polyvalent. The view of Christ/anti-Christ leading the procession merges the local context and the context of Christian history.

The historiosophic modality of some short stories by E. Zamyatin, written at the beginning of the twenties, particularly "Pishchera" [The Cave] and "Mamai" are very close to Blok's theme of the unleashed blizzard, the white shroud and the destruction of the spirit by frost. Zamyatin either refers to the return of man to the pre-Christian era in pre-civilized cave society (Pishchera) or equates 1917 with 1300 (the period of the Mongol Yoke) in "Mamai".

The understanding of contemporary history and the history of Russia in particular as Christian history, history which is still in motion and moving through cataclysmic occurrences, became even stronger during the years when literature was subject to political suppression. Even before disappearing from the reader's horizon for many years, Mikhail Bulgakov began his novel *The White Guards* with the words: "Great and terrible was the year of Our Lord 1918, or the Revolution the second".[3]   The stylistics of this novel, biblical and in places reminiscent of the Revelation of John, at the same time emerge from *The Primary Chronicle, Igor's Tale, The Last Testament of Vladimir Monomakh* and old Russian military tales.

From 1926 to the end of his life, Bulgakov was unable to publish anything. But during that time, the writer worked on a novel about the devil, which is known to us under the title *The Master and Margarita*. This novel, which relied on the tradition of Ernest Renan, puts the biographical life of Christ into narrative form for the first time in Russian literature. An apocryphal version of the Gospels is created within the framework of the novel. The juxtaposition of events in Jerusalem and Moscow in this gospel leads to their coexistence within a single time frame: the history of Russia is evaluated through the prism of Judea's history, and the Russian government is seen through the actions of the syndrion. But in this coexistence, one detail is seriously at odds: Jerusalem is the place of the last days of Christ's life, just as Moscow, though temporarily, is the residence of Satan and his followers. The similarity to Blok's poem is both evident and significant.

> January 4, 1899 in the Kievan newspaper Life and Art, appeared excerpts from a book by a well-known Parisian academician, France, which were published before in a Berlin magazine Die Zukunft: a guest comes to the aged Pontius Pilate; Pontius recalls events from the past; "Can you recall Jesus of Nazareth, whom you crucified?" "Well I can't," answered Pontius.[4]

Both Bulgakov and the master force him to recall the incident, to remember and never again forget. And according to the law of Bulgakov's novel, and according to the law of the eternally creating and unconditionally reciprocal history of Christianity, those in Moscow are doomed to recall and never forget about the new crucifixion of Christ. It might be that the Church of Christ the Savior which was blown up in 1932 finally convinced Bulgakov that his parallel was valid.

While Bulgakov still continued to work on and rework the final version of his novel, his contemporary Boris Pasternak already had begun creating his future novel, *Doctor Zhivago*, and published excerpts which he later reworked and included in the final corpus of the novel. Although the main concepts of the two novels were different, they shared a similar historiosophic idea of coexistence with the eternity of Christ and participation in the creation of Christian history, when "a single human life becomes inseparable from God, and partakes of eternity."[5]

The protagonist of each novel is an artist, a craftsman whose creative intention focuses upon the Gospel story, and each of whom creates a new apocryphal text within the novel. It is a mistake to isolate the Christian poems of Iurii Zhivago from the nature and love lyrics. In "The Secret Stream of Suffering," compassion for the passion of Christ is the symbol and embodiment of one of the key ideas of the novel, that only with the appearance of Christ does a genuine human being come into existence. This idea imbues the cycle with its total unity.

Certainly, one should take into account that both Bulgakov and Pasternak assimilated Christian symbolism into their prose in an underground fashion. However, this assimilation was built upon the foundation of Russian literature, Russian culture, and the Russian national tradition. Proof of this may be seen in the abundance of critical work concerned with both novels. Much has been said about the motifs and reminiscences of Dostoevsky in Bulgakov's novel, and references to Tolstoy, Solov'ev and Berdiaev in Pasternak's work. Recently work was published which demonstrates that some of Chekhov's short stories, particularly "Student" and "Arkhierei" influenced Pasternak's central idea in the novel.[6]

The christological tradition in Soviet literature appeared again only in the mid-1960s with the emergence of village prose, at first in an indirect fashion and later in broader scope. On the one hand, this was the result of the avalanche of influence from Bulgakov's novel, and to a lesser extent from Pasternak's novel, which was as yet unpublished. On the other hand, the reappearance of the christological tradition was due to a resurgence of the suppressed national consciousness and fear that the distortion of Russian culture was becoming irreversible. In our time these phenomena have enriched each other and have embraced something new: concern with the global consequences of nuclear and ecological catastrophes and with mutuality in the fateful problems that face mankind.

One should bear in mind the fact that many of the works written in the course of the sixties and seventies, which reflect the mood of that time, have only recently been published. Also, not everything, and possibly not the best work has been printed. However, published works, such as novels by Bulgakov and Pasternak have easily become a part of our time; their themes and stylistic devices are a wellspring for the ongoing process of literary creation.

Three trends can be identified in the mainstream of Soviet literature during the past quarter century. Each has assimilated the nostalgic mood and has attempted to reevaluate the present in this light.

The first and less generative trend is the historical novel about the formation of the Russian state across the centuries. Among these works are many which pretend to represent history and modernize one or another event or character in accordance with contemporary ideals and the intellectual fashion. However, in this mainstream, works can be seen which demonstrate a careful study of history, chronicles and saints' lives. These attempts to describe the past and bring historical characters to life without modernization, utilize methods of painstaking restoration and stylization of the language and reconstruction of the *zeitgeist* with an almost holy reverence for original sources. Among these, the most significant are the works of Balashov.

The second concentrates upon the search in our time for elements of national customs which have not been fragmented and features of national character which have not been lost. The mainstream of village and thematically similar prose belong to this trend. In these works the retrospective approach is a medium for the discovery in our time of customs, features of character and world view which can reconnect the lost links in the chain of tradition and at the same time show the absolute value of ideals which have nourished this heritage. The works of this type are maximally generative. Their sources grow out of the national tradition itself and are not spiritually bound only to our time. The stylistics of the best work in this movement have their roots in folklore, chronicles and saints' lives. At the same time it is a stylistics which bears traces of nineteenth century

Russian literature, Russian modernism of the twenties and many features of the best works of world literature. For example, in Rasputin's prose, one can easily trace the narrative technique of Faulkner and Marquez, but these influences in no way do harm to the power of his undeniably Russian style.

Even more interesting is the fact that in the works of this movement, the protagonists share particular features of the national character. These include asceticism, an inclination to poverty, meekness, love of work, compassion and readiness for confession and self-sacrifice. The saint's life, prayer and sermon can be seen in the framework of the short story and novella.

This trend is exemplified by A. Solzhenitsyn's "Matriona's Household", the works of V. Soloukhin, A. Jashin, V. Shukshin, F. Abramov, particularly his short story, "From the Family Tree of Avvakum", V. Likhonosov, V. Belov, V. Astaf'ev, B. Mozhaev, B. Shergin, V. Rasputin and others.

Within this trend one can name non-fictional works such as journalism and philosophical essays, the best of which may be Belov's *Lady and Sketches of Folk Aesthetics*. In this book, for the first time since the appearance of S. Maksimov's sketches, is a successful attempt to not only describe the northern Russian peasants' lives, but also to analyze their spiritual essence in terms of Christian ethics.

The third trend grows out of the second. At first it was represented by only a handful of works, possibly due to censorship. This movement shares thematics with village prose, enlarges its philosophical range by direct address of the protagonist and narrators to sacred texts through the introduction of theological dialogues and by the inclusion of contemporary events within Christian imagery.

The best examples of this group include the short stories by V. Shukshin, "The Thirst to Live" and Soloukhin's "The Icy Peaks of Mankind".

Soloukhin's short story, like another of his stories, "The Funeral of Stepanida Ivanovna", written in the late 1960s but only recently published, is written in the first person and closely resembles a journalistic sketch. But the structure is like a sermon; a thesis is presented to the readers, then a life story from the experience of the preacher is recounted. In conclusion, the preacher who has already led the readers to the answer, gives them an answer which is already self-evident. By this method, the narrator and the reader become allies in the argument and participants in it. The moral lesson is addressed to both.

The beginning of the story informs the reader of a book which foretells the coming victory of computer civilization in which there will be no unsolved questions and where all difficulties and shortcomings of contemporary society will be remedied. The style of this introduction is imitative of the pseudo-scientific language of popular scientific literature. The narrator tires of reading this book, and decides to take a walk in a nearby forest. On his way, as he ponders over what he has just read, he approaches a very old woman lamenting while she hobbles on with difficulty. The lament of the old woman is accompanied by weeping and "howls which tear the soul apart." This encounter inspires the narrator to recount an incident which was recently related to him. One of the village inhabitants, the son of this old woman, committed suicide by throwing himself under a train. Another villager whom he had offended while drunk refused to forgive him even though the man had begged. The old woman's son could not live any longer without forgiveness because he considered that his reputation as a good man had been destroyed.

The middle part of the short story consists of the lament and prayer of the old woman. The triptych composition of this lament develops, grows to tragic dimensions, and comes to a cathartic climax with the mother's tears. At first, the mother appeals to her dead son as if speaking to one living: "With whom are you angry, my dear one? Aren't you sorry to leave the world? Look at the world around you." This part of the lament is metrically organized as a series of repeating concepts: white, godly, light world on one side and offense, eclipse, blindness on the other. Having gone full circle, the mother directly addresses the Savior: "Lord, forgive his idiocy. . . . He didn't plan to leave the world." The stories about the everyday, domestic work of her son in the central part of the lament alternate with direct address to God, pleading with him to find a place there for her son "even on the edge." The third part of the lament is an address to the Theotokos: "Mother, our defender, tell me where I should go, to whom I should appeal? Who, if not you, knows what it means to bury your only son?"

As the climax is reached and the mother's prayer concluded, she acquires inner peace and repeats, "Glory to Thee, O God, glory to Thee."

The narrator is confused by the mother's tranquility.   If everything in the world has happened in accordance with God's will as this old woman thinks, the premature death of her son, a good person, is also a manifestation of this will. She should rebel, "shaking her fist above her head," but instead, she finds peace and reestablishes the harmony and unity of her being in God. She overcomes her suffering to such an extent that through prayer she finds peace with the world around her and accepts the fact that human beings are unable to overcome their limitations. The physical incapacitation of the old woman contrasts with her spiritual strength. The source of this strength is accessible to everyone, external to the conditions of everyday life and at the same time universal. "Does this mean," asks the narrator, "that in the place where nuclear physics, neuro-surgery and cybernetics are powerless, her blind, dark belief seems to be the most powerful?"[7]

This contemporary sermon is an example of an unusual new generic form which combines the sketch, short story and lament. Their stylistic and lexical features are very close to the established canon, but their combination produces a powerful new narrative. The apparent equality of the opposition, technological process versus religious belief, collapses. The icy peaks of the future to which progress is leading, are ultimately the pseudo-future because the technical future exists there only as a space and time category, but not as a category of consciousness. The future in terms of the spirit is at the same time past and present; it is out of time, spaceless and eternal.

Shukshin's short story, "The Thirst to Live", is truly unique in its artistic depth. Written in 1966, it was published during the author's life only with cuts. The plot of this story, based upon local events, is only the outer shell of a parable, shaped in the language and culture of its creator.   Only the evangelical motifs of Peter Breughel's winter paintings achieve a comparable harmony between the unifying idea and every detail. This idea is universal and congenetic with every moment in Christian history.

Among the possible ways to view this story, its analysis as a non-canonic form of theological debate may be both justifiable and very productive. Such an understanding permits one to describe the dialogical relationship between story content and Christian ethics in a similar way to the Sermon on the Mount and in works of Russian literature in which similar problems are stated, particularly in Dostoevsky's novel, *The Brothers Karamazov* and Bulgakov's *The Master and Margarita*.

The plot of the story revolves around a young criminal who is running from a concentration camp and finds sanctuary with an old hunter. The stage of the story is set in the winter taiga and in a hunter's hut. All day long, the two characters talk of their lives and touch upon subjects they have never before discussed with another person. After midnight, someone knocks at the door, and two more hunters enter the hut. One of them is the local police chief. The young man pretends to be asleep, and the policeman decides to reveal his identity only in the morning. In the middle of the night, the young man runs away, taking the hunter's rifle with him. The old man awakens at dawn while everyone else is asleep, takes a rifle from one of the newcomers and chases after the fugitive. For him, the experienced hunter, who knows the taiga very well, it is quite easy to catch the young man and disarm him. But after a short conversation, the old man pities the young man, returns the rifle and releases him. The young man kills the old hunter by shooting him in the back, but he has almost no chance to run away because those who stayed in the hut are already in pursuit.

From the start, both protagonists conduct themselves differently than their life's experience would dictate. The experienced old hunter, who normally cannot be fooled, loses his ability to discern truth from falsehood. He voluntarily ignores his native shrewdness and permits himself to be charmed by the young man. The fugitive, who hates everyone and everything in the world, is in his turn, more open and talkative than he ought to be. Whatever the criminal may say and however the hunter may argue with him, the dialogue develops against the backdrop of admiration of the old for the young. One witnesses a scene of temptation, in which the old man does whatever possible to bind himself to the point where he will be unable to turn back. But at the same time, the young man seems to be honestly glad that he may open his heart to another.

As soon as the dialogue begins, the voice of the narrator is dimmed, and all narration is conducted by the consciousness of the hunter. In this way, the reader is given a chance to witness how step by step the old man concretizes the image of the youth, in which iconic features of Jesus Christ may be identified. The old man, who in the sunset of his years still suffers from the guilt he feels because of sins committed in his youth (he seduced a young girl from an Old Believer's family), at times can see traits of the son he might have sired in the young man. While something draws the youth toward openness, the old man is drawn to make a confession, perhaps the last in his life. Might he not see the youth in this light so that he may entrust his confession to him?

There are certain key words which are encountered in the story. They are freedom (free will), life, thirst and fate. These key words frequently appear in the protagonist's and narrator's speech as conceptions and as a part of proverbs and folk sayings and create an ornamental style which is deeply rooted in Russian folklore. This feature of the text is interwoven with the evangelical text in the recollections of the old man and arguments with the Gospel by the young man/anti-Christ.

In this respect the most interesting argument between the two men concerns Christ. It develops as if reminiscent of the dialogue between Pilate and Yeshua in Bulgakov's *Master and Margarita*: "'So, Mark the Rat Killer, who is a cold and committed assassin, and the people, who, as I see it,' the procurator pointed at Yeshua's mutilated face, 'beat you because of your sermons, the thieves Dismas and Gestas, who killed four soldiers with the help of their gang, and finally the dirty traitor Judas, are all of them good people?' 'Yes,' answered the prisoner."[8]

In Shukshin's story, the old man tells the criminal, "If you kill, God will punish you, not the people. You can hide from people, but not from God." But the young man replies with such passion, as if what he is saying is close to his heart and well thought-out: "If I were to meet this your Christ anywhere, I would immediately stick him in the guts." "Why," asked the old man. "Why? Because he told fairy tales, lied. There are no good people."[9]

The young man continues to furiously blaspheme, even accusing the old man of hypocrisy because the hunter breaks a commandment when he kills animals. But while the argument continues, the old man falls more and more under the spell of "the man crushed by life, with such an attractive, such a heavenly face." The consciousness of the young man is also contradictory and ambiguous. He hates the world, seemingly, because of its inconstancy and because Christ's commandments are not incarnated in it. "I would think up a new Christ now," he screams, "one who would teach us to punch in the nose. You lie? You get it!. . . . Everybody lies! Everything smells like a morgue! We all pity clean, washed corpses; we like them, but try to like those dirty people who are still alive. There are no saints on the earth."[10]

In Shukshin's short story the many themes which were developed in the literature of the following two decades were crystallized. The loss of national roots, the generation gap, the loneliness of humankind in the world, moral degradation, the disintegration of the family, the betrayal of God and man are themes that more and more often can be seen beyond the confines of village prose. For example, in Bondarev's novel *Game*, the protagonist who has already stood on the edge of irreversible tragedy is brought by the narrator into a church before an icon of the Theotokos. Vasilii Bykov, from book to book, creates characters who are inclined to repentance and who seek spiritual freedom.

The christological notion in Soviet literature can be focused upon three basic themes tightly connected with the ideological crisis and attempts to overcome it. These themes may be formulated as liberation from God (*bogopreodolenie*), the search for God (*bogoiskatel'stvo*) and God's presence in life (*bogoprisutstvie*).

Three works published in 1986-87 in the magazine *Novyi Mir* represent the development of christological themes in contemporary Soviet literature in the most clearly focused way and embrace the whole spectrum of issues concerning the existence of the national ethos. These are *The Executioner's Block* by Aitmatov, *The Assassination of Mirages* by Tendriakov and *The Humble Cemetery* by Kaledin. Each work is an evident illustration of one of the issues raised although it is not limited by them. All these works share one extremely important characteristic in relation to Christian themes: their innovations are based on tradition, and they call to mind and interact with literature which has already been embraced by the culture. This interaction is generative.

Tendriakov dealt with one theme during his entire life: how can a religious consciousness rule an individual despite the seemingly invincible logic of atheism, the advances in scientific technology and changes in the conditions of human existence and the norms of social life? In defense of the author, one must admit that he did not rely on simplified conclusions drawn from Marxist doctrine. He studied the history of religion, and particularly Christianity, for years. He knew Russian village life and was familiar with the beliefs of the peasants from childhood. He cannot be faulted for his knowledge of Russian church history nor the rituals of Russian Orthodoxy. And, most importantly, he was a talented writer and relied no less on the rules of art than he did on his knowledge of the subject matter. It would seem that the atheistic propaganda would have been advanced on the banner of such a writer. But in reality, each of his works barely managed to pass by the censors. He named his last novel which preceded his death, *The Gospel According to the Computer*. It was rejected by the publishers in his lifetime and was published only in 1987 under a different title in *Novyi Mir*.

If one follows the evolution of the author's analysis of religious themes, one may see that the superficial theomachy, the undisguised aggressiveness of the author's position, gradually gives way to an attempt to understand the events and to overcome the difficulties from within the consciousness of the hero, and the author's voice is replaced by those of the heroes. And so, the atheistic and religious consciousnesses are not put into opposition; rather the former tries to converge with the latter and, without coercion, direct it into a new channel. In this way, theomachy is transformed into a complicated analytical system of liberation from God, and as a result, circumstances and situations which previously were seen as simplistic, become complex. This transformation also affects the hero.

In the novella *The Miraculous Icon* (1958), a village boy, Rod'ka, finds a lost, miracle-performing icon. The boy becomes a victim of the religious ecstasy of his family and the villagers. He believes, then does not believe, becomes ashamed of his faith in front of his school friends, then is ashamed of his weakness and sinfulness. The struggle goes on with the soul of the boy and between his family and the school. The boy, who tries to commit suicide by jumping into a river, is rescued, and a school teacher prepares to press charges against the boy's family. The novella ends with a conversation between the teacher and a priest who asks her to settle the matter without the interference of the government. However, the teacher is inflexible.

In the novella everything is rather simple: there are two opposing forces - blind faith and all-seeing atheism. Between them is a weak, inexperienced child's soul. The authorities are in possession of all means necessary to enforce their decision, so their flowery words about humanity are pure hypocrisy. The author's position is clear; the self-consciousness and world view of the protagonist is unformed and not to be taken into account. The propagandistic lining of the work is visible.

In the novella *Extraordinary* (1961), the situation is already more complicated. Once again there is a school, a believing child and a teacher. But this time the teacher is liberal, a democrat, and he defends the awakening self-consciousness of the school children. What is more, he succeeds in defending the believing girl from the extreme actions of her atheist father, and he defends a teacher of mathematics who is a quiet, deeply religious person. This person cannot be called either immature or fanatic. He has acquired his faith through suffering, and now he is at peace with the world; he is tolerant and compasssionate. Such a hero cannot be approached with proofs based upon popular accounts of the theory of evolution. Such a hero demands conversation in his own language, in this case, in the language of mathematics and theology.

In the novella, *The Apostle's Mission*, the author comes very close to using such language. The novella's hero is a physicist who is working for a popular scientific magazine. He is young but already established, married and passionately in love with his wife. But the more he thinks about the problems of eternity, the more he compares the absolute with his surroundings, and the more he thirsts for a different life and God. The whole novella is organized as a sort of diary of the protagonist's flight from home to a small village where there is an acting church.

The novella *The Apostle's Mission* is a brave and unusual attempt, for Soviet literature, to openly discuss religious problems. But despite this, the novella is artistically weak, and its points of view are not justified. The author's goal is to show how intellectual dissatisfaction of the protagonist with his surroundings pushes him toward religion and also how this religion, represented by old village women and a young poorly-educated priest, pushes him back to atheism. This new atheism, according to the author's idea, is modern and scientific because it acknowledges the existence of some sort of absolute divine power which has nothing to do with Christianity, nor with Russian Orthodoxy in particular. It is impossible to draw any conclusion about the protagonist's scientific and religious viewpoint from his endless confessions, permeated by the narrator's pseudo-scientific remarks. The description of liberation from God is shown in terms of destabilized false pride which is directed not from the self toward other people and God, but purely toward its own dissatisfaction within itself. The novella resembles a collage put together from details which lack ultimate unity. The main protagonist is unusual, but his character is not developed. The secondary characters, local atheists as well as the believers, are colorless. The psychological analysis of their character is shallow. In addition, the novella is very didactic and pseudo-philosophical. As in most novels of socialist realism, the ideological skeleton can be seen through the narrative structure. Nevertheless, Tendriakov's attempt to create a new type of non-militant atheistic consciousness, which mistakenly attributes religious qualities to any spiritual phenomena, is interesting and unusual. *The Gospel According to the Computer* is the next but a qualitatively different step toward developing the same type of consciousness.

The Assassination of Mirages, the editorial title of Tendriakov's novel, switches its intrigue from the historical perspective into the imaginative. But there is another dimension given to the novel by its new title. The imaginative perspective turns out to be so appealing, and history becomes so dependent upon this mirage that in order to understand the history, one enters into the mirage as if it were super-reality. And now, as soon as the word "mirage" is replaced by the word "Christianity," the complicated task of the novelist is revealed: to try to rationally analyze the phenomena which by their nature are opposed to the rational, or as they say, to test the harmony by means of algebra.

In particular, this is a task for the protagonist of the novel, a well-known physicist intrigued with the development of social thought. He takes it upon himself to reconstruct the historical evolution of mankind since the birth of Christ. Some historical data are put into the computer and the results are compared to the text of the Gospels and historically verifiable events in the history of Christianity. A group of young, well-educated scientists and pragmatists assists him, discusses results and proposes its own hypotheses. The leader does not inform his assistants about his new discoveries in advance, so that they may prove or disprove them by impartial methodology. The novel develops on three levels. One of these is a further development of the Renan/Bulgakov tradition, consisting of several legends related to the life of Christ, the Apostle Paul, Rome of Nero's time and the last days of Thomas Campanella. The second is a christological analysis and thought related to the data obtained from the computer. The third level is the personal life of the physicist. The fact that events of the first legendary level are narrated in the historical present, facilitates a certain unity with events of the novel's present. The legends incorporated in the novel are examples of good historical prose, but their significance in understanding the novel's central idea is much broader. The events and thoughts given in retrospect help to enlighten the christological hypothesis of the scholar and the outcome of the experiment.

Both the protagonist and the narrator follow the philosophy of dialectical materialism. For them, it is most important to understand how the social system works and how it acquires its determination. In accordance with this point of view, the opposition, Jesus Christ vs. the Apostle Paul, is unveiled in the novel. In the first proposed legend, Jesus Christ is stoned to death nearly at the beginning of his messianic path. His teachings are continued on a new ground by the Apostle Paul who "makes a very important discovery: that social mores depend not on the will of the individuals, but upon the societal structures within which they live. He is a dialectician who lived 2000 years ago."[11] The dialectic juxtaposition of the evangelical words of Christ with the text from Paul's epistles leads to the development of a biography and the evolution of Paul's ideology in the novel. The materialistic reconstruction of the historical and philosophical background appears to prove the logical necessity for the replacement of Christ by Paul. However, the narrator does not limit himself by the researcher's curiosity. He is still not a scholar of Christianity as a religion, but he already is a student of the history of Christianity for whom the search for truth is much more important than his own pre-determination. And when the computer resurrects Christ after the injunction in the program which forbids the repetition of data related to Christ is mistakenly erased, the protagonist is able to find an explanation for this phenomenon in his system of social development. "As Paul was necessary for the mission of Christ, so Christ was necessary for Paul's mission. Without each other, both of them would only turn out to be transient as are so many others in history who have been nearly forgotten. "The computer was programmed for the development of Christianity, but this movement could not be saved by Paul alone. Because of this, Christ whom we killed, must be resurrected again."

"No, this is not mysticism. Death is overcome by death. Evolution insisted on that."[12]

The historiosophic model of the author, the foundation of which is the idea that people are only participants "in the all-embracing human process" but not its creators, not only comes to terms with historical Christianity, but also recognizes it as the ideological ferment of modern culture. However, this model still remains atheistic in its essence. None of the scientists who are protagonists in the novel are influenced by the spiritual content of the sacred texts even though during the experiment they become experts on Christianity. Only in the scenes where the main protagonist visits his former commander, does a conversation about directed evolution and the divine nature of existence take place. As he approaches the end of his life, the old commander is unable to see the embodiment of his ideals and cannot find inner peace. Again, as in the previous novel, *The Apostle's Mission*, the young inexperienced priest arrives to hear the old man's confession. Finally, the commander chases the priest away, screaming "Come to teach? . . . . By what right? . . . . You see more? Experience more? . . . . What do you know about life, young pup?"[13]

Tendriakov's novel is symptomatic of contemporary phenomena. It indicates that atheism in its present form is undergoing a crisis, and the opposition of religion and atheism is no longer valid in the epoch of technocratic, computerized consciousness.

Contemporary poetry is full of motifs which in one way or another call for the need to search for God. The same tendency can be seen in the new novel of Chingiz Aitmatov, *The Executioner's Block*. It is interesting that this motif is found in the work of a Kirghiz writer, the author of many novels that are pantheistic in their approach and tightly connected with Kirghiz folklore. Even though Aitmatov writes in

Russian, his ethnic folklore and, to a certain extent, Moslem tradition are always present in his work, and the protagonists are usually Kirghiz natives.   But in *The Executioner's Block*, Aitmatov has chosen a protagonist who is unusual for both his work and Soviet literature. This hero typologically resembles Dostoevsky's Alesha Karamazov,[14] but at the same time, his character manifests features which are typical for hagiographic literature. But this is not an adaptation of typological features of the saint's life genre, rather an investigation into ascetic tendencies in contemporary history which is perceived as the history of Christianity.

There is already a great deal of critical literature on Aitmatov's novel.[15] Many critics agree that *The Executioner's Block* is an unusual and significant novel but are disturbed by its christological motifs and cannot recognize the social phenomena that stand behind the development of the main character. From their point of view, the scenes with Pilate and Christ paradoxically resemble those of Bulgakov's novel. They consider that the triptych composition of the novel is accidental and that the second christological part is weak and disconnected from the rest of the novel. Only Gachev's article breaks with the critical mainstream.

The Executioner's Block is a triptych on the theme of Christ's passion, which is experienced as Holy Week every Lent throughout the history of Christianity, i.e., literally as coexistence with Christ. And the fact that this redeeming coexistence embraces all creatures great and small is not a contradiction and not a weakness of the novel's composition, but evidence of an innovative artistic approach which leads to eschatological insight.

The novel begins slowly and peacefully. Nature is described as if in total harmony. The she-wolf Akbara senses the first movements of life within her womb. These moments of the novel are a lead-in to the tragic events that will take place in all parts of the novel. The first semantic and stylistic device which will be repeated with variations throughout the work is introduced. It binds together the pair of wolves, Tashchainar and Akbara with the people who bring both life and death.

Immediately after this overture, at the moment when a harmonious unity is achieved, the apocalypse begins. Helicopters chase flocks of wild antelope to certain points where they are met by a wall of fire from armored cars. Even the wolves are running among those crazed antelope, no longer as hunters, but as victims. The first litter of Akbara's children are trampled to death by the stampeding herd.

The irreversible catastrophe which takes place in the Mojukum Savannah is only the first sign of the global avalanche in which nations, countries and cultures may be buried. The time and space coordinates in the narration of the scene where the antelope are butchered are extended beyond their limits. The typographical space assumes a global significance. The comparatively short time of the slaughter becomes absolute, as in a parable. But time and space are limited by historical memory, by the presence of man and by his ability to do good and evil, to repent and be redeemed.

The tragedy in the Mojukums Savannah results from the actions of men whose understanding of the environment and therefore of themselves, is expressed with cannibalistic innocence in the famous words of the selectionist Michurin: "We cannot wait for mercy from nature; our task is to seize it." And if man will not stop, and if he will not take his sins upon himself, who will stop him, and who will repair what he has done?

And such a redeemer appears, a child of his time, who strives to follow in the steps of his teacher Christ in a militant, atheistic environment.

Avdii Kallistratov is the son of a deacon who was expelled from the seminary for heresy and who is presently a free-lance journalist writing for a young people's newspaper. In disguise he takes a trip to a desert to collect marijuana with a gang of young drug addicts. His task is to write a series of sketches on these drug users and pushers in order to warn young people away from the dangers of drugs. However, he is a missionary by nature, and the power of God's words, as he understands them, is unlimited. Thus, he preaches to these criminals and drug addicts. He begs them to look around themselves and think about the consequences of their actions before it is too late. They almost beat him to death and push him out of a railroad car travelling at full speed. He survives, but later on, using the words of God, he tries to adjure some drunken bums not to kill the antelopes. The bums ask him to leave them alone, then laugh at him, beat him up, tie him up with rope and throw him onto the truck on the still warm corpses of antelope. Later the same bums humiliate him, force him to ask for forgiveness, and when he refuses, they crucify him on a tree.

Avdii is searching for God even though his God has already been found, and his belief from childhood is rooted in Russian Orthodoxy. His search for God, which puts him between the church and the state, is of a specific variety. Avdii is a missionary and a preacher by nature. He does not want to submit to the conditions under which the Russian church exists in the atheistic state. Besides this, he is a child of his time in that he wants to interpret evangelic words in a way which can be understood by his contemporaries. He thinks that he has the right to do so.

This right is justified not only by the preaching activities of Avdii, but also by his facility to partake in the history of Christianity, not to reincarnate but to incarnate. Avdii lives in the history of Christianity which is still taking shape, and he is actively involved in its creation. His ego has value only when it takes part in this creative process. In this regard, one may look at one of the best scenes in the novel when Avdii visits the Pushkin Museum in Moscow before his departure for the desert. There he attends a concert of Bulgarian vocalists performing medieval church hymns.

> These ten young men united in God perform in order to help us look into the depths of our unconscious, resurrect the past in ourselves and the spirit and sufferings of generations already passed so that later we may rise above ourselves, above the world and find the beauty and meaning of our being: once we enter into life, we adore its miraculous manifestation.[16]

The evangelical parts of the novel are preceded by the ponderings of Avdii who has just been thrown out of the railroad car. He realizes that if he had asked for forgiveness, if he would retreat from his position, everything might be different. Avdii recalls the event which took place 1950 years ago and that it had also occurred on a Friday. And after that, the narration leads the reader to Jerusalem.

The historical-theological and historical-philosophical angle of the novel, as well as a comparison with Bulgakov's text, will not be dealt with here. But in order to understand the character of the main protagonist, one should note that the narration in the Jerusalem part of the novel can be linked with the hero's consciousness. The Jerusalem scenes are modernized and adapted by Avdii's consciousness. This consciousness, which overcomes its own death and humiliation, is at the same time thankful for and triumphant in its spiritual victory. And at this juncture, Avdii has a vision that he is running on the streets of Jerusalem, hoping to warn and save his teacher Christ. Avdii not only lives there in Jerusalem, and not only at that time, but also here in the desert, also in Russia, where he was born and where he lives. He is torn between despair and hope. One moment, it seems to him that it is already too late, and the next moment he suddenly "began knocking at the windows, all the windows which were on his way: 'People, arise, we are in trouble! Let's save the Teacher while there is time! I will lead him to Russia. In our river Oka there is a sacred island. . .'"[17] At the same time, Avdii calls out to the people in Jerusalem as well as to his own contemporaries.

Both liberation from God and the search for God as reflected in contemporary Soviet literature tap energy from a rejection of the established church; in the first case, there is full rejection and in the second, dissatisfaction.

The third theme, God's presence in life (*bogoprisutstvie*), deals with a type of consciousness which does not glorify or deny God, but dissolves itself in His Being as if the question of belief or non-belief did not exist. This consciousness manifests itself as if it were pre-Christian or non-Christian and is only revealed as Christian at critical moments in life. This type of consciousness is not a novelty for contemporary literature. It is often attributed to Russian peasants in short stories and novels of village prose writers. As a rule, it belongs to people with stable moral principles who exist in an easily recognizable environment, familiar to everyone. But from the pages of Sergei Kaledin's novella *The Humble Cemetery*, an entirely different consciousness emerges.

The protagonists of this novella are grave-diggers in an old Moscow cemetery. They are people with dark pasts, drunkards, former criminals and bums. The micro-world of the cemetery has very little in common with the world that surrounds it. The cemetery lives according to its own laws which are in total opposition to official law. The funeral business is profitable, but this profit is often milked from mourners. The humble cemetery lives according to the laws of a mafia; any break with these rules is punishable by beating, maiming or death.

The existence of this pit is guaranteed by the nature of life and death. The personality of the workers is not of primary importance. Someone may be sent to prison; someone might become a drunkard; someone is chased away; but others come to replace them, and the cemetery environment quickly reshapes these people according to its own rules.

The heroes of this novella are unusual for literature and particularly for literature of our time. There is no contrasting background or contrasting characters as found in Astaf'ev's novella *The Sad Detective*.[18] Some of Astaf'ev's heroes are bums who have lost their human face. They are cut off from society, and their spirituality is entirely atrophied.

In spite of their way of life, some of Kaledin's protagonists are somehow influenced by the sacral nature of their profession by association with the cemetery church and the priests. The Russian burial tradition is subconsciously incorporated in their souls. They think not only about the profit, but also about the necessity to be merciful and understand the fleeting nature of existence and the need for mankind to submit itself to the divine power.

The central character of the novella is Aleksei (Leshka) Vorob'ev with the nickname Sparrow (*Vorobei*). He had an alcoholic father who under pressure from his new wife was forced to send his son to a camp for difficult children. She hated the boy so much that while he was in the camp, she sent him jam with pieces of glass in it. After the camp, Leshka's life was not easy. He worked hard, drank heavily, often beat others up and was himself beaten, but now in his thirtieth year, he is an invalid with an ax wound in his skull, half-deaf, weak-sighted, embittered and suffering from seizures. But even after all that, he is still a very strong man and the best grave digger.

Even being what he is, he feels that he is limited in his egocentric whims, not by earthly power and is inclined toward mercy, self-denial and love not by earthly power, but by something else. His admiration for his mother, who was beaten to death by his father, introduces Leshka's religious sentiment. This sentiment is inseparable from his character in its good and bad moments.

> And because of this Leshka's words about God are not empty even though his religious sentiment is quite primitive. And therefore, no matter how one relates to Leshka's half-faith or half-disbelief, no

matter how one analyzes its social genesis, Leshka's inner world is undeniably centered around his religious sentiment.[19]

Kaledin's hero does not appeal for love, sympathy or understanding; he is not interested in the world beyond his closed circle. But this world, even without knowing him, has rejected him. For this world he is a bum, a thief who profits from people's grief. The only connection between the world of the humble cemetery and the outside world is the church. And the church, represented by the cemetery priests, unconditionally embraces him, accepts him as he is, and he in his turn, although sub-consciously, comes into the church and accepts the blessing of the priest.

And if more people from the world outside would come to the church and meet people such as Leshka there, the strife torturing the nation would be lessened, and the mutilated consciousness would be healed.

1. Andrei Nuikin, "The New Search for God and Old Dogmas," in Novyi Mir, 4, 1987, p. 255.

2. Dmitrii Likhachev, "From Repentance to Action," Literaturnaia Gazeta, September 9, 1987, p. 2.

3. Mikhail Bulgakov, The White Guards, New York: McGraw-Hill, 1971, p. 9.

4. Marietta Chudakova, "The Life of Mikhail Bulgakov," in Moscow, 6, 1987, p. 8.

5. Boris Pasternak, Doctor Zhivago, Milan: Feltrinelli Editore, 1957, p. 423.

6. N. Vil'mont, "Boris Pasternak," Novyi Mir, 6, 1987, pp. 216-17.

7. Vladimir Soloukhin, Mother/Step-Mother Stories, Kishinev: 1980, pp. 387-88.

8. Bulgakov, The Master and Margarita, Frankfurt/Main: Possev-Verlag, 1974, p. 42.

9. V. Shukshin, Stories, Lenizdat, 1983, p. 101.

10. Shukshin, Stories, p. 102.

11. V. Tendriakov, "Assassination of Mirages" in Novyi Mir, 5, 1987, p. 95.

12. Ibid., p. 118.

13. Ibid., p. 147.

14. Georgii Gachev, "Conscience! Be Brave!" in Iunost', 387, 1987, pp. 82-87.

15. The most comprehensive discussion aside from Gachev's article is "We discuss Chingiz Aitmatov's Novel, The Executioner's Block" in Voprosy literatury, 3, 1987, pp. 3-82.

16. Chingiz Aitmatov, The Executioner's Block, Riga: 1986, p. 57.

17. Ibid., p. 165.

18. Viktor Astaf'ev, "The Sad Detective," in his book To Live a Life, Moscow: 1986, pp. 4-124.

19. Igor Vinogradov, "About the Novella of Sergei Kaledin, The Humble Cemetery," in Novyi Mir, 5, 1987, p. 84.

10

CHRISTIANITY
IN RECENT SOVIET FILMS:
THE CASE OF RUSSOPHILE IDEOLOGY

Dmitry Shlapentokh

Until now films have not attracted much attention from either Soviet or western social scientists. They have appeared in Soviet sociological studies mostly as items in time-budget studies[1] or in studies of cultural activities of Soviet people.[2] Movie-goers were the subject of a few studies.[3]

However, with the availability of video recorders, scholars of Soviet society received a powerful new source of information about the processes underway in the USSR. Until now neither western researchers, nor even Soviet social scientists have analyzed the Soviet films as a source of information about the USSR. In a few cases social researchers studied only single films, usually the most popular, with the goal of understanding why they gained such public recognition and what feelings and ideas of their audiences they reflected.[4] In general, the analysis of films has so far been monopolized by Soviet critics who very rarely considered them a source of information on the major social developments in the USSR. Soviet films produced in the late 1970s and the 1980s, however, are an important source of information about the image of Christianity in the context of the general major ideological processes underway in the country.

The situation of stagnation into which Soviet society lapsed in the 1970s aroused various reactions in the country. These reactions took the form of several ideologies - systems of more or less cohesive values and beliefs that define the goals and moral standards of behavior of a society.[5]

Along with official public ideology based on Marxist postulates, at least four other ideologies have been operating in the country in the period preceding the Gorbachev "revolution" and have continued in its wake: Russophile, neo-Leninist, neo-Stalinist (or Andropovian) and democratic. To be sure, a number of other ideologies also function in the USSR: "pure" religious (Orthodox) and various nationalistic (non-Russian) ones although they have been much less vocal than the first four.

The borders between some ideologies are rather vague and some of them strongly interact and overlap with each other. This is the case with the neo-Leninist and democratic ideologies, the Russophile and religious ideologies, and the neo-Leninist and neo-Stalinist ideologies.

If the study of official public ideology is not difficult because, by definition, it has always been abundantly presented in the mass media, the speeches of politicians and the works of hack writers, the situation with the other ideologies is much more complex. Films, along with novels, and to some extent letters to editors (particularly in the period of glasnost) provide us with glimpses into the world views of various segments of the Soviet population.

However, not all ideologies are evenly reflected in films, novels or letters to editors. Censorship, even in Gorbachev's time, has been strong enough to prevent democratic as well as nationalistic ideologies from finding outlets.

It is hard to exaggerate the importance of the study of ideologies in the USSR. Unlike opinions on current issues, ideology is a relatively stable construct which influences people's behavior over long periods of time. The study of ideology in this crucial period in which Russia is attempting to free itself from the Stalinist model imposed upon it is of special significance because it can help us understand the degree to which Soviet society is capable of entering a new stage of modernization of its economy and other spheres of social life.

MAJOR IDEOLOGICAL TRENDS:
SUMMARY OF CHARACTERISTICS

Soviet ideologies differ from each other in various ways. First of all, some of them - Brezhnevian and Russophile - are conservative, whereas others - neo-Stalinist, neo-Leninist and democratic - are dynamic. Each has its own central value; for Brezhnevian and neo-Stalinist ideologies it is the might of the state; for Russophile ideology it is Russian patriotism and traditions; for neo-Leninist, social progress; and for democratic ideology it is individual freedom.

Dynamic ideologies offer different explanations for the unsatisfactory state of society. Russophiles point to the moral decadence and the obliteration of Russian tradition and religion; neo-Leninists blame bureaucratization, and democrats point to the lack of democracy. The various ideologies also differ in their designation of the major culprit behind the problems of Soviet society; for Russophiles it is the West and alien elements in Russia; for neo-Stalinists it is the masses; for neo-Leninists the bureaucrats; and for democrats it is the "system," per se. Of course, each ideology also has its own vision of a better future. Russophiles look toward a resurgence of Russian traditions with their emphasis on Christianity; neo-Stalinists seek a restoration of order; neo-Leninists favor the active participation of the masses in economic and political activity; and democrats hope for increased freedoms.

Soviet films made in the late 1970s and 1980s can be used as a source of information about three ideologies: Russophile, neo-Leninist and neo-Stalinist. Two other primary ideologies - official and democratic - have only rarely found their way into Soviet films. Because even the most obedient authors in Brezhnev's time wanted their films to be widely viewed (in the Soviet Union films as well as theaters are far more dependent on public reaction than novels or articles), they often included heterodox elements - mainly Russophile or neo-Leninist - in their films. Less than 10 percent of all films included in the sample can be considered to be ideologically consistent. Democratic ideology, as mentioned earlier, with its focus on pluralism and individual freedoms, could sneak into Soviet films only when cloaked in the garment of its closest relative - neo-Leninism. In some cases, neo-Leninist phraseology can be a vehicle for a veiled expression of an author's democratic sympathy as, for instance, in such films as "My Dear Edison" (1986) or "Repentance" (1984).

This study is based on an analysis of seventy-six films. The sample can hardly be regarded as random. The major factor which influenced the sample's composition was the availability in the U.S. of videocassettes of Soviet films. The selection of films from those available was further affected by information about the films. Movies which were popular in the USSR were given priority in order to enhance the quality of the analysis since the popularity of a film indicates that its ideology is shared by large segments of the Soviet population.

The artistic quality of the films included in the sample was not very high although the overall quality of films produced by the Soviet film industry is even lower, a fact which has been clearly revealed during the period of glasnost (see the materials of the congress of filmmakers in Isskustvo Kino, 1986). Of the films included in the sample, only 3 percent were assessed as "very high" in quality while 13 percent were considered "very trivial." Between these two extremes, 48 percent were treated as "relatively original" and 36 percent as "rather trivial."

Given the study's focus on the ideological trends in the country, it was necessary to determine the political orientation of the films which were the subject of our analysis.

Of course, there are many films whose ideological character is absolutely clear. Such films as "Shore" (1984) and "Do Not Shoot the White Swans" (1982) are clearly representative of Russophile ideology whereas "We, the Undersigned" (1979), "Repentance" and "My Friend Lapshin" (1985) express neo-Leninist ideology while "Confrontation" (1985) reveals a neo-Stalinist perspective. At the same time, a number of films, even if they have a prevailing political orientation, are nevertheless mixtures of various ideological perspectives. Thus, labelling a film as having a particular ideological inclination does not exclude its use in a discussion of other ideologies.

With these reservations about our sample, about one-quarter of all the films which clearly deviated from official public ideology can be treated as Russophile with more or less religious overtones. Neo-Leninist films with various elements of liberalism make up about two-thirds of the sample, while less than one-tenth fall into the neo-Stalinist category.

As with novels, some films, usually those of higher quality, are much more important sources for understanding social phenomena than are mediocre or simply bad ones. Keeping this in mind, we gave these more important films extra attention.

For the purposes of this paper, we will concentrate on Russophile films in which Christian themes play an important and, in some cases, crucial role.

Russophile Ideology in Soviet Films

Russophiles are traditionally viewed as those who stress the basic differences between Russia and the rest of the world, mainly the West. This traditional view of Russophilism also implies that Russophiles view Russians as the only Christian people who demonstrate the qualities of meekness, natural nobility, devotion to lofty spiritual principles and a willingness to sacrifice. With such characteristics, Russians do not need technological progress and economic growth to lead happy lives, which explains why Russophilism in the 1970s was so eagerly accepted by Brezhnev's regime and was, to some extent, incorporated into the official ideology as a rationale to justify stagnation.

Russophilism, like any other ideological trend, is a complex phenomenon with at least two main schools - the extremist and the liberal. The first preaches hatred of non-Russians and shares with Stalinism a focus on the might of the state (e.g., "The Legend of Princess Olga", 1983) whereas the liberal wing emphasizes Russian religious traditions and manifests some tolerance toward others, although not without a feeling of superiority.

War and Peace in Russophile Films

Soviet films which we consider as primarily Russophile in perspective usually reflect the liberal tendency in this ideological trend. One of the most important subjects for these films is war, which, as a religious experience, provides abundant opportunities to reveal such Christian qualities as willingness to sacrifice and meekness, contrasted to peacetime with its earthly temptations (e.g., the pursuit of a career and material well-being) when Russians often deviate from the Christian model of behavior. During wartime the Russian national character manifests itself fully as the major base for the nation's strength. The victory in World War II is seen as due primarily to this character.

Russophile films about the last war present soldiers and the civilian population mainly as suffering and making sacrifices for others, in a sense repeating the ordeal of Christ. Film directors avoid presenting Russians in the act of inflicting suffering on others, for example, killing foreign soldiers on the battlefield. We will consider separately two categories of heroes in films of this type - soldiers and civilians.

"Shore," based on Bondarev's novel (1975) presents Russian soldiers as martyrs who follow Russian Christian traditions. One of its main heroes often recalls the images of his childhood - particularly a sunken church - as being crucially important to his future behavior. The church appears as a symbol of the Christian nature of the Russian people. The water which covered the church symbolizes all the evils inflicted upon the Russian church in the previous periods - the civil war, the collectivization and the purges. However, this flood of hatred and violence was not able to destroy the church. In the depth of their souls the Russian people remained as kind and meek as Christian saints. This was emphasized by the filmmakers by their depiction of the icons of saints and angels in the church remaining unscathed under water.

Of no less importance in this connection is the fact that the main hero, Lieutenant Kniazhnin, emulates the ordeal of Christ. He sacrifices his life not for his friends, but for his enemies. A detachment of German youths desperately resisted the onslaught of Soviet troops in the last days of the war. Their position is hopeless, and they will be imminently crushed by the victorious Soviet army. Kniazhnin understands that a Soviet attack would lead to the death of all these poor youngsters, and he decides to save them. He marches to their position with a white flag, hoping to convince them to surrender. He was about to reach them but is shot by a German. However, his mission is fulfilled. His death, a sort of mystical sacrifice, saves the lives of the youths. The film implies that the Soviet troops' attack did not cause the deaths of the German youth, who, instead, were taken alive as prisoners of war.

The same presentation of Russian soldiers as people inclined to sacrifice and forgiveness was seen in the film "Back Home" (1983) based on a story by Andrei Platonov. In this film, an officer returns from the front to his family. Upon his arrival he finds out that his wife has not been faithful to him. He gets quite angry and prepares to leave his family. However, at the request of his son, he decides to forgive his wife. As in the case of "Shore," the film's director notably ignores the hero's military valor. Despite the fact that the hero wears a captain's uniform with military decorations and, as he himself acknowledges, often faced death in battle, the film's director pays no attention to his military feats. The forgiveness of his wife is the culmination of the film, portraying the hero in a clearly positive light and demonstrating that he is indeed worthy to be a "defender of the motherland."

If in "Shore" and "Back Home" the directors focus on particular individuals as martyrs or near-saints, in another film, "Children's Home" (1982), the director, Evgenii Evtushenko focuses on collective martyrdom. One of the film's episodes depicts boys from the countryside, fresh recruits ready to be dispatched to the front in the midst of the battle of Moscow. The film underlines the youths' wholesomeness and desire to live. Just before being sent to the battlefield, they get married and barely have time to consummate their marriage. The film implies that all of them are destined to die. Their apparent ill fate is emphasized in another episode: a newly-wed, just a few minutes after her wedding, meets a married woman who just received a letter informing her that her husband had perished in battle. Many scenes in the film are accompanied by the sound of church bells. The recruits' performance on the battlefield is utterly ignored.

The makers of Russophile films often present soldiers not only as willing martyrs, but also as victims who bear their fate with dignity and courage. These films also often take place far away from the battlefield. As examples, we can point to "Fall of Stars" (1980) and "I Will Never Forget You" (1983). In both films soldiers are presented as hospital patients who stoically suffer their wounds.

Russophile films only rarely touch upon Russian soldiers' collaboration with Germans, and if so, portray them as nevertheless still behaving according to the Christian model. In the film "White Snow of Russia" (1980), a Russian emigre begins to collaborate with the Germans. However, when his superiors send him to participate in repressions against the Czech resistance, he can no longer stand the Germans' cruelty and openly rebels. Though one might have expected him to then join the resistance himself, the film implies that, as a Russian, he was disinclined to shed anyone's blood and instead chooses to commit suicide, thus preferring moral to physical resistance.

Films with Russophile themes tend to display civilians as also willing to endure suffering. In "Fall of Stars" we see nurses who organize a party for wounded soldiers. Though some of the nurses ostentatiously demonstrate their promiscuity and cynicism, it becomes clear that this is not their true essence. Under the veneer of cynicism one can see the souls of Christians, full of love and ready to sacrifice for others. It is notable too that the party takes place in a church. The filmmakers constantly draw the viewers' attention to the images of saints on the church's walls. The Christian mood of the film is also revealed when one of the nurses recites a religious poem. However, even more important is the readiness of the nurses to donate their blood to help the wounded soldiers. We also see nurses who donate blood at evident risk to their own lives in the film "I Will Never Forget You."

As in the case with soldiers, Russian civilians are quite magnanimous to their enemies. In "Wounded" (1977) one sees German prisoners of war in postwar Russia. Only notorious war criminals are executed; whereas the vast majority of prisoners live well in prison camps, which appear to be more recreation areas than correctional institutions.

Such Christian meekness and willingness to suffer do not, however, diminish Russia's military might. In fact, these qualities secure for Russia a spiritual superiority over her enemies which leads to their final defeat. The episode from "Children's Home" serves as a good example.

The film depicts the period of the battle of Moscow when Soviet troops were in retreat. One of the movie's main heroes is taken prisoner by the Germans. He is presented as a victim and martyr. No information is presented about how he was captured and how many German soldiers he might have killed. When the viewers meet him, he is suffering - a wounded young prisoner in the grip of the powerful and victorious enemy. The German soldiers push him into a building for interrogation. The building happens to have once been the home of Leo Tolstoy, and one of the German officers who interrogates him is a specialist in Russian literature.

The entire episode is reminiscent of the interrogation of Christ by Pilate and was inspired either by the biblical story or Bulgakov's *Master and Margarita*. The power of the advancing German army is behind the officer, and only the legacy of Tolstoy, the humanistic Russian culture, is behind the helpless prisoner. Nevertheless, it is the prisoner who completely dominates the scene and puts the officer in an uneasy position. The officer, like Pilate, tormented by doubts, implicitly recognizes the spiritual victory of the prisoner - of humanism in general - over him and the brutal force which he represents. By the end of the film the viewer is informed that the Germans are beating a hasty retreat.

While "Children's Home" does not elaborate on the reasons for Russia's victories, "Shore" does. As that film implies, Westerners, including Germans, see Russians as liberators. They also see Russian culture, imbued with highly spiritual and humanistic Christian values as the only alternative to the materialistic, depraved and cruel world. The film implies that such benign Russian characteristics not only explain Russia's victory over Germany, but also Russian influence in contemporary Europe as well.

The film's plot revolves around a German girl who falls in love with a Russian officer who saved her from a rapist's attack. The officer then left to return to Russia. The girl later married a prosperous West German businessman and seemed to live well from a material point of view. However, the material well-being which she and other Westerners enjoyed did not make them happy. On the contrary, it deprived them of lofty values, love and care of others and was associated with cynicism and cruelty.

To demonstrate the rotten character of western lifestyles the film's director places the hero, the Russian officer-lover, in post-war Germany. The depravity and cynicism of the West is represented by a brothel in which the hero accidentally finds himself. The film suggests that the best people in the West do not want to tolerate the degradation of their world and look to Russia for guidance. The German girl, who by the end of the film becomes a middle-aged German matron, is among them. With all her material comforts she feels frustrated and lonely. The memory of the caring Russian officer and the Russian army which brought him to her is the only positive feeling she enjoys. She finds the officer (by this time he has become a writer) and arranges for him to visit West Germany. Her encounter with the hero is quite comforting. Her affection for him is not the only reason for this. He brings to her the spirit of the great Russian culture. There is no sexual encounter between the former lovers, and their new relationship is purely spiritual, based on common values, in clear contrast to the cynical sexuality prevailing in the West.

Before his departure from West Germany, the hero takes part in a press conference where he speaks about the humanistic tradition of Russian culture and Russia's desire to save the world from nuclear catastrophe. The film points to the cultural roots of the hero's proposals for peace - Christianity. Meditating upon the future of mankind and the role which Russia is destined to play in its salvation, the hero once again remembers the sunken Orthodox Church which fascinated him so much in his youth.

Because of the special role of war in Russophile ideology, the soldier is presented as one of the most moral figures and the army, even in peacetime, is portrayed as a national sanctuary, a sort of national church which people join to purify themselves of the egotism of their civil life, to experience a kind of religious catharsis.

In "Relatives" (1982), the army appears as a sort of national sanctuary. A hero in the film, apparently a war veteran, is shown as quite a vain person and a drunkard, abandoned by everyone, including his wife, whom he constantly cheated. His daughter is also pictured as a shallow person infatuated with the western style of life. Her brother is not much better. The single positive character is her mother who continues to live in the countryside.

The conscription of the young man becomes the turning point for all members of the family who come to say goodbye to him. The event reveals the true essence of their souls. The scene at the railway station where recruits are assembled is the culmination of the film. The old drunkard-veteran is particularly affected by the event. He puts on all his war medals and in an emotional scene, urges his son to serve the motherland well. The recruit himself and his sister are overcome with emotion. Purged of their petty interests, they demonstrate their deep affection for each other and for their parents and the people around them. The entire scene becomes a sort of religious ceremony in which people repent and attempt to redeem their sins.

The same role of the army as purgatory is depicted in another film "Peasants" (1982), although not as strongly as in "Relatives." In this film a man does not marry his bride-to-be who allegedly has not been faithful to him. He also does not accept a girl born by this woman as his daughter. His elderly parents urge him to adopt her, but the hero remains stubborn. However, he soon changes his mind. This occurs at the wedding party. Right after the party, the bridegroom will be going into the army, a fact central for those attending the gathering. After the party the man talks with the young girl and finally decides not only to accept her as his daughter, but also to adopt two boys, children of other fathers, including one who is mute.

The long quarrels between spouses in the film "Love and Pigeons" (1984) also come to an end when their son enters the army. Again, this sacred institution inspires the loftiest sentiments in the film's characters.

Although war is the best period for the manifestation of the noble and spiritual values of the Russian people, in peacetime they are also shown as behaving in accordance with the requirements of Christian morals. However, there are quite a few people who deviate from these requirements, and it is the task of society to bring them back to these Russian values.

The true repository of the highest national virtues is, of course, the countryside. Thus, Russophile movies in various, mainly indirect, ways praise the technological backwardness of the countryside. However, liberal Russophiles tend to be more lenient with all types of Russians, allowing every Russian individual the opportunity to redeem themselves and return to the virtuous life.

Russophile Characteristics in Soviet Society

We will now consider how some of the main actors in Soviet society are portrayed in Russophile films.

Bureaucrats are the people who, with their consumerism and cruelty, deviate more often than others from the ideal Russian national character. Of course, not all Russian officials are evil. "I Will Never Forget You" and "Stepmother" (1978) present industrial and agricultural managers whose main positive characteristics are kindness and care for their subordinates. Bureaucracy is presented somewhat positively in "The Peasants" as well. However, in many Russophile films, perhaps even the majority, the bureaucracy is presented negatively, particularly in such films as "Fruzia" (1983), "Do Not Shoot the White Swans" and "Shore." In these films officials abuse women, destroy nature and demonstrate their indifference to ordinary people.

In contrast to the bureaucracy, intellectuals are presented by liberal Russophiles as sharing Russian values. Even if they make false steps in their life, it is not very difficult to bring them back to traditional values.

Intellectuals demonstrate their inclination to make sacrifices for the sake of the Russian people in a number of films, particularly "Do Not Shoot the White Swans," "Married for the First Time" (1978) and "The Last Meeting" (1983).

In "Do Not Shoot the White Swans," a young female teacher reveals in various ways her allegiance to Russian values, beginning with a book on medieval Russian art with a picture of an icon displayed on the front of her bookshelf. She also has an opportunity to show her strong interest in Russian classical literature with its strong religious overtones. Most important, of course, is her self-effacing behavior and selfless service. In "Married for the First Time," the main hero is a self-taught countryside intellectual who is busy with the creation of a museum in the local church. In "The Last Meeting" a scholar is praised for serving the public good.

The repentance of an intellectual is shown in the film "Turn" (1979), explicitly influenced by Dostoevsky's *Crime and Punishment* and imbued with strong religious overtones.

The hero of the film, a middle-aged scholar, is a prosperous intellectual who apparently neglected Christian values and became absorbed with vain and petty issues like his scientific career and prestigious vacations.

An accident in which an old woman is hit by the hero's car becomes a turning point in his life. At the very beginning of the ordeal he continues to care about his career and desperately tries to avoid imprisonment. However, with the evolution of events he comes to the conclusion that he is guilty not only of hitting the woman, but in a broader sense. He begins to realize that his life has been emotionally cold and meaningless. Like Raskol'nikov, he is ready to be imprisoned and hopes that suffering will purify him. However, the hero is acquitted by the court, and he seemingly returns to his old life. Yet his spiritual awakening during his time of trial and uncertainty is not completely lost, and the viewer is led to believe that he is on the path of moral rehabilitation. This theme of moral recuperation of intellectuals who have gone astray amidst a life full of temptations can be seen in other films as well, for instance, "Relatives."

Western lifestyles are the major threat to the Russian intelligentsia and to Russian youth. Western values clearly destroyed the life of a young girl who, like her mother, is completely under the influence of the West, and too much absorbed with the roaring sounds of a western song with the constant refrain "I love you" to take the time to answer her mother.

A female professional in "Love and Pigeons" is depicted as a successful career woman and an admirer of western culture. However, she is deeply unhappy and alone. The same theme is found in "Married for the First Time": young people craving western pleasures find themselves empty and frustrated.

In all Russophile films western culture is mainly identified with consumerism and sexual promiscuity. These movies do not ignore the efficiency of the western economy and science. However, these achievements are not praised. What is more, by portraying village life as more virtuous than urban life, Russophiles see technological progress as an enemy of high moral values. For this reason, it is ultimately not the intelligentsia with its close links to science and to the West, but rather ordinary people, who are the true bastions of Christian values and the hope of the country.

The genuine hero of Russophile films as presented in "Do Not Shoot the White Swans," is the individual with little or no professional training. He is not an achiever and not a particularly hard worker. He is not without creative skills, but exercises them only when he is in a good mood or if he likes his job. If both these conditions are not present, his professional performance is terrible. In spite of this, the hero is endowed with many very positive qualities. He is absorbed with love, not only for human beings, but for all living creatures, and he is extremely generous and absolutely free of vanity and ambition. What is more, these qualities, despite his low professional level, allow him to be extremely efficacious when a noble purpose demands it. In fact, this individual is a "holy fool," a hero from Russian fairy tales. It is he who, along with soldiers, is the embodiment of Russia's Christian spirit and the guarantor of her leading role in world history.

The hero of "Do Not Shoot the White Swans" is a resident of a village and apparently has no formal education beyond elementary school. He does not read books and does not go to movies and, in general, does not display any interest in the outside world. Similar to Tolstoi's Karataev from *War and Peace*, he is absolutely content with his daily life. He definitely possesses artistic talents, but does not exploit them, not only because of his resistance to any bureaucratic routine but mostly because of his carelessness and childish irresponsibility. Not only is he unable to perform well any official job, he also cannot even sustain his family, the poorest in the village.

Yet this village fool is shown to be the sole defender of nature against the offenses of civilization. Being appointed as a forester he decides to repopulate a lake with swans which had left it many years ago. Using money given to him for buying various goods in the capital where he was sent to take part in an ecological conference, he buys swans for his lake and dies defending them from poachers. His death, full of religious allegories (similar to Christ, he, by his death, gave life to others), was not in vain; civilization retreated, and the lake, as in the remote past, was once again filled with life.

In the film "Valentine" (1980) it is the simple uneducated peasant girl who plays the role of the "holy fool." The girl is absolutely unselfish, in clear contrast to the urbanized bureaucrat and the youngster enchanted with western culture. Her Christian patience and belief in the influence of a good example make her a cornerstone of rural society. The Christian spirit of Russophile heroes, their abhorrence of western and, more generally, of urban values, not only makes them saviors of society, but also guarantees personal happiness for them.

The hero in "Love and Pigeons" belongs to the same class of people so highly regarded by Russophiles. The same low level of education, unfitness for modern life and passionate love of nature and of living things, in this case, of pigeons. Like his equally unsophisticated wife, the hero is happy, in contrast to the tribulations of those who try to live by western standards.

This film also demonstrates the strong anti-feminist feelings typical of Russophile ideology, which regards the emancipation of women as one of the greatest vices of western civilization. This theme is strong in a number of other films, such as "Quarantine" (1983), "Twenty Years Later" (1980) and "Married for the First Time." In all these films, poorly educated and unpretentious, but kind and warm women are contrasted with westernized modern females.

The film "Scenes from Family Life" (1980) approaches family problems in a similar way. The only difference is that it is the man who is presented as the main partisan of family values. Although a professional, he is a content person with practically no career ambitions. This unpretentious family-oriented man is contrasted to the vain behavior of his ex-wife.

One can see definite Christian motives in these films, especially in "Stepmother." The film centers around family affairs, and its principal heroine is a simple peasant woman. The woman adopts a child whom she treats very well, but who repays her with hostility. The woman, however, is not discouraged, and with Christian patience continues to care for and comfort the child. Finally her Christian all-forgivingness triumphs, and the child calls her "mother."

CONCLUSION

Russophile ideology provides a comforting vision of Russian political reality. It presents the view that Christianity is the very essence of the Russian national character and culture regardless of all the changes which the Bolshevik revolution have brought to Russia. This Christian essence is portrayed as the willingness to sacrifice and love. Wartime provides the best opportunity to exercise these benign qualities.   In this sense war is presented as akin to a religious experience and the army as a sort of substitute for the church, a role which it continues to play.

In peacetime and outside the army the Russian people are not without faults, exhibiting such anti-Christian traits as cruelty, egotism and consumerism. It is the bureaucracy which is most affected by these negative tendencies.

However, intellectuals and especially the simple folk are able to preserve their benign Christian character. Even the bureaucracy is not totally polluted, as kind individuals sometimes appear within its ranks. Those who are tainted by western values are also not beyond hope because their adoption of western values leads them into suffering, thus opening the door to their redemption and rehabilitation.

Russophiles are not only hostile to manifestations of western lifestyles such as consumerism and sexual promiscuity, but also to the work ethic and to technological progress. These are regarded as responsbile for the erosion of Christian values and for leading Russia and mankind in general toward self-destruction. According to Russophiles, the Russian victory in World War II and the Russians' high position in the world, is a result not of Russia's industrial potential or even of its soldiers' valor, but rather of its spiritual wholesomeness.

Such an ideological stance actually glorifies stagnation and technological backwardness. It was apparently accepted quite benevolently by the authorities during Brezhnev's reign, but appears sharply at odds with Gorbachev's current approach to the Russian political reality. However, the popularity of writers Astaf'ev and Rasputin (both extreme Russophiles) and of the society "Pamiat'" [Memory] demonstrate that Russophile ideology in its various forms is far from being outmoded. Moreover, the further westernization of Soviet society, emphasizing hard work and professionalism, is likely to cause further social polarization affecting large segments of the population and may end up stimulating a resurgence of Russophilism and a renewed interest in religion.

The author wishes to thank Vladimir Shlapentokh of Michigan State University for his contribution to this article.

1. See V. Artemov and V. Patrushev (eds.), Budzhet vremeni zhitelei Pskova [Time Budgeting in Pskov], Novosibirsk: Institut ekonomiki, 1973; V. Patrushev (ed.), Problemy vneproizvodstvennoi deiatel'nosti trudiashchikhsia [The Problems of Leisure Activities of Workers], Moscow: Institut Sotsiologicheskikh Issledovanii, 1976; V. Patrushev (ed.), Tendentsii izmeneniia budzheta vremeni trudiashchikhsia [Trends toward Changing the Time Budgeting of Workers], Moscow: Institut Sotsiologicheskikh Issledovanii, 1979; A. Maksimov, Rabochie i svobodnoe vremia v usloviiakh razvitogo sotsializma [Workers and Free Time under Conditions of Developing Socialism], Moscow: Nauka, 1981; D. Dumnov, et al., Budzhet vremeni naseleniia [Time Budgeting for the Population], Moscow: Finansy i Statistika, 1984; V. Swinnikov, Sotsializm i svobodnoe vremia: Pravo na Otdykh [Socialism and Free Time: The Right to Rest], Moscow: Vyshnaia Shkola, 1985.

2. See L. Kogan and V. Volkov (eds.), Sotsiologicheskie issledovaniia problem dukhovnoi zhizni trudiashchikhsia urala [Sociological Studies of the Problems of Workers' Cultural Life in the Urals], Sverdlovsk: Ural'skii Tsentr AN SSR, 1974; L. Kogan (ed.), Kul'turnaia deiatel'nost: Opyt sotsiologicheskogo issledovaniia [Cultural Activity: The Results of Sociological Research], Moscow: Nauka, 1981; N. Mansurov, et al. (eds.), Sotsiologicheskie problemy kul'tury [Sociological Problems of Culture], Moscow: Institut Sotsiologicheskikh Issledovanii, 1976; Ia. Kapelush et al., Uchrezhdeniia kul'tury v nebol'shom gorode i naselenie [Small Town Cultural Institutions and the Population], Moscow: Finansy i Statistiki, 1985; K. Khabibullin (ed.), Razvitie dukhovnykh potrebnostei v sisteme sotsialisticheskogo obraza zhizni [The Development of Spiritual/Cultural Needs in a Socialist System], Leningrad: Pedagogicheskii Institut, 1980; L. Kogan and A. Sharova (eds.), Issledovaniia i planirovanie dukhovnoi kul'tury trudiashchikhsia Urala [Research and Planning of Spiritual Culture of Workers in the Urals], Sverdlovsk: Ural'skii nauchnyi Tsentr, 1975.

3. See S. Iosifian, Problemy massovosti kinoiskusstva [Problems of the Mass Character of Film Art], Moscow: Institut Kinematografii, 1977; M. Zhabskii, Metodologiia prikladnogo sotsiologicheskogo issledovaniia (Problemy sotsiologii kino) [Methodology of Applied Sociological Research (Problems of the Sociology of Film)], Moscow: Institut Teorii i Istorii Kino, 1976; I. Rachuk and Z. Kutorga (eds.), Sotsiologicheskie issledovaniia kinematografa [Sociological Research in Cinematography], Moscow: Institut Kinematografii, 1971.

4. See V. Volkov, "Fil'm i ego auditoriia" [Film and its Viewers], in Kogan and Volkov (eds.) Sotsiologicheskie issledovaniia problem [Sociological Problem Studies], pp. 94-131; T. Zudilova, "Zamysel'-fil'm-zritel' [The Concept, the Film and the Viewer]," in Kogan and Volkov, Sotsiologicheskie issledovaniia problem, pp. 132-159.

5. See C. Geertz, Interpretation of Culture, New York: Basic Books, 1973; C. Kluckhohn, "Values and Value Orientations in the Theory of Action," in T. Parsons and E. Shills (eds.), Toward a General Theory of Action, Cambridge: Harvard University Press, 1951; V. Shlapentokh, Soviet Public Opinion and Ideology: Mythology and Pragmatism in Interaction, New York: Praeger, 1986.

11

THE ICON IN RUSSIAN ART, SOCIETY AND CULTURE

Oskar Gruenwald

THE ICON AND SPIRITUAL RENAISSANCE

The inspiration for this paper comes from the confluence of three phenomena evident during the last two decades: 1) the rising western interest in icons, especially Russian iconography; 2) the burgeoning dissident movement in the Soviet Union; and 3) the growing religious renaissance in the Soviet Union. At the heart of these phenomena is modern man's quest for meaning, for touchstones of judgment, for values and for faith. Thus, Aleksandr I. Solzhenitsyn confirms that a total moral and spiritual revolution is needed if modern man is to escape the thrall and disillusionment of secular culture, rampant materialism, and moral/ethical relativism in the West and an equally deadening nihilism and atheism of Soviet totalitarianism in the East.[1]

The growing religious renaissance in the Soviet Union since the 1960s appears to corroborate Solzhenitsyn's thesis. Thus, Anatoly Levitin-Krasnov, who represents the Christian wing of the Democratic Movement in the USSR, wrote in his Letter to Pope Paul VI (c. September 26, 1967) about the quest for moral and spiritual values, distinguishing between three generations under communism. He claimed that the third generation under communism no longer hates the church for its association with tsarism (as did the first generation) and is no longer indifferent to religion (as was the second generation). Rather, the third generation is an "unhappy generation for whom religion is part of its passionate search for truth. This new type of believer is young and concerned."[2]

There is a growing consensus among observers, East and West, that the spiritual vacuum left by the disillusionment with the official ideology has propelled people on the quest for new values, ideals and faith. As Michael Meerson-Aksenov points out, many Russians are turning from Marxism to the Russian religious philosophy and existentialist literature of the late nineteenth and early twentieth centuries - to such philosophers as Vladimir Solov'ev, Nicholas Berdiaev, Sergei Bulgakov, Semen Frank, Lev Shestov and Nicholas Lossky, and such writers as Fedor Dostoevsky and Lev Tolstoy.[3] Thus, Dmitrii Nelidov's famous samizdat essay on "Ideocratic Consciousness and Personality" recovers the essential idea of Russian Christian existentialist thought that man is a spiritual being and that spirituality is the ultimate source of his freedom and dignity.[4]

In fact, the religious renaissance is playing an ever increasing role in the dissident movement, so much so that since the 1960s, it has become one of the three major currents along with national and human rights and democracy and rule of law. Crucially, as Barbara Jancar intimates, the concern for civil rights is central to religious dissent.[5] Hence, Jancar perceives religious dissent as a potential "link that could unite the intellectual currents of opposition with latent popular dissatisfaction."[6]

Religious dissent has deep popular roots in Russia, both among the intellectuals and the masses. While the other currents of dissent in the USSR are confined to relatively small groups composed mostly of intellectuals, religious dissent strikes a receptive chord among the population at large, regardless of nationality, as exemplified by the 17,000 signatures collected for a 1972 memorandum protesting religious persecution.[7] It appears also that Nikita Khrushchev's anti-religious campaign of the late 1950s, which began a systematic closing of churches and monasteries, has had the opposite effect of that desired by the authorities; namely, it renewed the popular quest for meaning and faith. As the people of the Zanosychi village, whose church was destroyed on Easter Sunday, 1979, put it:

> The shameful authorities continue to search for ever more ways of forbidding the faith, but Orthodox Russia lives on and will do so as

long as the devout carry on serving the Lord as fervently as in the Rovno region. Their hearts have become a temple for the Lord, and there is no hellish power capable of destroying such a temple.[8]

The late Boris Talantov's letters to N. V. Podgorny, Chairman of the Presidium of the Supreme Soviet, and to Pope Paul VI indicate that educated young people may still be afraid to be seen in church, even though they seek to return to religion.[9] On the other hand, the ranks of those willing to suffer persecution for the sake of their beliefs are increasing. Thus, a group of prisoners of various faiths in the Sosnovka concentration camp, Mordovia, issued "An Appeal to Christians Throughout the World" on July 3, 1979, demanding freedom for political prisoners in the USSR, and asking for freedom of conscience and religious worship, including permission to wear a cross and to possess a Bible, prayer books and icons.[10]

My thesis is that the icon represents an integral link between Russian art, society and culture; and that a genuine spiritual renaissance in the USSR awaits a rediscovery of the central ethical, cultural and spiritual values embodied in the representational art of the icon, which constitutes the Russian identity or national character. Such a rediscovery of the icon would also bolster the rationale for the separation of church and state - one of the major demands of religious dissenters first voiced by Reverend Nicholas Eshliman and Reverend Gleb Yakunin in 1965.[11] The rediscovery of the icon would speed the much-needed inner revival of the Russian Orthodox Church, urged by Levitin-Krasnov.[12] Its rediscovery would also corroborate the scriptural injunction to distinguish betwen the flesh and the spirit, the secular and the sacred, thus leading to a reconciliation between freedom and faith, and allowing for religious tolerance and freedom of conscience for all believers, implied by the "Founding Statement of the Christian Committee for the Defense of Believers' Rights in the USSR" of December 27, 1976.[13]

Finally, by rediscovering the icon, Russians and others would likely rediscover their own souls. Pavel Korin, who allegedly boasts the best private collection of icons in Russia, could thus advise his friend, writer and icon collector, Vladimir Soloukhin:

Always remember that they (icons) are great works of art. A collection of shells or butterflies is just that and no more, but when

you collect old Russian paintings you are collecting the nation's
soul.[14]

How can art, even great works of art, have anything to do with
the human soul, spiritual renaissance, personal identity or national
character, separation of church and state, inner revival of the Russian
Orthodox Church, a reconciliation between freedom and faith,
religious tolerance, and freedom of conscience? What, indeed is an
icon?

THE ICON AS RELIGIOUS ART

The essence of the icon is its representation of the Holy and
participation in the Divine. Hence, the icon is quintessentially religious
art. The Greek word *eikon* means image. Indeed, the phenomenon of
the icon cannot be understood apart from the traditions and symbols of
Eastern Christianity, developed in Byzantium, and reaching their
pinnacle in Russian iconography.

Western scholars of iconography agree that the rich and
peculiar artistry of the icon derives its significance from Eastern
Christian spirituality. George Galavaris notes that the icon was related
directly to the doctrine of Incarnation at the Council Quinisexte in 692
A.D., a doctrine central to the Gospel and the Christian faith: "The
Word became flesh, dwelt among us, and therefore an image must
represent that which was revealed to man."[15] Following the
iconoclastic controversy, 726-843 A.D., the icon became fully
integrated in the liturgy of Eastern Christianity, and found its flowering
in Byzantine art and architecture. Egon Sendler maintains that
Byzantine art was preoccupied for a millenium with the spiritualization
of forms and subjects. The objective of Byzantine art was to express
the very idea of spirituality and the truth of faith.[16]

Hence, the themes of Greek, Byzantine, and Russian
iconography are the great themes of Christianity: the Incarnation of
God as man, His suffering, Crucifixion, death and descent into Hell,
His Resurrection, and the consequent Redemption of sinful man, the
Great Commission to His disciples to preach the Word and gather His
flock, the lives and struggles, and martyrdom of the Saints, life-in-

Christ, man's sanctification and pilgrimage to salvation. Vladimir Lossky thus sums up the essence of iconography as setting forth "in colours what the word announces in written letters."[17] Since the purpose of the icon was to represent the spiritual reality of Christian faith, it necessarily became a symbolic art. Leonid Ouspensky writes that the icon as an art form strove to reflect the glory of God by a new symbolism. He also reminds us that the icon was not meant to serve religion, but, rather, was considered from its inception as "an integral part of religion, one of the instruments for the knowledge of God, one of the means of communication with Him."[18] Thus, the icon is simultaneously a work of art and a religious phenomenon.

According to the Eastern Orthodox tradition, the icon is not merely a representation of the Holy. The Holy - the represented - is thought to become present through the icon. Galavaris recalls that the Council of Nicea of 787 A.D. urged the faithful to say, "this is Christ the Son of God," when adoring the icon of Christ. In this way, the icon becomes a means for the faithful to participate in divine life, whereas the icon itself is considered as a "gate through which this world is bound to the other. The people, through these icons, participate in it and are transferred into the divine world."[19]

Another characteristic of the icon, rooted in Eastern Orthodox Christianity, is the notion that it helps man grow "into the eternal life, already here on earth acquiring the beginning of this life, the beginning of deification, which will be made fully manifest in the life to come." This sanctification of the human body, continues Ouspensky, testifies to the "manifestation of man as a living icon of God."[20] In sum, the icon is "theology expressed in the image."[21] And that is the reason why the art of iconography developed according to specific rules laid down by the magisterium of the Church in Byzantium, Russia and elsewhere.

Dissenting from the official Soviet view of iconography, Sendler in the West and Soloukhin in the East contend that church doctrine did not impede iconography in its perfection as an art, its search for new forms, or its introduction of novel themes.[22] The Church did insist that the artist paint icons following ancient models and symbols anchored in the faith. The calling of the icon-painter's art was to portray the transcendental, spiritual aspect of their subject. Thus, an ordinary portrait of a saint in his natural, physical state would not qualify as an icon. The icon was expected to express the saint's transfigured state, reflecting his spiritual qualities. Ouspensky remarks that the beauty of an icon "is the beauty of the acquired likeness to God, and so its value lies not in its being beautiful in itself, in its appearance as a beautiful object, but in the fact that it depicts Beauty."[23]

The nature of the icon, which sets it apart from other art forms, is recounted by Soloukhin in his quest to find and restore old Russian paintings. In a novel about old Novgorod, he read about an episode in which a merchant commissioned an icon of St. Paraskeva. To please his client, the icon-painter asked the merchant's young wife, Domasha, to pose as the model. When the icon was finished and shown to the merchant, its spirit of beauty painted on a clumsy coal-black board left him speechless:

> Oleksa gazed at it, and gradually became deaf to all around him. St. Paraskeva was looking at him with Domasha's eyes, full of suffering, compassion and wisdom. The face was somehow different and more elongated; the nose too was longer, after the Byzantine style, and the mouth narrower. . . The artist had made her look older; yet the face was not old, but as though everything fleshly and ephemeral had been purged from it, leaving only the beauty of a mother's face that endures till old age, till the hour of death.[24]

Since the vocation of the icon-painter was to express in his art that which could not be conveyed in words, and to represent that which could be reflected only imperfectly in the material world, the church tradition expected the icon-painter to be merely an instrument of the Holy Spirit, illumined by divine grace. Ouspensky and Sendler concur that the true iconographer was meant to be a man of asceticism and prayer.[25] The iconographer worked not for his own glory, but to the greater glory of God. Hence, an icon was never signed.

An icon fulfilled its mission and attained fully to its essence as a holy image only after benediction and an appropriate ceremony symbolizing its acceptance by the Church as a work which henceforward would become a source of grace for all who contemplated it. Sendler concludes that it was this sanctification of the icon which signified its accomplishment: its purpose of representing the world of God in terrestrial form.[26] Galavaris expounds that through the icon the beholder became a "participant of divine life."[27] Icons were thus to be found not only in churches and chapels, but in homes, at crossroads, and believers wore them around their necks and on travels.

THE ICON AS A SYMBOL OF RUSSIAN CULTURE

In his seminal study, *The Icon: Image of the Invisible*, the French Jesuit, Sendler, refers to the icon as "a universe of beauty and of faith."[28] The consensus among scholars, East and West, holds that Russian iconography perfected this unique art from Byzantium and in the process added new, distinctively Russian features. Nikodim P. Kondakov compares the quality of Russian icon-painting with West European works of art of the High Middle Ages.[29]

In the year 988 A.D., Prince Vladimir of Kiev, the founder of the Russian state, adopted Orthodox Christianity from Constantinople as the official religion, and imported from Byzantium doctrine, priests and ritual as well as artists and craftsmen. Thus, it was Greek artists from Byzantium and their iconography which became the model for the Russians. David Talbot Rice argues that there were actually three major influences on Russian iconography: 1) polished Constantinople; 2) forceful Asia Minor (via the Caucasus); and 3) enigmatic pre-Christian Russia. These influences blended into a new synthesis of features which came to distinguish Russian art: "notably elongated proportions, great delicacy of detail, bright tones and a markedly rhythmical composition."[30] In Galavaris' view, the Russians added another dimension of mysticism to the icon: "a new treatment of form: a visionary abstraction and fiery colours."[31]

Furthermore, the essential Christian symbolism of the Church's unity in Christ became amplified in Russian writings and the iconostasis (the screen, decorated with icons, dividing the Sanctuary from the nave in an Orthodox Church). Galavaris contends that the Russian iconostasis came to express "the union in love of all creatures with their creator - *sobornost*'; it manifests a transfigured world and the eternal presence of Christ (Mt. 28:20)."[32]

But how did the icon become a symbol of Russian culture? After all, very few of the early Russian icons survive to this day. Moreover, the first icons in Russia were of Greek-Byzantine origin. One of the great marvels of old Russia was that of the Virgin Mother of God, an eleventh century Greek icon imported from Constantinople, venerated at Vyshgorod, and later transferred to Vladimir, hence the icon's designation as "Our Lady of Vladimir" (*Wladimirskaja Bogomater*).

It was Russia's acceptance of the Christian faith - of Eastern Orthodox Christianity - and its underlying moral and spiritual values which were the fertile soil for the development of Russian iconography, and which, in turn, became the mirror image of the Russian soul - its piety, suffering, patience, its expectation of the consummation of the millennium and man's purification and ascent to God. Of all the Russian icon themes, it was the Virgin Mother of God which became the most popular and venerated object of devotion among believers in old Russia. Soloukhin observes that "not a hut, not a shrine was without her image."[33] The Vladimir Virgin inspired generations of Russian iconographers and became a model for many later works, a yardstick by which to measure the excellence of icon-painting.

Russian iconography itself dates from the twelfth century. St. Alipy (died c. 1114), a monk of the Kiev Monastery of the Caves, is regarded as the father of Russian iconography.[34] Several distinct schools of Russian icon-painting developed in Kiev, Novgorod, Pskov, Suzdal and Moscow. The Tatar invasion of the mid-thirteenth century laid waste to the greater part of Russia, destroyed many old icons, and hindered the creation of new ones. There is substantial agreement among scholars that the fourteenth, fifteenth and the first half of the sixteenth centuries represent the flowering of Russian iconography.

Historians agree also that Andrei Rublev's Old Testament Trinity is considered a masterpiece of Russian iconography at its best. Successive church synods held up Rublev's work as an example for other Russian icon-painters, so that his influence reaches up to the eighteenth century. Rice characterizes Rublev's art as follows:

> Rublev is essentially a Russian of the new age; his faces are modelled and the severe highlights are absent; his figures sway with the delicate rhythmical movement of dancers, they no longer have the angularity and violence of Greek work; the style is humanistic rather than expressionist or symbolic.[35]

From the fifteenth century onwards, the popularity of icons in the home increases. This also is an indication of the icon gathering into itself the rich symbolism of Russian spirituality as an integral part of everyday or popular culture. By 1517, Sigmund Freiherr von Herberstein, the Kaiser's diplomatic envoy to Russia (1517-1518, 1526-1527), could observe that the icon had become a symbol of Russian culture in that every home had an icon. As soon as a guest entered a home, he would first look around to catch a glimpse of the icons, thereupon baring his head, cross himself three times, after their custom, and only then would he greet the host: "Good health to you!"[36]

Kondakov relates that by the sixteenth century, there were more than twenty types of icons, depending on the place which they occupied in the church or in the home or according to the specific role assigned to them in the cult or in private life.[37] The number of icons in old Russian churches as well as homes grew enormously. In addition to depicting the Mother of God, icons were drawn to represent Christ and the Trinity, the great feasts of the church, stations of the Cross, angels, martyrs and saints. St. Nicholas became a national trademark as did St. George the Victorious, Martyr - the bearer of light and patron of farmers and herdsmen. Galavaris writes that the worship of icons influenced the personal lives of the worshippers even when they did not always understand the fine theological points of the underlying doctrine.[38]

Some icons were accorded special status as miracle-working or wonder icons. Thus grew the worship of saints and martyrs as protectors of cities, and icons were carried in procession into battle. Soloukhin discovered during his search for lost icons that an icon of St. George the Great Martyr was used in his village in old times to bless cattle with in the spring. He also refers to the Galitsky Mother of God - a wonder-working icon which allegedly stopped a cholera epidemic in a village.[39]

Above all, icons became principal places of, and occasions for, prayer, deepening Eastern Slav spirituality noted for its spiritual exercises, asceticism, and the monastic way of life of the most devout. Hence, Ouspensky concludes that for an Orthodox man today, an icon is not "an object of aesthetic admiration or an object of study; it is living, grace-inspired art which feeds him."[40] There remains a western misconception that the Orthodox believer venerates or worships the icon itself. Stefan Jeckel, a German scholar of Russian metal icons, quotes Pierre Pascal to the effect that the Russian believer who prays before a wonder-working icon, knows well that the icon is not itself the source of physical or spiritual healing, but only an intermediary or medium through which God's grace is at work.[41]

The decline of Russian iconography is commonly set in the latter part of the sixteenth century and attributed to the growing secularization of Russian society due to western influences of humanism and the Enlightenment. This process was completed by Peter the Great (1672-1725) who introduced western ideas and techniques in wholesale fashion in order to modernize Russia. Ouspensky records that by the seventeenth century, church art became secularized. This reflected a deep spiritual crisis, a secularization of religious consciousness, and the influence of nascent secular realistic art by the famous iconographer, Simon Oushakov.[42]

To arrest the decline of church art, the Hundred Chapters Synod (*Stoglav*) decreed in 1551 that icon-painters should follow tradition and keep to the established types, rather than follow their own whims. H. P. Gerhard recounts that at the 1553-1554 Synod, the *d'iak* [clerk] Ivan Mikhailovich Viskovati objected to icon-painters' repainting of Moscow churches destroyed by fire, for their portrayal of Christ as a lamb and not in human form, and enjoined them to return to the iconographical canon.[43]

By the eighteenth and nineteenth centuries, secular art had completely eclipsed church art in Russia. This religious art was largely forgotten, only to be rediscovered at the end of the nineteenth century. The old religious themes became replaced by miniature-like portraits.[44] But the decline of old Russian painting in the seventeenth century coincided with the renaissance of metal icons, a variation of traditional iconography, and a unique art form in itself, rich in motifs.[45] The total eclipse of Russian iconography, irrespective of medium, came with the October Revolution of 1917.

THE RUSSIAN SOUL CRUCIFIED

The whirlwind of October 1917 swept away many Russian treasures and traditions and cost incalculable human lives and suffering. It touched the very soul of the nation in announcing the imminent arrival of the Christian millennarian hope of Heaven on earth. But the promise of an earthly Jerusalem, ushered in by force and built on the ideological enslavement of Man-God, was in fact an inverted Christianity leading to distopia - totalitarianism and terror. A student of Soviet Russia cannot escape the conclusion that the Bolshevik Revolution crucified the Russian soul itself.[46]

If the icon truly mirrors the Russian soul and the nation's conscience, and is a symbol of Russian culture, rooted in deep spirituality, then the fate of the icon in post-revolutionary Russia may serve as a reliable guide to the fate of the nation. The Bolsheviks pledged to sweep clear the national and religious consciousness by removing icons, destroying churches and monasteries and killing or imprisoning the priesthood. They succeeded in subverting the Russian Orthodox Church, which became even more dependent on the all-powerful state than in tsarist times.

Russian children were taught in school - as Pioneers - to report their parents to the authorities, and some became militant destroyers of icons, as Soloukhin remembers.[47] Religion, said Karl Marx, was the opium of the people; it held up progress and, hence, had to be swept away, confined to the dustbin of history. The new Soviet man was, thus, brought up to loathe or ignore icons and all religion as things of the past. Icons, which in the eighteenth and nineteenth centuries were suffering from benign neglect, were now seen in the twentieth century as something completely useless and even inimical.

What happened to all those Russian icons, that universe of beauty and of faith? At the beginning of the Revolution, two railway wagons full of old icons found at the Nizhnii Novgorod station were burned. After the Revolution, the destruction of icons continued. Thus, at Ryazan, icons were burned to make room for storing milk bottles. A most insightful account concerning the fate of the icons is the dispassionate tale of Vladimir Soloukhin, a collector of icons. He found out to his amazement and disgust - from the standpoint of an art lover (but not a believer) - that icons were: used as barrel-lids, bars for doors or windows in closed churches, or as crates for potatoes, tables, firewood or even horse troughs. And they were even left lying on the floor or in the attic to rot.[48]

An old woman, a character in Soloukhin's story, perhaps summed up best the fate of the Russian icon in the twentieth century:

"The icon came down to us from the bright days of antiquity, and now, as you can see, it's been swallowed up by the darkness of ignorance."[49] Yet, there is hope that the icon may survive and even become a catalyst for the growing religious renaissance in post-Stalin Russia.

THE RE-CHRISTIANIZATION OF RUS

In this godless twentieth century, which has already suffered two world wars, the icon was saved from total extinction thanks to its duality as a work of art and a religious object. Throughout Russia, private collectors like Soloukhin have been drawn to icons by the sheer beauty of their art and craftsmanship while believers snatched them from the jaws of destruction among church ruins as holy objects. Even the new Soviet state realized the inestimable value of the icon as an irreplaceable national treasure of old Russian art. The art and science of restoring ancient surviving icons has developed apace.

New schools of Russian iconography, such as early Tver painting, have come to light.[50] The Soviet state brought together great collections of Russian icons in such museums as the Tretiakov Gallery, the Russian Museum in Leningrad, the Hermitage and the Rublev Museum at the Andronakov Monastery. It has funded the study of Russian iconography and its restoration, the exhibition of state collections abroad, and even bilingual publication in Russian and English of lavishly illustrated books by such official historians as Viktor N. Lazarev, E. Smirnova and S. Yamshchikov, and L. M. Yevseyeva, I. A. Kochetkov and V. N. Sergeev.[51]

The problem with officially approved Soviet studies of Russian iconography is that they reduce the icon to its artistic component, or worse, misinterpret its spiritual dimension. Thus, Rublev's Old Testament Trinity, where Abraham and Sarah entertain the three angels who symbolize the Christian trinity - Father, Son and the Holy Ghost - is given the following secularized misinterpretation in Lazarev's volume:

> the symbolism extends far beyond the ecclesiastical aspect. It is of infinitely greater significance as a concept of human love and amity. We find in the Trinity, as in medieval social utopias, the incarnation of the Russian peoples' dream of peace and accord which they vainly

sought in the life that surrounded them. Since the ideals are so pure, so noble and humane, they reverberate in the composition with exceptional force.[52]

As we have learned above, if Lazarev's musings were true, Rublev's Trinity would clearly not qualify as an icon. The time is ripe for the re-christianization of Rus. But the road is a long and arduous one since what it requires is the rediscovery of faith as well as Russian national identity, along with pluralism, tolerance, and human rights. Happily, these are precisely the wellsprings of the religious, national, and human rights dissent in contemporary Russia.

The icon may again become a symbol of, and a catalyst for, moral and spiritual regeneration advocated by Solzhenitsyn and others as the only way out of the physical (pollution and war), moral (relativism), and spiritual (godlessness) morass of the twentieth century, East and West.[53] Much, indeed, needs to be rehabilitated: the value of free thought, respect for human dignity, love of God, love of neighbor, and care for God's creation, the strengthening of individual character, prayer, and the Christian vocation of restoring both man and nature in accord with the will of God. What is needed is clearly a process of healing. The icon, of course, is a symbol of spiritual healing. The frequent themes of physical welfare and spiritual healing in Russian iconography are central, not peripheral and have recently drawn the attention of western scholars such as Jorgen Schmidt-Voigt in his study of Russian icon-painting and medicine.[54]

It is also obvious that the conceptual distance between the Russian icon and Soviet reality can only be measured in light years. This Soviet reality is based on an adamant doctrinal enmity toward freedom and faith and is backed by the power of a modern, totalitarian state. Soviet propaganda at home is just as pernicious as that directed for foreign consumption. The former creates the illusion of progress, the latter the illusion of glasnost' and of peace. While imprisoning believers, peace groups independent of the state, and human rights activists at home, the Soviet state encourages "peace" movements and "dialogue" between the captive Russian Orthodox Church and well-meaning if misinformed western Christian churches abroad.

The true Soviet attitude toward believers, freedom of conscience, freedom of religion and peace reveals itself in the persecution of all believers and the closing of churches and monasteries. And there is a method to this Soviet madness, that is, specific procedures worked out for the closure and destruction of churches and monasteries over long periods of time in order to overcome popular resistance. Soloukhin enumerates three steps followed by the authorities in closing a church: 1) an invitation to the diocesan clergy to inspect a church (visit just a formality); 2) inspection by two or three members of the local department of culture (who look for precious metals); and 3) the church is then made over to the nearest collective farm to serve as a garage, storehouse or carpenter's shop.[55] The authorities padlock the church and leave it that way for years on end in an effort to acclimatize the local population to the fact. Ultimately, the church is destroyed (only the bricks are salvaged) or converted to more "practical" uses noted above (church buildings of architectural value are sometimes made into museums).

The spiritual barrenness of the official Marxist-Leninist ideology finds its truthful mirror in the ruins of a typical old church, ransacked, abandoned and boarded up. Soloukhin describes the scene in chilling detail:

> The candlesticks had been thrown down, the lampchains were broken, the cupboards were overturned and the books scattered page by page. The windows were broken; so was the glass in the icon frames and the coloured lamps, and at every step we took it crunched under our feet. Bronze overlays had been wrenched from the icons and were lying about, twisted into every conceivable shape. The oak altar table in the sanctuary had been turned upside-down and the underside hacked about with a crowbar. In the iconostasis there were gaping sockets where the icons had been, and its carved and gilded cross-beams, piled high with pigeon droppings, completed the picture of devastation.[56]

In the face of such militant Soviet atheism, how can there possibly be any hope for a re-christianization of Rus? It is precisely the senselessness and suffering inflicted by the Soviet reality upon the *narod* - the man in the street - which constitutes the wellspring of the contemporary religious renaissance in Russia. Among the intelligentsia, there is pervasive religious imagery in the work of some of its best poets such as Iosif Brodsky, Boris Pasternak, and Anna Akhmatova, and such writers as Solzhenitsyn.[57] Akhmatova's iconic imagery of crucifixion in her poem, *Requiem*, testifies to the truth and the power of the Christian faith. It recalls one of the treasured themes of Russian iconography, "Mother, weep not for me," in which the half-buried Christ gives the promise of the resurrection to His Mother.[58]

The exiled Russian poet, Brodsky, the 1987 Nobel laureate in literature, encompasses well the suffering, yet hopeful, spirit of Russia in the twentieth century:

> In villages God does not live only in icon corners as the scoffers claim, but plainly everywhere. He sanctifies each roof and pan, divides each double door. In villages God acts abundantly - cooks lentils in iron pots on Saturdays, dances a lazy jig in flickering flame, and winks at me, witness to all of this. He plants a hedge, and gives away a bride (the groom's forester), and, for a joke, he makes it certain that the game warden will never hit the duck he's shooting at. The chance to know and witness all of this, amidst the whistling of the autumn mist, is, I would say, the only touch of bliss that's open to the village atheist.[59]

The underground church is alive and well in Russia. Believers gather in homes, in the forest, anywhere and everywhere where they hope to pray and worship, while dodging official surveillance, the Secret Police (KGB), intimidation, threats, blackmail and firing from jobs. The more outspoken among the faithful, unafraid to witness openly, are, of course, given long prison sentences or sent to psychiatric hospitals.[60] The phenomenon of underground churches in the Soviet Union and Eastern Europe has been captured in documentaries (filmed clandestinely) and distributed by such western Christian missionary organizations as Open Doors and Christian Missions to the communist world. Thus, "Christians Behind Bars," a film smuggled out of the Soviet Union in 1975, showed the world of a Soviet prison camp to western audiences for the first time (aired on American television).[61]

Equally notable is the growing disillusionment of the young and the technical intelligentsia with the sterility of the official ideology which fails to answer such crucial questions as: is there a God, good and evil, justice, meaning of existence and death. Even atheist intellectuals are beginning to have gnawing doubts about official dogma, especially the deification of man in the concept of Man-God, whose iron logic leads ultimately to suicide, as confirmed by

Mayakovsky, the poet of the revolution, and other idealistic communists.[62] Aleksandr Zinoviev's novels are also instructive in this regard.[63] Yet, the road is open to one and all, including Marxist intellectuals, to find their way back to God.[64]

Surprisingly, iconic imagery conveying Christian values of suffering, self-sacrifice, love and redemption are increasingly surfacing amidst the themes of Russian cinematography.[65] For example, the film, "Pokaianie" [Repentance], by Tengiz Abuladze, a Georgian director, which won a special jury prize at Cannes in 1987, is the story of Stalin told in fantasies and nightmares. What is unusual for a Soviet film is the explicitness of its religious imagery. It depicts the heroine's father with a Christ-like face, hanging from wrist irons under torture as in the traditional scene of Christ's crucifixion. Even more direct is the symbolism at the end of the film, where an old woman asks directions to the church from the heroine, but is informed that it is Varlam (Stalin) Street, upon which she remarks: "Oh, what good is a road if it doesn't lead to the church?" and trudges off disconsolately.

It is also apparent from the samizdat literature, explored by Jancar, that the Russian believer is not looking for a new religion, but the old one, "purged of its complicity with power."[66] Here again, Russian iconography may point the way to a genuine separation between church and state, by teaching contemporary man the timeless spiritual truth of Christianity - namely the duality between the flesh and the spirit, and the necessity of distinguishing the sacred from the secular realms. It will be recalled that it was the very mixing of the church image and the worldly image, of church and the world, as a result of a deep spiritual crisis and the secularization of religious consciousness, which corrupted Russian iconography itself.[67]

The prospects for the inner revival of the Russian Orthodox Church are also directly related to the rediscovery of the central message of Eastern Christianity, symbolized by the icon: the sinfulness of man and the need for deliverance. Galavaris captures the specific hallmark of Eastern Christianity in its emphasis on free will and the struggles and the ultimate triumph of the saints venerated in the icons.[68] That the Church is in need of such a revival is attested to by a group of believers in Russia, who addressed their plea to the World Council of Churches, with copies to Patriarch Athenagoras, Pope Paul VI and the International Committee for the Defense of Christian

Culture. The letter by J. Vishnevskaia, B. Dubovenko, V. Kokorev, V. Lashkova, E. Stroieva and Yu. Titov, dated September, 1969, testifies to their courage and the indomitability of the human spirit:

> We deeply deplore the fact that the Russian Orthodox Church finds its supporters amongst laymen and ordinary priests, and not among the bishops of the Russian church, many of whom are barren fig trees, completely under the control of the Council for Religious Affairs. . . Anatolii Emmanuilovich was doing his duty as a Christian, and none of his activities, which were all in defense of the Christian faith, infringed Soviet laws. . . We, Christian believers and citizens of the Soviet Union, are deeply disturbed by the arrest of the Orthodox writer A. Levitin-Krasnov and the teacher B. Talantov. We join with them in their protest against the abnormal relations which exist between Church and State, and we demand the opening of the forcibly closed churches, monasteries, seminaries and houses of prayer.[69]

The question which concerns many believers and democrats in the West is whether the national and religious renaissance in Russia can be anything but a return to dogma, tradition and autocracy or theocracy, which would necessarily again suppress basic human rights and freedoms, including freedom of religion and freedom of conscience - this time in the name of religion, instead of scientific socialism. Solzhenitsyn's response to this question is disquieting to many, East and West, believers, agnostics and nonbelievers.[70]

But the icon can provide a more felicitous answer and point the way beyond all human dogmas to the fundamental Christian truth embodied in the icon: God created man in His image, and, hence, human dignity, freedom and responsibility originate in the Creator, and, as such, should not be abridged by man. That the national and religious renaissance in contemporary Russia can be reconciled with freedom, pluralism and tolerance, is underlined by Talantov's notion of the indivisibility of freedom. It is Talantov's greatest legacy to civil rights and to the national and religious movement in Russia to have stated the simple truth that freedom for the Orthodox requires freedom for the Baptists and intellectuals as well.[71] Equally, Levitin-Krasnov shall be remembered for his passionate defense of civil rights.[72]

It is in this light that the icon assumes its full significance in the classic sense, namely as a bridge between God and man and as a symbol of Christ's two great commandments in the New Testament: love of God and love of neighbor (Matthew 22:36-40, John 13:34-35). It is also in this light that Meerson-Aksenov's call for spiritual renewal, for sobornost', understood as the whole people and the church together forming the body of Christ and becoming witnesses, may be fully understood.[73] Such a genuine moral and spiritual revolution would clearly indicate that Russia has become an icon for the rest of the world, if not God's chosen nation in the twentieth century.

---

1. Aleksandr I. Solzhenitsyn, A World Split Apart, Commencement Address delivered at Harvard University, June 8, 1978, New York: Harper & Row, 1978, pp. 21, 23.

2. Anatoly Levitin-Krasnov, "On the Situation of the Russian Orthodox Church" (Letter to Pope Paul VI, c. September 26, 1967), cited by Barbara Wolfe Jancar, "Religious Dissent in the Soviet Union," in Rudolf L. Tokes (Editor), Dissent in the USSR: Politics, Ideology, and People, Baltimore: Johns Hopkins University Press, 1975, p. 205.

3. Michael Meerson-Aksenov and Boris Shragin, eds., The Political, Social and Religious Thought of Russian Samizdat: An Anthology, Belmont, MA: Nordland, 1977, p. 505. See also Mihajlo Mihajlov, "The Great Catalyzer: Nietzsche and Russian Neo-Idealism," in Bernice G. Rosenthal, ed., Nietzsche in Russia, Princeton, NJ: Princeton University Press, 1986, pp. 127-145.

4. Dmitrii Nelidov, "Ideocratic Consciousness and Personality," in Meerson-Aksenov and Shragin, p. 290.

5. Jancar, "Religious Dissent," p. 208.

6. Ibid., p. 228.

7. Ibid., p. 191.

8. "Church Destroyed despite Villagers' Protests," in Michael Bourdeaux and Michael Rowe, eds., May One Believe, In Russia? Violations of Religious Liberty in the Soviet Union, London: Darton, Longman & Todd, 1980, p. 43.

9. Boris Talantov, Letters to N. V. Podgorny and Pope Paul VI, cited in Jancar, "Religious Dissent," p. 227.

10. "An Appeal to Christians Throughout the World," in Bourdeaux & Rowe, pp. xii-xiii.

11. Jancar, p. 213. English trans.: A Cry of Despair from Moscow Churchmen, New York: 1966; shortened version in Michael Bourdeaux, Patriarch and Prophets: Persecution of the Russian Orthodox Church Today, Oxford: Mowberg, 1970, pp. 189-223. See also Gleb Yakunin and Lev Regelson, Letters from Moscow: Religion and Human Rights in the USSR, Jane Ellis, ed., San Francisco: Dakin, 1978.

12. Anatoly Levitin-Krasnov, "The Situation of the Russian Orthodox Church," Letter to Pope Paul VI, as reported by A Chronicle of Current Events, No. 5, in Peter Reddaway, ed., Uncensored Russia: Protest and Dissent in the Soviet Union, New York: American Heritage Press, 1972, p. 323.

13. "Founding Statement of the Christian Committee for the Defense of Believers' Rights in the USSR," December 27, 1976, in Bourdeaux and Rowe, pp. 32-33.

14. Pavel Korin, quoted by Vladimir Soloukhin, Searching for Icons in Russia, New York: Harcourt Brace Jovanovich, 1971, p. 33.

15. George Galavaris, The Icon in the Life of the Church, Leiden, Netherlands: E. J. Brill, 1981, p. 2.

16. Egon Sendler, S.J., L'icone-image de l'invisible: Elements de theologie, esthetique et technique, Paris: Desclee de Brouwer, 1981, p. 59.

17. Leonid Ouspensky and Vladimir Lossky, The Meaning of Icons, Rev. ed., Crestwood, NY: St. Vladimir's Seminary Press, 1982, p. 22.

18. Ibid., pp. 29, 31.

19. Galavaris, The Icon, pp. 3, 7.

20. Ouspensky and Lossky, The Meaning of Icons, p. 36.

21. Ibid., p. 45.

22. Sendler, L'icone, p. 60; Soloukhin, Searching for Icons, pp. 119-120.

23. Ouspensky and Lossky, The Meaning of Icons, p. 35.

24. Soloukhin, Searching for Icons, p. 151.

25. Ouspensky and Lossky, The Meaning of Icons, p. 42; Sendler, L'icone, p. 230.

26. Sendler, L'icone, p. 231.

27. Galavaris, The Icon, p. 4.

28. Sendler, L'icone, p. 9.

29. Nikodim P. Kondakov, The Russian Icon, 4 vols., Prague: Seminarium Kondakovianum, 1928-1933, III, p. 182.

30. David Talbot Rice, Russian Icons, London: King Penguin Books, 1947, p. 17.

31. Galavaris, The Icon, p. 3.

32. Ibid., p. 45.

33. Soloukhin, Searching for Icons, p. 127.

34. Ouspensky and Lossky, The Meaning of Icons, p. 45.

35. Rice, Russian Icons, p. 30.

36. Sigmund Freiherr von Herberstein, cited by Stefan Jeckel, Russische Metall-Ikonen - in Formsand gegossener Glaube, 2nd rev. ed., Bramsche: Rasch, 1981, p. 18.

37. Kondakov, The Russian Icon, III, p. 184.

38. Galavaris, The Icon, p. 19.

39. Soloukhin, Searching for Icons, pp. 34, 77.

40. Ouspensky and Lossky, The Meaning of Icons, p. 49.

41. Pierre Pascal, cited in Jeckel, Russische Metall-Ikonen, p. 13.

42. Ouspensky and Lossky, The Meaning of Icons, p. 48.

43. H. P. Gerhard (pseud), The World of Icons, New York: Harper & Row, 1971, p. 181.

44. Rice, Russian Icons, p. 38.

45. Jeckel, Russische Metall-Ikonen, pp. 24, 38-41.

46. Anyone who doubts this thesis need only read the Solzhenitsyn corpus, especially Aleksandr R. Solzhenitsyn, The Gulag Archipelago, 1918-1956, 3 vols., New York: Harper & Row, 1974-78.

47. Soloukhin, Searching for Icons, p. 13.

48. Ibid., pp. 14, 18, 30, 77, 155.

49. Ibid., p. 73.

50. L. M. Yevseyeva, I. A. Kochetkov and V. N. Sergeev, Zhivopis drevnei Tveri [Early Tver Painting], Moscow: Iskusstvo, 1983.

51. Viktor N. Lazarev, Moskovskaia shkola ikonopisi [Moscow School of Icon Painting], Moscow: Iskusstvo, 1980; E. Smirnova and S. Yamshchikov, Drevnerusskaia zhivopis [Old Russian Painting], Leningrad: Aurora Art Publishers, 1974; Yevseyeva et al.

52. Lazarev, Moskovskaia shkola, p. 24.

53. For an assessment of Solzhenitsyn's thought, see O. Gruenwald, "The Essential Solzhenitsyn: The Political Nexus or the Russian Connection," Thought, 55:217, June, 1980, pp. 137-152.

54. Jorgen Schmidt-Voigt, Russische Ikonenmalerei und Medizin, 2nd rev. ed., Munich: Karl Thiemig, 1983.

55. Soloukhin, Searching for Icons, pp. 100-101.

56. Ibid., pp. 90-91.

57. Josef Brodsky, Less Than One: Selected Essays, New York: Farrar, Straus & Giroux, 1987; Boris Pasternak, Doctor Zhivago, New York: New American Library, 1964; R. McKane, ed., Anna Akhmatova, Selected Poems, New York: Penguin, 1969; Aleksandr I. Solzhenitsyn, Cancer Ward, New York: Bantam, 1972.

58. McKane, Anna Akhmatova, p. 102.

59. Josef Brodsky, "In Villages God Does Not Live," in Selected Poems, New York: Harper & Row, 1973.

60. Sidney Bloch and Peter Reddaway, Soviet Psychiatric Abuse: The Shadow Over World Psychiatry, Boulder, CO: Westview Press, 1985; Harvey Fireside, Soviet Psychoprisons, New York: Norton, 1982.

61. "Christians Behind Bars," distributed by Christian Missions to the Communist World, Middlebury, IN 46540; "Freedom Held Hostage," distributed by Open Doors, Orange, CA.

62. Marc Slonim, "Vladimir Mayakovsky: The Poet of the Revolution," in Soviet Russian Literature: Writers and Problems, 1917-1967, New York: Oxford University Press, 1967, pp. 19-31.

63. See Libor Brom, "The Soviet Man as an Atheist and Believer: Alexander Zinoviev's Spiritual Stratum," paper presented at the conference on "Christianity, the State and Society in Contemporary Russia: Sources of Continuity and Change," Monterey Institute of International Studies, Monterey, CA, January 17-20, 1988.

64. For a group of Marxist humanist thinkers who have travelled far down this road, see O. Gruenwald, The Yugoslav Search for Man: Marxist Humanism in Contemporary Yugoslavia, South Hadley, MA: Bergin & Garvey, 1983.

65. See Dmitry Shlapentokh, "Christianity in Recent Soviet Films: The Case of Russophile Ideology," paper presented at the conference on "Christianity, the State and Society in Contemporary Russia: Sources of Continuity and Change," Monterey Institute of International Studies, Monterey, CA, January 17-20, 1988.

66. Jancar, "Religious Dissent in the Soviet Union," p. 206.

67. Ouspensky and Lossky, The Meaning of Icons, pp. 47-48.

68. Galavaris, The Icon, p. 9.

69. Letter from Six Christian Believers to the World Council of Churches, September, 1969, in Reddaway, ed., Uncensored Russia, p. 325.

70. See, e.g., Mihajlo Mihajlov, "The Return of the Grand Inquisitor," Chronicles of Culture, 9:6, June 1985, pp. 20-26.

71. Talantov, assessed by A Chronicle of Current Events, in Reddaway, ed., Uncensored Russia, pp. 326-327.

72. Levitin-Krasnov in Reddaway, Uncensored Russia, pp. 322-324.

73. Meerson-Aksenov and Shragin, eds., The Political, Social and Religious Thought of Russian Samizdat, pp. 535-541.

12

THE RESURGENCE OF CHRISTIANITY AND RUSSIAN-JEWISH RELATIONS

(An Examination of Soviet Literary Prose)

Mikhail Heifetz

In his polemical article, "Russian Nationalism, Marxism-Leninism and the Fate of Russia" (1979), Canadian Professor Dmitry Pospielovsky wrote the following thoughts on Russo-Jewish relations as they developed in the 1970s:

> ... One notes with a certain consternation the anti-Jewish sentiments that exist among some contemporary Russian nationalist circles in the USSR. One would think that when these groups assert that aspersions had been cast upon the Russian people, they should realize that the Jewish people in the USSR had perhaps been vilified even more because of the forced substitution of true Jewish culture with the Evsektsii (TN). ... Even worse, while the Russianness of Russians was destroyed by the communists and Communist Youth League members of all nationalities, those who led the destruction of the Jewishness of Jews were exclusively Jewish communists, i.e., Jewish renegades. This no doubt led to an even greater demoralization among the Jewish people. It is amazing that the overwhelming majority of Russian nationalists do not seem to realize this tragedy of the Jewish people. Instead of mutual understanding between these two slandered peoples, more often than not we unfortunately encounter mutual hostility and distrust.[1]

Russian Soviet literary prose, including both officially published materials and those appearing in *samizdat*, explains to a great extent how this "surprising" hostility and distrust, to use Pospielovsky's words, arises. Socio-political factors include the Russian nationalists' need to adjust to a Brezhnevian and Andropovian Party apparatus which has traditionally been anti-Semitic; and the Jewish nationalists' desire to morally justify their split with their troubled native land. Ideological factors include the conflict between the Russian, essentially Populist progressive tradition and the Jewish tradition of socialist universalism. In other words there is a conflict between the Slavophile Russian tradition typical of Russian nationalists and the Russian Westernizer tradition of the Jews. Herein lies the contradiction between the newly revived nationalist and religious trends, which are burdened by the anti-Semitic past of Christianity and the anti-Christian attitudes of Jews. Herein also lies the contradiction between the Russian and Jewish mentality because both are trying to preserve completely identical Russian cultural roots. This has led to an unnatural cultural dichotomy at a time when both sides are on a religious search.

Why was it that only in the 1970s and 1980s material appeared in Russian prose which could be used to analyze these complicated relations? The phenomenon can be explained by years of artistic repression during which Party authorities ordered editors and censors to remove Jewish characters and plots from artistic and literary works. As proof of this, let me remind you of the 1940s ban on Yu. German's story, *Podpolkovnik meditsinskoi sluzhby* [Lieutenant Colonel of the Medical Service]. This story was banned simply because the hero was called Levin. The story's conclusion had already been typeset for the journal *Zvezda* [Star], and, based upon a ruling of the court, the author had to pay the journal's costs (even in the annals of censorship a unique event!). Another example is the film "Kommissar" [Commissar] by Director Askol'dov. In the 1960s it was not only banned, but the director himself was deprived of his right to work in his profession; he was classified as unfit simply because the plot involved a Jewish family helping a commissar. On many occasions this "general rule" permitted some fluctuations both in favor of and against Jewish characters and plots. For example, the positive characters such as Zalkind in V. Azhaev's *Daleko ot Moskvy* [Far from Moscow], Officer Farber in Nekrasov's *V okopakh Stalingrada* [In the Trenches of Stalingrad], and Jews in stories by the Leningrad writer Ermogaev; or the negative Jewish characters in Panferov's novel, *V strane poverzhennykh* [In the Country of the Defeated], and especially in I. Shevtsov's novels in the 1960s.

The following episode, however, completely epitomizes the situation. In his well-intentioned poem, "Babii Yar," the poet Evtushenko dared to expose the anti-Semitic feelings of the enemies of

Soviet power - Hitlerites, Black Hundreds, etc. The very mention of the taboo term "Jew" [*evrei*] was so shocking to society that the editor and the poetry department of *Literaturnaia Gazeta* were immediately fired, and top leaders of the CPSU began to publicly persecute the poet himself. After years of deliberate silence, the very word "Jew" had acquired such a compromised connotation that even now when Soviet political figures speak out loud about Jews they use the euphemism "a person of Jewish nationality," in order to be tactful and not insult the given individual with the degrading label "Jew."

In the 1970s the situation changed. The campaign against Zionism conducted in socio-political literature was not successful ("Those dirty souls did not believe our warnings," said the prominent anti-Zionist L. Korneev).[2] Therefore, it was decided to use more emotionally forceful and effective devices in the campaign against Soviet Jewish emigration and repatriation. Jewish characters and Jewish plots could now legally appear on the pages of prose fiction. And, naturally, various social groups tried to make use of these new opportunities to express their own position and mold public opinion, just as Russian literature has traditionally done.

Which public groups tried to influence public opinion in Russia in this period? The CPSU program had declared 1980 to be the year in which the necessary financial and resource base would have been laid for a communist society. This tenet of the official ideology should not be underestimated. Since it logically flowed from Marxist-Leninist doctrine, not achieving it meant that the failure of the historical experiment, conducted on a living, breathing Russia, had to be recognized. As this date approached, the ideological collapse of the official doctrine became more and more apparent, and on the ruins of this doctrine, new ideologies arose to fill the void. As one would expect of the 20th century, these new ideologies were primarily nationally-oriented ideologies, i.e., ideologies of ethnic rebirth.

As early as the 1960s the first signs appeared that the Russian consciousness of itself as a nationality was reawakening after a long period of inactivity. In and of itself, this rebirth merely meant a restoration of the old habits and traditions of the Russian people, and a revival of interest in the traditional Russian religion, i.e., Russian Orthodoxy. However, this whole turn of events was complicated by the Russians' need to disassociate themselves from a people who were for a long period of time a form of "shadow culture", i.e., from the Jews of Soviet Russia.

The reasons for this dissociation are a separate topic, outside the parameters of this discussion. Within the framework of this symposium, however, it should be noted that the need for dissociation placed the "Russian party" on difficult terms with Christianity. After all, Christianity is not a religion associated with one ethnic group; it is an international phenomenon, and moreover, its basic values are closely tied to Judaism. Consequently, as early as the 1960s some "Russites" developed an interest in paganism as an ethnic religion. However, it would be best to trace this development by using a concrete example, found in the works of one of the strongest supporters of Russian nationalism, the prose writer Valentin Pikul'.

Even in his earliest works Pikul' was an advocate of "the Russian idea." His early novels, however, contained absolutely no anti-Semitic overtones. For example, in his novel *Iz tupika* [Out of the Deadlock] (1968), Pikul' depicted the civil war as a skirmish between opposing groups of Russian people who did not understand each other. For the author, these Russians were all citizens of the Russian Empire and were all fighting to strengthen the forces and the might of the empire, no matter whether the blood flowing in their veins was Russian, German, French, or Jewish. The enemies of Russia were those people who encroached upon the empire (the Finns, for example). However, during the 1970s, the tone of his novels began to change. For example, in the novel *Bogatstvo* [Riches] (1978), about the Russo-Japanese War, there was still no disdain or hate for the "vassal" people of the empire; however, his characters of Russian nationality had already started acting like elder brothers, patrons to the "natives," who repay this suzerainty with touching loyalty. The only exception is the Jew. For example, the main reason the Russian Army was defeated at Kamchatka, according to the plot in *Riches*, was the fact that a tsarist civil servant committed treason. His name was Gubnitskii, a Jewish convert to Christianity. It should be noted, however, that Gubnitskii was not accused of being Jewish but of cosmopolitanism. He is "a man cut out of the contemporary mold who simply could not understand how one could love any land just because one was born there." Therefore, he was accused of cosmopolitanism. Pikul' clearly imitates the trend of the "Suslov group" in the party apparatus with its traditional pro-Stalinist stance on the nationality question.

A new turn in Pikul's works appeared in the novel *U poslednei cherty* [The Last Trace], which treats the fall of the Romanov dynasty. This work was published in the journal *Nash sovremennik* in 1979. According to the author, the fall of tsarist Russia was in no way the result of an uprising by workers and peasants dressed as soldiers, as it is depicted in communist textbooks. The main reason for the downfall of the dynasty was the decay of the ruling elite. For example, Sabler, a descendant of Swabian rabbis and a minion of Rasputin, supposedly controlled the spiritual administration (Holy Synod). The army was commanded by Sukhomlinov, who was ruled, unbeknownst to himself, by Jewish agents of the Central Powers. For a long time the government was headed by Witte, a friend of the Zionist bankers who entangled Russia in debts and befuddled it with vodka. Even the tsar and the tsarina were pawns of Rasputin, himself a tool in the hands of the Jewish merchants - Simanovich, Rubinshtein and Marius (the latter at the same time "a prominent German spy"). They either killed the true Russians opposing them (such as Stolypin) or ruined them (like Kokovtsov). The way Pikul's work portrays events, it is not surprising that the empire, which was in the hands of Jewish minions, fell like overripe fruit.

Two special features of Pikul's novel should be mentioned. First of all, Pikul' is not only anti-Semitic, but anti-Christian and anti-Orthodox as well. He depicts members of the clergy as being almost worse than Jews. They are deceitful, corrupt, crooked and homosexual (the "synod of Sabler pederasts"). These people used deceit and cunning to advance themselves in Rasputin's court. The only member of the clergy who has any merit at all in the novel is the ordained monk Iliodor (a "highly complex figure"), who is a well-known member of the Black Hundreds. He is meritorious because in the end he renounced Orthodoxy and became a proponent of "the true pagan faith!"

The second special quality of this novel is that it is not a consistently anti-Semitic work. The author did not unmask Jews in general, but only those Jews who participated in imperial matters and who were somehow connected with the ruling elite. There is no libel too dirty or despicable for Nicholas II and his wife. The heir to the throne, Pikul' alleges, was not the tsar's son, but General Orlov's, the tsarina's lover. The tsar is the patron of homosexuals, the organizer of Stolypin's murder and so on. Strangely, Pikul' does not make use of the historically undisputed fact that the tsar patronized the Zionist movement. After all, according to Pikul', it is not Jews per se who are a danger to Russia, and especially not Jews leaving Russia. The really dangerous ones are the "wheeler dealers" of southern Russia with close ties to the ruling elites of the empire, like the sugar factory owner Brodskii, the intelligence agent Manasevich-Manuilov, or Simanovich, the "landlord of an establishment which exploits human vices," and so on.

Pikul's novel was condemned by the party ideologues since Suslov and his assistants figured out that Pikul's period novel was an allusion to themselves. These people had also married Jewesses, some of whose close relatives had been implicated in "diamond swindles" and other financial machinations in which Southern Russian "wheeler dealers" took part. As a result the empire has sunk into "stagnation and regression." After Pikul' fell into disfavor, the anti-Semitic tones completely disappeared from his later novels published in the 1980s.

The trend which Pikul' was the first to portray did not, however, disappear but continued at the end of the 1970s and the beginning of the 1980s. It was the most clearly embodied in a series of biographical novels published as *Zhizn' zamechatel'nykh liudei* [The Lives of Exceptional People] (by *Molodaia Gvardiia*). Anti-Semitic plots appeared in many books of this series, often using the following device: some well-known negative historical personality would appear, and through a slight theme change he would be associated with Jewry (most often in a completely untrue way). False Dmitrii II turned out to be a Jew (R. Skrynnikov's *Minin i Pozharskii*). It is hinted that Biron was a Jew (A. Kuz'min's *Tatishchev*), or at the very least Biron's banker Lipman ruled Russia during Anna Ioannovna's time (in the same book).

The same type of innuendoes were made about the singer Polina Viardo, who was depicted as an evil genius by Turgenev. It is insinuated in *Ostrovskii* by M. Lovanov and in *Dostoevskii* by Yu. Seleznev that Kankrin, Abasy, Grieg and other ministers who brought Russia to ruin were of Jewish origin. The latter two books are especially interesting because they describe the historical convictions widespread among that faction of Russites referred to as "National

Bolsheviks," (although they prefer the term "Statesmen").   The Statesmen do not so much oppose Jews, who at most play a secondary role in their thinking, as they oppose their main competitors in the Russite camp, i.e., the supporters of "conservative nationalism." These more moderate Russites are sometimes called "Revivalists". Alexander Solzhenitsyn is the most outstanding member of this group.

The revivalists represent the historical development of Russia on the rise. Despite all the acknowledged minuses of national and state development, the country was gradually becoming more civilized. And this natural, albeit complex development was interrupted by the outbreak of madness in Europe in 1914 that ended with the disaster of 1917. For the Statesmen (or National Bolsheviks) by contrast, the ideal Russian state can be deemed the end of the eighteenth and beginning of the nineteenth centuries, i.e., the era of Suvorov and Derzhavin. Since then Russia has been eaten away by the germ of bourgeois infection, particularly as the result of Jewish money. Already Nicholas I, it would appear, trembled before a Rothschild, while a certain Epstein nearly bought up the entire mother river Volga and its tributaries![3] The undermining of the peasant culture began as early as Alexander II's reign and was completed under Stalin in the "year of the great turning point".[4]

The Statesmen's "anti-bourgeois" though not thoroughly anti-Semitic ideas, had important political advantages for its members. On the one hand it allowed them to establish contacts with and display loyalty towards the traditionally anti-Semitic party apparatus. On the other hand this idea propitiously allowed October 1917 to be presented as a people's uprising against the power of the Rothschilds. It legally allowed tsarist rule to be discredited and the liberal opposition to be stigmatized as patrons of this bourgeois and foreign movement. It also allowed all revolutionary excesses to be written off to foreigners who had attached themselves to the revolutionary, thoroughly positive Russian-Bolshevik movement. (The party subsequently eliminated these positive elements during the purges.)   Solzhenitsyn was completely right when he defined this group as people who are engaged in a last ditch effort to save communism by merging it with Russian nationalism.[5]

I am not trying to deny the fact that the Statesmen's anti-Semitic feelings are authentic. However, I believe that this trend is not so much a part of their spiritual quest, as a part of their political orientation. Among some Russites this idea is seen as an integral part of the new ideology of the ruling class. Their anti-Semitism serves as an attestation of loyalty to the Party apparatus. In any case, the anti-Semitic trend in the series, "Lives of Exceptional People," became more pronounced after various ideological echelons of the Communist Party checked up on its activities in 1980.

Judophobic trends in the literature of the 1970s and 1980s sometimes had curious and unexpected consequences. For example, the Soviet classicist Valentin Kataev published a short story called "Uzhe napisan Verter" [Werter Is Already Written][6], which is his unique condemnation of the revolution and Soviet rule, made just before his death. He had faithfully served the regime his whole life. For him it was enough to depict the Chairman and investigator of the Regional Extraordinary Commission for Combatting Counterrevolution and Sabotage, and the special representative of the All-Russian secret police [Cheka] as Jews and associates of Trotsky's. This was done in order to conform to the ideas of the Statesmen and to publicly damn the Soviet regime, the revolution and the secret police! I think Kataev, the "most ignoble of the Soviet writers," according to Solzhenitsyn, was not an anti-Semite. Kataev simply made use of the ideological situation in order to tell the Soviet regime what he thought about it before his death. "May you all be damned!"

Another example is Ivan Shamiakin's historic novel *Petrograd-Brest* concerning the Brest-Litovsk peace of 1918. The author's attitude toward his Jewish characters can be summed up as follows. The Jews do not carry any type of ontological evil in and of themselves. Among Jews there are indeed some completely decent people. Due to their foreignness to "the soil", however, they cannot understand the historical and political realities which guide the native population. Even the most positive Jewish characters do not understand, for example, that the "Teutonic hordes" have always coveted Slavic lands. The Jews truly believe in the brotherhood of workers of all countries, including Germans and Slavs. It is this which leads to catastrophe for Jews in countries in which they can influence political decisions.

Finally, it is worth mentioning Yu. Sergeev's novel *Stanovoi khrebet* [The Mainstay], published in *Nash sovremennik* in 1987, which has become famous for its portrayal of "polytheism."

> Polytheism is the true belief of Russians - a religion of marvellous beauty which was defiled and butchered. In its place we have been given a slavish religion; Nikonian icons with foreign faces have been imposed upon us. These icons are mocking and sickly-sweet in their biblical loathsomeness, venality, drunkenness, and lust; in their bestial desire to subjugate this, our land.[7]

As we see, the whole system of Pikul', including the "true religion of paganism" and the damnation of Christianity, has been continued and expanded by writers of this bent.

The most significant and influential group opposing the Statesmen is the other wing (or faction) of the Russites, sometimes called "Revivalists" or even "National-Liberals." Among them two people should be mentioned. The first is Leonid Borodin, who is one of the most rapidly maturing contemporary prose writers. The second is Feliks Svetov, a well-known activist in the Christian revivalist movement who unexpectedly made his debut in prose.

Leonid Borodin is one of the most talented "pens" of the Russian Party. He is a poet, essayist and prose writer and was a political prisoner for eleven years each in jail and the camps. His Jewish characters are accurate, placed in contemporary and true-to-life situations and are unique in their own way because the image of a contemporary Russian Jew is recorded through the eyes of a Russian, who dispassionately assesses the important aspects of the social process happening before his very eyes.

In the story "Pravila igry" [The Rules of the Game],[8] Borodin portrays a contemporary Russian Jew as a man who completely blends in with Russian life. He has nothing Jewish left in him, neither Jewish traditions, nor an elementary knowledge of his people's history, nor any social recollections. Even his first and last name are Russian - Valerii Osinskii. Yurii Plotnikov is his prison comrade (the action takes place in a camp) and is the hero of the story. Osinskii is so Russian that when Plotnikov wants to convince Osinskii that his human rights tactics are incorrect, he appeals to Osinskii's nationality feelings and announces "Ne po-russki vse eto!" [All this is not the Russian way!] having completely forgotten that he is speaking to a Jew. What he encounters in return is an unexpected outburst from Osinskii: "Then how should it be? The way yids do it, right?" Plotnikov is accused of being an anti-Semite and the plot conflict begins. As this conflict develops, Plotnikov talks with Moiseev, one of the Judophobic dissidents, and to the writer Ventsovich who is a Judophile. During these conversations the author reveals the sources of the Russian-Jewish national conflict.

Moiseev (the Judophobe) embodies the typical Russian populist tradition. He firmly believes that there is only one value for which a person can sacrifice himself, even to the point of being sent to the Gulag, and that is for the interests of his own people. It is precisely for the sake of their own, the Russians, and especially for the sake of the sufferings of the peasants, that Moiseev sacrifices his own freedom. And therefore the Jew Osinskii, who is meddling in Russian affairs (that is to say, matters foreign to Osinskii), arouses almost mystical suspicions in Moiseev. This misunderstanding of Osinskii's true goals (and the goals of other Jews) is not only due to Moiseev's narrow-mindedness, but, perhaps more importantly to Osinskii's own narrow-mindedness. Osinskii is a Marxist ("with a human face"), but socialism never required renouncing the interests of one's own people, especially those who are considered to be oppressed. As defined by N. Syrkin, one of the founders of the Jewish socialist movement, only among the Jews, who have an especially distorted view of socialist theory, has there appeared a mass movement repudiating one's own people and sacrificing oneself for the sake of the common rights of the native nationality groups of the countries inhabited by the Jewish Diaspora. This renunciation of intrinsic national feeling, this conscious national suicide, as Borodin so correctly portrays it, avenges its possessors, however, in that Jews are abnormally quick to take offense and to be suspicious of their comrades. This suspiciousness creates a paradoxical feeling of solidarity among Jews. They unite not for the natural reason of defending the interests of their own people, but to do battle against real or imagined anti-Semitism, including the anti-Semitism of their own comrades. This seeming contradiction is heightened by the fact that some comrades, like Moiseev, observe this solidarity of the Jews on the one hand, but on the other hand see that the Jews have repudiated their own national interests and have become preoccupied with Russian matters. They begin suspecting the Jews of harboring secret, incomprehensible designs, mystical ravings and perverse anti-national feelings. Indeed they really do become anti-Semitic, fulfilling the abnormal suspiciousness of people like Osinskii. Thus the vicious cycle of mutual suspicion and lack of mutual trust is complete.

Plotnikov, who embodies the positive ideals of the author, spurns both Moiseev's suspicions of all Jews and the Moiseev-like (as he sees it) defense of the Jews as a national group, set forth in Ventsovich's monologues. Plotnikov feels that it is completely unacceptable to judge people by their nationality, and he contrasts this judgement with saving a person's soul and consciousness, preferring this yardstick to determine the "rules of the game of life." Although religious persuasions are not mentioned in the story because the action takes place before the religious revival in the country, Plotnikov's further evolution towards religious rebirth seems inevitable.

Another trend which has fostered anti-Semitism in the Russite camp can be found in V. Belov's novel *Vse vperedi* [It's All Ahead]. In Russia, as in practically all countries of the world, the last four centuries have witnessed the gradual europeanization of society. This is the process of assimilating and putting into practice the standards of civilization initially worked out in Great Britain and the Netherlands, and which then spread throughout Western Europe. This process is complicated and often painful; its success depends not only upon what a society has gained, but also what it has lost. European standards often do not coincide well with the traditions and outlook of a particular society. They may evoke very strong feelings of rejection. As an example we need only recall the romantic reaction in Germany against French influences in the nineteenth century. It is this painful process of adopting the European heritage in nineteenth century Russia which gave rise to a conflict between the Westernizers and the Slavophiles and later between the liberals and the reactionaries (from "reaction," the retaliatory response to the European invasion). This process has continued in our time, evoking the very same romantic reaction as it did in the nineteenth century.

The "village prose writers," in particular, belong to this camp which rejects European influence. This is where the anti-American feelings of V. Astaf'ev came from in *Pechal'nyi detektiv* [The Sad Detective], and V. Soloukhin's fear of captivity in *Kameshki na ladoni* [Pebbles on the Palm], and Belov's negative reaction to Jewry in *Vse vperedi*. It is worth noting the Jewish professor A. Voronel's remarks in *Trepet zabot iudeiskikh* [The Tremor of Judaic Concerns], that "Jews tend to have Westernizer mentalities, and tend to be more like a Shtol'ts than an Oblomov." Voronel' adds, ". . . if a Jew is not like this, he must then explain why he does not think like a Jew." This leads to conflict between the Jews and the Russite writers. For example, in Belov's novel *Brish* [Brish], it is no accident that the main negative hero is a Jew. He personifies the very western inspiration which Belov feels is threatening to destroy modern-day Russia. The traditional "city of dark intrigues" - Paris - becomes the location for his dark schemes.

This circle of writers was pointedly silent while the National-Bolsheviks led their anti-western propaganda campaign in Soviet literature. The "village prose writers" did not wish to play into the hands of the government. But since the appearance of "glasnost and perestroika," many of them have voluntarily removed their self-imposed restriction and come out with anti-western works, including anti-Jewish ones.

The variety of relations between Jews and Russians is portrayed in F. Svetov's novel, *Otverzi mi dveri* [Open the Door to Me]. Although the novel did not appear abroad until 1978, it was written in the USSR in the first half of the 1970s. It is a genuine encyclopedia of character types, situations and conflicts between Russians and Jews. It was written by a young man in a unique position. He is a Jew who had entree in any Jewish circle in Moscow who then became a Christian and experienced the influence of the most varied Russian circles. Unfortunately the novel's artistic rendition is considerably weaker than the possibilities which the plot afforded the author. Therefore Svetov's novel (like his other prose works) did not attract much public attention. However, for historians and sociologists the information contained in the novel is very valuable.

At the center of the novel is the image of the literary critic Gol'tsev, who is the son of a well-known historian repressed during Stalin's time (this image is somewhat autobiographical - Svetov himself was a critic for *Novyi Mir* and the son of Ts. Fridliand, a purged historian). Gol'tsev is an honest, kind and conscientious Jew who, however, has no recollections of Jewish nationality in an historical sense. To a great extent he also has no recollections of Russianness in an historical sense since, as a Soviet, he is also deprived of a knowledge of Russian history, just like any other Russian person. This means that his general lack of historical recollections is only worsened by a total lack of ethnic roots. This lack is so complete and absolute that he can't even guess at what these roots are like. Gol'tsev, motivated by his newly awakened conscience, decides to become Russian Orthodox. The twist to becoming baptized is that when the convert joins a persecuted church, this not only does him no earthly good, but on the contrary the convert is also threatened with persecution (Gol'tsev is driven from work by the joint efforts of a Russian boss and his Jewish deputy). In accepting baptism, Gol'tsev did not intend to reject his people, so even after he is baptized, Gol'tsev continues to feel and act like a Jew even though his faith is now Russian Orthodox. However, he soon finds that the situation of being a Russian Orthodox, Muscovite Jew is very complicated and confusing.

As a man completely lacking any sense of historical tradition, Gol'tsev does not realize the complicated situation he has put himself in by becoming baptized. He does not know that Judaism has an anti-Christian tradition, nor that Christianity has an anti-Semitic tradition. At the same time he has absolutely no notion of church religiosity. As a man who is culturally Russian, Gol'tsev can only understand religion in its cultural sense without a commitment to the church or knowledge of its ceremonial tradition. Accordingly, his behavior irritates and embarrasses not only Jews, but Russian Christians as well.

For example, at a Jewish cemetery, he is deeply moved during the burial of his favorite Jewish uncle and makes the sign of the cross over him, which is something that a true Christian would never do. The *samizdat* journal *Chasy*, which is published in Leningrad, several years ago distributed speeches from a religious seminar held there. The journal included a speech by B. Ivanov entitled "Sovremennoe khristianstvo" [Modern-day Christianity], which bears witness to just how typical the portrait drawn by Svetov is. Ivanov notes that the "new Christians" (i.e., those who chose Christianity for themselves, despite the traditions of their family or nationality), share the following characteristics. First, they do not believe in personal immortality. Second, they have a weak prophetic sense of the faith, i.e., dual ethics and dual understanding of the world. All this brings the "new Christian" closer to Manichaean heresy. Third, they distrust the authority of the historical church. Trust in the church's authority is viewed as a personal choice, and not as a sacred attribute of divine authority. Finally, they doubt that confession and repentance are necessary.[9]

The hero of Svetov's novel possesses all these traits, especially his habit "in the middle of casual conversations of touching upon those things which a traditional Christian in essence sees as holy."[10] For example, in the novel's denouement, he invents his own version of the conversion of St. Paul, the "Jew from Tarsus," which he obviously sees as an analogy for himself. This legend, which tells that St. Paul was actually betrayed by Christ's remaining apostles to be executed by the Romans, is, of course, incredibly sacrilegious for any Christian. However, this thought doesn't enter into the hero's head.

New converts are difficult for any church to absorb, but if people convert when the church is mature and strong, it can accept them with relative ease. It is a completely different situation today when the church is weaker and is demeaned by persecutions. It must literally resolve issues on the run, even issues which cannot be resolved easily under the most favorable conditions. Svetov's hero truly does not notice that for his beloved church he is only a burden, and that is probably true for his ardently beloved Russia, too.

For their part his fellow Jews maliciously repudiate him. No other contemporary prose work has so accurately traced the evolution of the Jewish community in the USSR. According to Svetov, Jewish emigration from Russia was brought about not by an increased Jewish awareness of themselves as a nationality (at least for the overwhelming majority of the capital's intelligentsia). These Jews were completely Russian from the standpoint of culture and habits, accepting Russian history and Russian society as their own. They fled Russia because they smelled the ruination or, at best, the decay of society (now officially termed "the period of crisis and stagnation"). They had a unique opportunity to use their national origins to abandon this sinking ship, and their choice was based not upon nationality but on their life situation.

The main positive heroine of the novel is a Russian woman who forsakes her beloved in Russia and leaves with her Jewish husband. The main negative heroine is a Jewess who remains in Russia with her Russian husband, despite the fact that she reviles and derides his country. The Jewish situation is so complex because all their intellectual, psychological and cultural traits tie the Jews to Russia.

Therefore in order to break with their homeland, they become inordinately inflamed against it.

It is precisely their close tie with Russia that causes their Russophobia, and ignorance of the complexity of nationality-related issues plays no small role in this. As they encounter the arguments of nationalist ideologists like Jabotinsky for the first time in their lives, they could not be further removed from the benevolent, liberal atmosphere which gave birth to these ideas. As a result, they make use of these ideas to mimic the National Bolsheviks (or later, Pamiat'), i.e., they force them into a reverse, anti-Russian direction. Their aggressiveness, as Svetov notes, is exacerbated by their amoral choice of life in the United States over life in Israel. In today's Russian spiritual context it is considered unworthy of an upstanding person (and especially an intellectual) to have as his main concern his personal welfare and fate. Lev Gol'tsev, who reminds them of this, is hated by them more than they hate anyone else because he was a Jew who chose another alternative. At the novel's close, therefore, one of the emigrating Jews cruelly beats him up.

Yet he is even hard for the Russians to understand. In the Russian environment the religious revival is integrally tied to the revival of national feelings and the return to one's roots. It is not surprising therefore that his old friend the philosophy professor has such a sharply negative attitude towards Gol'tsev. This old friend had gladly accepted him and even befriended him as a Jew but deliberately and spitefully begins to insult him when he finds out that Gol'tsev accepted baptism. After all, Russian Orthodoxy is the only undefiled, sacred object which the Russian people have left. A non-Russian intruding into this area, into the holiest of holies, leaves the Russian people without any hope, according to his old friend.

The philosophy professor is depicted as a particularly negative character in the novel. The novel's most positive hero is Father Kirill, who baptized Gol'tsev. Father Kirill is esentially of like mind with the professor, but he does not insult Gol'tsev, trusting in the latter's good intentions. Father Kirill feels that religion is also a way to bring about a national revival of Jewish people. He therefore advises Gol'tsev to leave for Israel and defend his country and his people with a machine gun in his hands. To the priest's way of thinking, serving one's people and one's homeland is the primary duty of every religious person.

Gol'tsev proudly informs the priest that he will serve Russia, but he does not understand that Russia once again today faces the tragic situation which Lev Tolstoy wrote about in *War and Peace* through the mouthpiece of Andrei Bolkonskii: "While Russia was healthy, a stranger could serve her, and he was indeed a remarkable minister. But as soon as she falls into danger, one's own, native countryman is needed."[11] Gol'tsev and those like him with the very best and noblest intentions wind up in a very grievous situation, just like Barclay de Tolly did. This unhealthy situation of instinctive distrust is described by Svetov in a story which serves as a sort of continuation to his novel - "*Khorosho poguliali*" [We had a Nice Walk][12]. Two baptized Jews are touchingly concerned about their religious brothers, the Russians, who look upon this concern with views ranging from sympathetic bewilderment to incredulous suspicion; it is something not needed and an intrusion.

I think the greatest writer of contemporary Soviet Russia is Venedikt Erofeev, who is the author of the tragic poem *From Moscow to Petushki*. Erofeev is one of the most profound philosophers among contemporary Russian writers and a man of great culture and erudition, especially on religious matters. His best works reflect the influence of the Old and New Testaments. The tragedy, *Val'purgieva noch', ili shagi komandora* [Walpurgis Night, or the Knight Commander's Steps], was the last work published by Erofeev and concerns the eschatology of Russian-Jewish relations.[13]

The fact that there are Jews on Russian territory at all is an historical accident brought about by the partitioning of the Polish Kingdom. However, the fact that both peoples are very interested in each other is clearly not historical happenstance. This can be seen in the fact that there have been many joint inroads into both cultures. The fact that many Jews have taken part in furthering Russian culture, and that the Russians have an exceptional interest in the Jewish question (which makes little sense considering the actual size of the Jewish population in Russia) is a riddle to be solved. It is precisely this riddle to which Venedikt Erofeev's play is devoted.

The action of *Walpurgis Night* takes place in ward No. 3 of psychiatric clinic No. 31. Ward No. 3 is analogous to Chekhov's Ward No. 6. It is a symbolic representation of Russia enslaved. The clinic's inmates symbolize certain sides of the Russian national consciousness (or subconsciousness), including the exclusion of the rural areas from contemporary life (the little old man Vova), the dream of communism (Serezha Kleinmikhel'), uncontrolled protest (Alekha), and finally the sober understanding of the tragic hopelessness of one's own situation and an agreement to accept imposed rules of life (the psychiatrists). All of these personalities are parodied and mocked by the elder Prokhorov. The "crazy cart" (ambulance) brings a new patient named Lev Gurevich to the psychiatric clinic (he is partly modelled after Boris Pasternak). The ward has a prejudicial attitude towards Gurevich because tradition teaches that, "Wherever you find Jews, you should expect a disastrous plot."

At the same time, however, the inmates, especially Prokhorov, are curious. After all, Gurevich is the only one among them who physically fights back against the hospital orderly Boren'ka (who symbolizes penal institutions) and exhibits a "sense of honor and other throwbacks."

Gurevich plans to take vengeance on his tormenters and free the ward. "I will blow them all up," he says about the psychiatrists. In order to draw the tormented and depressed souls together and console them, Gurevich steals alcohol from the pantry and convinces them to have a feast on the eve of the uprising. It turns out they got methyl alcohol. All the characters in the ward go blind and then die, among them Gurevich himself, whom the orderly Boren'ka begins to beat to death right before the witnesses' very eyes during the denoeument. Prokhorov's prediction is thus justified: "These Jews are good to everyone. The only bad thing is, they just don't know how to live. Just look at what happened to Gurevich. He was beaten to a pulp. Yes he was." But even before this, during the feast, it becomes clear that not only Gurevich and Prokhorov, but the other inmates of the ward as well dream about refashioning mankind, recreating the world, and making it a happier place. In their drunken dreams they create a Russian empire over the whole world. However, the Russians are constantly afraid of intrigues by their Jewish "strategic ally". It eventually becomes clear that their suspicions are justified because, having drawn a picture of the future Russian victory over the world, Gurevich suddenly foretells: "However, afterwards, the conquerors will get all the ailments of the conquered, and their health will begin to decline. They will disperse like ashes across the face of the Earth. . .

and while the Russians fly to their appointed abyss, the people of Jehovah will. . ."

The Russian characters in the play fear that the future victory of Russia will in the end turn into a Jewish victory for the Jews! For Gurevich, himself, however, this future kingdom of Jehovah's people is not a Jewish kingdom, but a kingdom "which binds hearts together." Its capital will not be Jerusalem, but Cana in Galilee, the desolate village where Jesus performed his first miracle by turning water into wine. The miracle was bestowed upon the people before the prescribed time for his miracles. It was not granted because it was deserved or because the wedding guests lived upright lives but simply out of divine goodness and at the request of Jesus' mother, Mary, by tradition the patronness and protector of Russia. In other words Gurevich is prepared to erect the Kingdom of Goodness on the ruins of the worldwide Russian empire.

For Venedikt Erofeev, Russians and Jews are united by an identical longing to recreate the world, to make it their own, and to make it good. It is only the Russians, however, who are in constant fear of the consequences. They ask: "If we alter the world, what are we doing it for? What will become of those people who realize that they are unworthy?" For the Jew, however, recreating the world simply means recreating it in the image and likeness of God.

Consequently, Erofeev feels that the general idea of the two peoples and the reason for their interest in each other and for their mutual fate is contained in the belief in the Messiah inherent in both people's beliefs. Antagonism, alienation and suspicion, however, result from a lack of trust in the true goals of their "ally." The Russians, especially, are suspicious that the Jews have some kind of other, hidden goal.

It is particularly symbolic that the play ends with the destruction of both peoples. Both Russian and Jewish Messianism are equally responsible for the death of the ward!

It is, of course, also possible to find novels and stories in Soviet prose by Jewish writers who are striving to prove that the Jews are equal to any other Soviet nationality - that they have taken part in building socialism, have been at war, and so on (see A. Rybakov's novel *Tiazhelyi pesok* [Heavy Sand], and D. Kalinovskaia's story, "O subbota" [Oh Saturday]). It is also worth mentioning the clever plot twist used by Yu. Semenov, the celebrated writer of spy novels. In his unconventional works he expresses the thought that hostility toward Jews is incompatible with imperialistic ambitions and goals. As his model he used either Nazi Germany in his series of novels about the escapades of the ace of Soviet intelligence Shtirlits, or tsarist Russia, especially in the story "Version II", about Russia during Stolypin's time. The story points out the controversial nature of Solzhenitsyn, but is much more aimed against Pikul's thesis of Jewish responsibility for the revolution.

In summary, the national and religious revival in Russia in the 1970s and 1980s has led to complex processes in Russo-Jewish relations. The self-conscious, false and hypocritical anti-Semitism of Party bureaucrats began to be replaced with openly declared anti-Semitism, similar to traditional European Judophobia. In turn the "Jewish side" responded with outright Russophobia. Still, in bringing these mutual accusations out into the open, and openly revealing nationalist and religious myths, they are now being discussed and better understood. In the end it is understanding which gives birth to tolerance and even cooperation.

Distinguishing between nationalities clarifies the dialectics of nationality relations. At the same time, it promotes the elimination of national and religious prejudices on a new, more modern level. Certainly in any situation, clarity in relations is better than hypocritical confusion. Having to live together on this small planet of ours teaches us tolerance and how to gradually repudiate the dilapidated traditions of hate and contempt one step at a time. The presence of a safety valve for these complex relations, such as Israel, promises to make the final outcome of these mutual relations peaceful and worthy of all civilized peoples. Renouncing messianic ambitions, certainly possible in the long-term perspective of history, will hopefully place Erofeev's eschatological prophecy of historical tragedy beyond our reach.

TN (p. 183) Evsektsii refers to Communist Party departments which were established to deal with Jewish affairs in the USSR.

1. D. Pospielovsky, "Russkii natsionalizm, marksizm-leninizm i sud'by Rossii" [Russian Nationalism, Marxism-Leninism and the Fate of Russia], <u>Grani</u>, West Germany, No. 111-112, 1979, pp. 422-423.

2. See L. Korneev's afterword in Tarasov's story Posidi na kamne u dorogi [Sit on the Stone by the Road], Novosibirsk, 1981, p. 203.

3. This episode can be found in Iu. Seleznev's Dostoevskii in the series, "The Lives of Exceptional People," Moscow: Molodaia gvardiia, p. 244.

4. A certain Jewish merchant talks about this in M. Lobanov's Ostrovskii in the series, "The Lives of Exceptional People," Moscow: Molodaia gvardiia, 1978. He says that they were preparing to boil the Russian peasant in foundation pits. This is a clear reference to A. Platonov's novel Kotlovan [The Foundation Pit], which depicts the horrors of collectivization.

5. See A. Solzhenitsyn, Dve press-konferentsii [Two Press Conferences], Paris: YMCA-Press, 1975, p. 49.

6. Novyi mir, No. 5, 1980.

7. Yu. Sergeev, Stanovoi khrebet [The Mainstay], in Nash sovremennik, No. 1, 1987, p. 76.

8. L. Borodin's story "Pravila igry," in the journal Grani, No. 140, 1986, pp. 5-77.

9. Quoted from excerpts from B. Ivanov's report published in the journal Grani, No. 113, 1979, p. 324.

10. Ibid.

11. L. Tolstoy, Voina i mir [War and Peace], Vol. III, Shkol'naia biblioteka, p. 198.

12. F. Svetov, "Khorosho poguliali" [We Had a Nice Walk], Grani, No. 126, 1982, pp. 5-48.

13. Kontinent, No. 45, 1985, pp. 96-182.

CHALLENGE OF THE "RUSSIAN IDEA": REDISCOVERING THE LEGACY OF RUSSIAN RELIGIOUS PHILOSOPHY

Nicolai N. Petro

Overshadowed by the cataclysmic events of 1917, Russian political-religious thought of the turn of the twentieth century has been greatly neglected in the West. Until quite recently, the same could be said of Soviet scholarship concerning this period. Today, however, the Soviet leadership is beginning to realize the extent to which the process of perestroika, or restructuring, is hindered by the widespread ignorance of the country's own political traditions. The rediscovery of Russian religious thinkers of the early twentieth century can therefore be considered one of the most significant contributions of glasnost' to the restructuring of Soviet society.

The origin of Russian religious and philosophical thought can be traced back to Peter Chaadaev's famous "Philosophical Letter" of 1836, in which he attempted to give a religious interpretation of the divergent historical development of Western Europe and Russia. By the 1850s, however, the intelligentsia had begun to address itself almost exclusively to the socio-political problems facing the country. The majority became infatuated with the positivist social theories of their age and abandoned their religious heritage in favor of religious indifference and sometimes even militant atheism.[1] Not until the turn of this century, following the partial fulfillment of the demands for constitutional reform in 1905, did certain prominent Marxist intellectuals rethink their original assumptions and search for solutions to pressing social problems based not on positivism, but on a sense of aesthetics, culture, and philosophy rooted in Christianity.

These "religious philosophers," as they came to be known, represented a turning point in the social attitudes of the Russian intelligentsia. Their evolution "from materialism to idealism" led them to reject calls for the violent overthrow of the monarchy. Their skepticism about materialism and reason as the sole arbiters of the Good eventually led to their ostracism from the ranks of respectable intellectuals.[2] Even the Constitutional Democrat Pavel Milyukov, who had earlier broken with the Marxists, described this religious re-orientation as "pernicious and repulsive," a betrayal of the intelligentsia's revolutionary calling.[3]

What was it that these thinkers proposed that aroused such ire? Deeming Marxism and all other forms of positivist thought to be a dead end, they called for a return to Christianity, and specifically to Eastern Orthodoxy with its strongly defined sense of the Church. They embraced patriotism and political activism imbued with a strong sense of Christian identity. They sought to restore a sense of public service to the intelligentsia and hoped that their personal example would help heal the rift between the political cultures of Petrine and Muscovite Russia which still haunted the intelligentsia.

However, this healing process was interrupted by the October 1917 Revolution. After the victory of the Bolsheviks, nearly two million people either fled the country or were expelled. Lenin banished many intellectuals, particularly social theorists and philosophers who disagreed with the new regime.[4] By decapitating any intellectual opposition to the new order, Lenin hoped to clear the way for a new breed of intellectual, dedicated to the humanist ideals of the October Revolution. But even though the search for an alternative path of political development was broken off inside Russia, it continued in the Russian diaspora. A number of the most prominent religious philosophers managed to obtain prestigious positions in the West, which allowed them to continue writing.

The Russian religious thinkers who survived the revolution and escaped abroad lived with three objectives. First, to continue their personal search to find the true meaning of a Christian life combined with social activism. Second, to give meaning and purpose to the Russian diaspora and to Russian history after October 1917. Third, to leave a legacy which could be rediscovered and reintroduced into Russia after communism had run its course there. Working in close contact with one another, these Russian religious philosophers devoted much of the interwar period to the first two tasks. The final task of restoring these ideas to their native soil is taking place today. The eagerness with which religious philosophers like Vladimir Solov'ev, Nikolai Berdyaev, Lev Shestov, Father Sergei Bulgakov, Father Pavel Florensky, Semen Frank, and Giorgii Fedotov are being welcomed back into Russian culture by the contemporary Russian Soviet intelligentsia is a telling comment on the effect of seventy years of communist rule.

Why are these writers, who died as relative unknowns in foreign countries, now being published in leading Soviet journals? The answer lies in the fact that Russian religious philosophy presents a clearly defined historical and philosophical alternative to socialism. The vexing issues of democratization, modernization, and the shattered ideals of the October Revolution are today the subject of soul-searching debate in the Soviet Union. In exile, these religious thinkers likewise sought to explain why the October Revolution had occurred, and tried to delineate a path of personal and social action that could put their country back onto the road of peaceful and prosperous historical development. At the same time, Russian religious philosophy is attractive to Russian intellectuals today because it is seen as the last expression of a truly Russian national approach to politics.

Today, many leading Soviet intellectuals argue that the re-acceptance of this rejected religious-philosophical heritage is essential if the country is ever to return to the path of normal historical development. To those who view a strand of Christian politics emerging in the Soviet Union as a utopian fantasy, literary critic Igor' Vinogradov replies:

> Were they alive now, V. Solov'ev or N. Berdyaev, S. Bulgakov or S. Frank, they would likely ask in return: well, what of your level-headed, clever idea of erecting a happy social paradise on earth without God, without absolute moral principles rooted in Christian commandments, without belief in the unconditional meaning of good and of moral norms? What has it brought us over the last 70 years in the life of our unfortunate country, [except] bring us to the brink of catastrophe?[5]

It is difficult to categorize these individuals as either political or religious thinkers, for in their writings and in their personal lives, religion and politics became inseparably intertwined. The very fact that the present generation of Russian intellectuals is turning to the legacy of Russian religious philosophy in its search for political and social alternatives to socialism, makes the study of the socio-political aspects of Russian religious philosophy particularly relevant today.

This discussion focuses on the socio-political ideals elaborated by three prominent Russian religious thinkers: Anton Vladimirovich Kartashev (1875-1967), Giorgii Petrovich Fedotov 1886-1951), and Ivan Aleksandrovich Il'in (1883-1954). Each comes from a different social and intellectual background, and offers a distinct socio-political ideal which, however, maintains the basic unity of concept characteristic of Russian religious philosophy. They express most clearly the socio-political ideals of Russian religious philosophy, which are finding a strong resonance among nationally oriented Russian intellectuals in the Soviet Union today.

THE "HOLY RUSSIA" OF KARTASHEV

A son of serf factory workers, Anton Kartashev demonstrated an early propensity for religious studies. Completing the Perm' seminary at 19, at the age of 25 he was offered the cathedra of Russian Church History at the St. Petersburg Spiritual Academy, where he taught for five years. His move to the capital gave him the opportunity to meet many of the most brilliant Russian religious thinkers of his day, including Sergei Bulgakov and Semen Frank. At the same time, he contributed actively to contemporary journals and participated in various Christian philosophical societies. After the overthrow of the Tsar, the Provisional Government asked Kartashev to become High Procurator of the Synod, then the highest government office supervising Church activities. His first act was to change his title and functions to Minister of Faiths, and within ten days he had done away entirely with the last vestige of government oversight over the Church. His entire activity after this was geared toward convening the Church Council, which commenced August 15, 1917, and was the first and last such council held in Russia. Escaping Russia in 1920, he settled in

Paris and taught at St. Sergius' Theological Academy until the end of his life.[6]

Kartashev begins his monumental essay "The Recreation of Holy Russia": "The Russia of St. Vladimir - christened, Orthodox, Holy Russia - is our banner. Immersion into this heart of hearts of our russianness will never cease to be the task of our national self-awareness."[7] In these two sentences he affirms the inseparability of religious consciousness and national self-awareness, both essential to the well-being of Russia. Re-establishing this vital tie is the most urgent task of "Holy Russia."

The term "Holy Russia," Kartashev acknowledges, might seem pretentious, but it is an expression which has existed in Russian popular lore even before written annals. For Kartashev the phrase is merely evidence of the extremely close connection between Christianity and national self-awareness in Russia, an oft-repeated theme in writings of twentieth-century Russian religious thinkers; it is the *vox populi*.

For Kartashev the lives of both individuals and collectives hold within themselves the entire organic fullness of past experience. "Thus is formed, and *exists in actuality, the collective will of peoples*, with their particular interests, callings and spiritual fates. . . . Thus, Russia is an organic *whole* as a spiritual type - the living spirit of the Russian people with a single common [*sobornoe*] self-awareness."[8] Nations may organically incarnate their spirit in only one form particular to them. They are, "fated to live out their historical life in this form, developing, enriching, transforming, but never exchanging or betraying it if they wish to live up to their full potential."[9] This view of historical evolution has important implications for the path of development the nation chooses, for it presumes that any path that attempts to override native tradition will invariably fail. In an obvious reference to her current communist rulers, Kartashev states that "Russia cannot be planned anew, thought up and constructed according to a plan alien to her nature."[10]

The calling and responsibilities of nations may differ. Russia's calling, says Kartashev, is clearly tied to her Christian heritage. Both as individuals and as a group, Christians must serve the aims of the Kingdom of God and are responsible to God for this. As with individuals, it is a matter of free choice as to whether a country follows its natural path or not. Still, Kartashev asserts, the task of creating Holy Russia is today a holy task of worldwide significance. "As a Christian culture of worldwide significance, we are called to create an imperial peace - *pax Russica* - in those areas delegated to us by Providence, strengthening the activities of Russian culture in them and *internally transforming them in the spirit of Orthodoxy*. . ."[11] Appealing to Russian patriotic sentiment, Kartashev insists that a great people do not have the right to shirk off their greatness. A communist Russia can never be truly great because she will never be able to accomplish the tasks for which God created Russia.

Kartashev recognizes that the past order is irretrievably lost. The current task is therefore one of creative renaissance, of creating a new social and political ideal as yet unknown, but which is rooted in its Russian historical traditions. Holy Russia is to be a state "lit up from within by the Orthodox spirit, Christianized; or, more directly, a Christian state."[12] Kartashev stresses that this task requires "realism as to the paths and means by which an ideal can and must be accomplished."[13] Consequently, the first question he asks is whether there is room for Holy Russia in a modern secular state. His answer is yes, as long as it is not merely an attempt to restore the past.

THE TASKS OF CHURCH AND STATE

Despite its quintessentially other-worldly focus, Kartashev argues that the Church has nothing to apologize for in concerning itself with people and governments in this world. "This is not her 'fall,' as it appears to many Protestants and to which many of our emigre adherents to 'the purity of Church [separateness] from politics' succumb; it is her elevation to a new level of human salvation."[14] This is not to say, Kartashev adds, that the Church has not committed errors along this path but only that the apostolic path itself is fundamentally correct. Hence, the church is called upon to "spiritually guide the world, establishing the Kingdom of Christ on earth as it is in heaven. It is in this sense essentially theocratic and Christocentric."[15]

It is through the Incarnation of Christ, an act which united heaven and earth, that the path of ascendancy is opened for government. All forms of government are "born, according to the

Bible, in egotism and rejection of God, and built on sin and violence. They can *and consequently must become God-fearing*, Christ-loving, the collective Son of God, *nearing itself* to a freely chosen, fulfilling union with the *church, churchifying itself [otserkovliat'sia]*."[16] Kartashev realizes that this is a tall order for mankind. Indeed, the only indication that this can occur at all, he concludes, is the "eternal burning hurt of our conscience over the sinfulness and inadequacy of our personal and collective activities."[17]

A good part of this inadequacy stems from the church's abandonment of social activism, letting humanistic ideology and legalistic governments be at the forefront of social reform. It is precisely this lack of a church presence in social reform movements, and its support for certain reactionary movements, that has led to the principle of the separation of church and state becoming commonplace in modern societies. Kartashev, however, reminds his readers, that the canonical commandment of Eastern Orthodoxy to be in "symphony" with government is not tied to any specific form of government.[18] In pursuing the goal of human salvation, the validity of the separation of church and state must therefore continually be re-examined to assess its effect and desirability.

CHURCH, STATE, AND SOCIETY

Having held the highest Church-related government position in pre-revolutionary Russia, Kartashev saw first-hand the evils of government controls over the church and worked hard to abolish them. At the same time, he questioned whether Christianity ought to withdraw entirely from such a significant form of collective existence as the government and passively accept whatever it dictates.

In the Orthodox tradition, says Kartashev, the antinomy of the two cities *civitas dei* and *civitas terrena* is not seen as an absurdity or paradox, but as consistent with the postulate of the Incarnation, as the ultimate unity of two poles of existence. There is a division of labor between the two arms of God: the government's highest goal is to lead the people to material welfare and the accumulation of the values of human culture; the church's highest goal is to save souls from the limitations of this secular ideal and to point them toward eternal salvation. In this dichotomy the two are never on equal footing. Just as the flesh listens to the spirit, so the church must guide the State because it, not the state, sees the higher end of mankind.[19]

This division of labor is known as "symphony." The Latin term *consonantia* perhaps gives one a flavor for the musical quality of the term, in which the church plays the main tune and the state is relegated to playing the harmony; each would, however, be incomplete without the other. Without idealizing the various manifestations this symphony has had throughout history, Kartashev argues that this perspective helps to clarify the Christian understanding of some contemporary political phenomena. Totalitarianism, for example, is to be judged as "the violent revolt of the 'flesh' against the spirit, of God against man, of the anti-Christ against Christ. The concept of the State as god goes against the very first principle of the evangelical and Old Testament commandments."[20]

For Kartashev, the basic principles of symphony still hold true today. The church can work toward christianizing all spheres of society, even government itself although it must do so independently of the government.[21] Kartashev recognizes that *de facto* legal equality of the church as an autonomous social group alongside other groups would be more appropriate today than church domination. This requires a new and broader symphony, therefore, to take the place of the traditional one between the church and government: a symphony between the church and society.

Symphony between the church and society will encourage the *"realist-theocratic transformation."*[22]   This "new theocracy," says Kartashev, must come to grips with secular government by, in effect, recognizing a trade-off between separation of church and state and subjection to the church's spiritual authority. But won't formal separation lead to the extinction of the church role in social life? Kartashev believes not because today's social conditions have not altered the church's eternal message; they are merely the "tactical directive of the moment" to be free from close ties with government that "distort [the church's] image and weaken its prophetic strength."[23]

At the same time it would be absurdly naive, says Kartashev, to suppose that the church hierarchy could christianize the world by itself. Church brotherhoods, therefore, must assist the "collective [*sobornoe*] activity in the church. These brotherhoods comprise all groups of people. Every social group, profession, and faith should get together to imbue with Christian meaning issues related to their specialty. They should especially focus on how to direct one's expertise in the light of church teachings, and toward the good of the church."[24] Kartashev likens the lay branches of the church to bridges between the antinomous spheres of heaven and earth. While influencing the heart of the individual believers is the main form of church action, it must also take up organized forms of social activism. For Kartashev this is true even for party politics; not the church itself, but lay Christians who happen to be politicians must strive to christianize their profession, preparing it for "churchification."[25]

To clarify his ideas Kartashev modifies a famous metaphor: he sees Roman Catholicism as placing the sword of government in the hands of the papacy, granting it authority to direct every aspect of human activity; Protestantism places the sword in the hands of monarchs, thereby threatening to place the word of God at the service of the state; Eastern Orthodoxy has the church bless the sword of secular rule in the hands of the state, while keeping it under strict evangelical censure, cognizant of its sinful origin.[26]

Kartashev pursues two tasks as theologian and political thinker: the first is clarifying the type of Christian ideal to be pursued; the second is determining how this ideal is to be achieved under present conditions. He does not, however, assume that these ideals can ever be entirely achieved. He views the affirmation of Christianity's social gospel as incremental and evolutionary, rather than reaching completion in millennarian fashion. This view stems again from Orthodox doctrine, which views mankind as having already been saved *on this earth* through the Crucifixion and Resurrection, and which therefore allows for human deeds to be untainted by sin even now, even though these deeds will always be incomplete until the second coming. The construction of the Kingdom of God is therefore the most appropriate social activity of Christians. It is the task which ultimately gives meaning to Christian political life because, when freely chosen, it affirms men's freedom of choice and requires the *joint* (symphonic) efforts of man and God.

Kartashev stresses the enormous variety of Christian solutions to the social problem which, none the less, ought always to be guided by the transcendent purpose of salvation. The particular expression of

Christian politics will differ given historical circumstances, but it will always, for Kartashev, maintain a sense of organized purposefulness. One is tempted to call him a Christian militarist, in that he has set up a plan by which Christianity can conquer the world; only its army is to be bound by a discipline of consent and compassion, rather than compulsion. The church is the backbone of his strategy, and his political system might well be called *raison d'Eglise*, for all things must eventually come under the church's spiritual guidance.

FEDOTOV AND THE PROBLEMS OF REVOLUTION AND DEMOCRACY

Giorgii Fedotov was a more secularly oriented contemporary of Kartashev's. An active member of the Russian Social Democratic Labor Party from 1904 to 1906, he was arrested and deported for his revolutionary activities, giving him a chance to study history in Germany. Ten years later he returned to Russia and to Christianity and became active in religious-philosophical circles. Emigrating in 1925, he spent the next fourteen years as an instructor at the Orthodox Academy in Paris and was a leading member of the Russian Student Christian Movement. During World War II he was evacuated to the United States and became a visiting fellow at Yale Divinity School where he wrote *The Russian Religious Mind*, and *A Treasure of Russian Spirituality*. Fedotov spent his last years teaching history at St. Vladimir's Theological Academy in New York.

Concerned with the tragedies of a person's social existence, Fedotov strove to define the inadequacies of contemporary political consciousness. The solutions, he believed, could only stem from a Christian worldview. The problem with contemporary politics, he felt, lay in the misunderstanding and misapplication of the terms democracy and revolution.

According to Fedotov, contemporary defenders of democracy use the term to mean twentieth century bourgeois-parliamentarian democracy, but democracy has taken different forms at different times. The essential, historically transcendent element of democracy, says Fedotov, is that it embodies the rule of the people. "In a democracy the people do not shirk their concerns for 'the common good' - *res publica*, but, along with all its citizens, assume complete responsibility for government service."[27]   Politics is more than just the struggle for personal rights, privileges, and interests, says Fedotov, it is also the struggle for social ideals, it is the sphere uniting spiritual culture and economic and technical existence.

Far too often, however, the democratic ideal becomes "formal democracy," a mere caricature of true democracy. Election campaigns turn into "grandiose epics of lies and hypnotic befuddlement of the masses." Politics has come to be identified with the basest instincts of mankind--the art of shysters and sycophants. As a result, says Fedotov, "the populace does not recognize itself in its rulers." [28]

One major reason our democracies are so helpless and weak-willed (Fedotov is writing this during the period between World Wars I and II) is because of the party system. It is obvious to Fedotov that party politics demands totally different qualities (among them careerism, demagoguery and intrigue) from government leadership. Strict adherence to the party line characterizes the vast majority of party activists, especially at election time. Statesmanship, by contrast, requires impartiality and the ability to rise above factions and pursue the common interest. Parties, concludes Fedotov, pose a fundamental dilemma to political life. They are an essential component of contemporary democracies, but at the same time they constrain individual expression of political will and disrupt the construction of a national consensus. Still, democracy is preferable to a monarchy, he says, since the latter exerts even greater control over the choice of personal vocation and is too inconsistent in the hereditary transmission of the gift of leadership.[29]

The scourge of revolution, in Fedotov's view, stems largely from the inadequate social guidance given by contemporary democracies. Most revolutions are not inspired by the desire for freedom, but by the pursuit of some "new order" that can rationally organize all of life under government aegis. Such centralization, argues Fedotov, destroys the spiritual and material prerequisites for a truly constructive revolution. Today's secular revolutions are distinguished by their particular violence and cruelty. They aim not merely at changing the government or political structure, but the intent of life itself. They seek to be as "the first people on earth," overcoming original sin; hence the "immorality of current revolutions. . . Slavery and lies are the result of the triumph of might, inevitable in the war of all against all. The great revolution, beginning in the name of freedom, ends in universal slavery."[30]

Fedotov's thinking was strongly influenced by the October Revolution of 1917, but he sees similar errors in all modern revolutions. including the French Revolution of 1789. He decries its "mechanistic, lifeless character - the stamp of bureaucratic centralism, thinly veneered with a democratic mantle."[31] Fedotov sees secular revolution as neither a normal evolutionary development, nor the cure to a diseased society as Marxian dialectic would have it; it is instead "the most acute stage of the disease itself--a national calamity."[32] Revolution as a political alternative is therefore totally unacceptable.[33]

CHRISTIAN RESPONSIBILITY
AND THE CHRISTIAN IDEAL

Fedotov realizes that it is no easy task to eschew evil and to do good in a sinful world. The political sphere bears the particular brunt of evil in the form of violence, and the tragedy of mankind is that it must be a part of this evil *volens nolens*. Violence can be justified under only one condition, that is if a person can say with a clear conscience that all peaceful, lawful means of reform have been exhausted, and that tyranny will not cease before it destroys all the people with it. Then, says Fedotov, the Christian may draw his sword, but only for the clearly defined and limited objective of removing the tyrant: "One does not transform the world and build a new society with a sword. A sword is to free one from tyrants, and only that."[34]

Fedotov sees Christianity as offering a qualitatively different solution to the dilemmas of social existence. Very early on the Christian Church had to choose between two paths: remaining a small community of saved souls awaiting the second coming of the Lord; or saving the world, conveying whatever it could of the Christian ideal. The Church correctly chose the latter path, even though an "ascetic indifference to the whole world of Caesar" arose among certain Christians. Fedotov seeks to reminds his readers of the importance of Christian positive social activism, i.e. of "benevolent Christian resistance to evil," which requires that Christians be at the forefront of social renewal.[35]

Christianity requires a constant affirmation of social values, says Fedotov. It calls for "an entirely new and different order of existence - the Kingdom of God."[36] According to Fedotov, the Kingdom has at least three scriptual meanings: it is in the hearts of men, in heavenly life, and in the secular kingdom of the Messiah.[37] Christian social activism is therefore clearly in the tradition of the early Christian Greek Fathers, of the messianic sermons of Jesus, and of the prophetic revelations of the Old Testament: "the prophetic religion of Israel and the New Testament church was social before it became personal, and the Kingdom of God was prior to the kingdom of the people of God, prior to the kingdom in men's soul."[38]

Social interaction lies at the heart of the Christian Church, and consequently the social order cannot be a matter of indifference to Christians since it educates for good or evil. Acknowledging that there are no absolutely just social institutions, Fedotov argues that some institutions are clearly to be preferred from a Christian perspective, and Christians should support these with a clear conscience. The value of any social reform thus depends on its moral context, on how well the spirit of love, justice and freedom are incorporated in them. Christians should strive for a social order "where the beginnings of brotherhood and justice are best exemplified, where the struggle with evil is easiest, and where the individual is placed in the best conditions for his own spiritual development."[39]

But Christianity is called to do more than just advocate social reform. It also rejects secular social relations and offers instead a new social concept which asserts the equality of part and whole, of the persona and the world, of the church and a person's spirit. Such goals do not fit easily into a parliamentary framework, hence Fedotov concludes that "Christianity is infinitely higher than social truth."[40] The Christian social ideal is sobornost', "the organic equilibrium of personality and society."[41] Sobornost' is inimical to totalitarian collectivism and to formalized democracy, both of which are based on "the number and equality of social atoms." "The ideal of sobornost'," writes Fedotov, "is an organism of love, similar to ideal family or friendly relations, where subjects subject themselves freely, where the rulers do not rule but serve all. . ."[42] Fedotov sees this solidarity and brotherhood exemplified in the following description given by the fourth century Christian writer St. John Chrysostom:

> Let us not be satisfied with the search for personal salvation; this would mean destroying it. In war and in the ranks, if a soldier thinks only of how to save himself by flight he will wind up destroying himself and his comrades. A dedicated soldier who fights for others and with others saves himself as well.[43]

Fedotov urges that Christians work to shape an "organic democracy," characterized by three conditions. First, participation in government should be a common obligation and a common sacrifice, rather than an individual right. Second, popular representation should mean the selection of the wisest and most just for the determination and creation (rather than simply expression) of the popular will. The creation of political order from chaos is a creative task which requires more than the simple compilation or balancing of opinions. Third, government should be the leadership of the people, not the service of a slave to his master (Fedotov approvingly cites the examples of American presidents and Roman consuls). In an organic democracy, says Fedotov, the only binding mandate will be the government's conscience and its understanding of the common good.[44]

In 1932 Fedotov felt that if fascism could overcome its extreme centralism and evolve democratically, so as to allow leaders to rise from the bottom to the top, it might constitute the basis for "a new corporativist or social democracy."[45]   Actually, the term "socially concerned Christian democracy" might better describe Fedotov's ideal. He hoped his ideal would eventually incorporate "the best elements of fascism, communism and other systems and enlighten and spiritualize them with the breath of the single Truth."[46]   He also saw his government as highly de-centralized, since "moving toward the kingdom of God means restricting the power of Caesar."[47]

At times, Fedotov concedes, the enemies of the Church may be nearer to the truth than their opponents. Still, this did not vitiate what he saw as the fundamental truth of Christian political involvement,

> Christianity has something to say in history and in politics. Certainly there is no single program for all time, except the maximalist one - the Kingdom of God, but inasmuch as Christianity has an ethical relation to personal life, there is a general ethico-religious

framework to the social world . . . the ethics of the least evil or . . . the greatest good.[48]

Fedotov, however, idealistically lumps rulers and ruled into one category in his Christian society, a pitfall that Kartashev was careful to avoid by acknowledging that Christians would for a long time remain a minority in any modern day government. His recommendations seem more applicable to a society where a high degree of social and religious harmony around principles has already been achieved, rather than to the fractious world we know. But while he felt that his ideal was probably unattainable, Fedotov still believed that the Christian social ideal was more worth striving for than any man-made cause because it raised its sights to the Kingdom of God. As he put it, "we are not for the old or the new, we are for the eternal."[49]

IL'IN'S CRITIQUE OF DEMOCRACY
AND THE PARTY SYSTEM

One of the most overlooked contributors to Russian political and religious thought is Ivan Il'in. After finishing classical academy and Moscow University's school of jurisprudence with honors, he spent two years studying philosophy in France and Germany. Returning to Russia he wrote on a wide variety of subjects, from the nature of the ideal state in Plato, to the idea of the general will in Rousseau. Later he become a leading scholar of Hegel. In the field of jurisprudence he wrote about the concept of state sovereignty and the nature of international law. Exiled in 1922, he moved to Germany and shortly afterward became a corresponding member of the London School of Slavonic Studies. From then until 1938, when he was forced to flee Germany as a result of Hitler's rise to power, he lectured throughout Europe on Russian and Soviet affairs. His Christian faith was a constant source of sustenance throughout his life, and his many writings are devoted to the apposite role of the Christian in the contemporary world. His books include, *The Religious Meaning of Philosophy: Three Speeches* (1924), *The Path of Spiritual Renewal* (1935, revised in 1962), *The Bases of Christian Culture* (1937), *Axioms of Religious Experience*

(1953), *The Path to Clarity* (1957), and *The Singing Heart: A Book of Quiet Meditations* (1958).

Like Fedotov, Il'in imbues politics with broad responsibilities. "Politics," he writes, "is the task of the lawful and just organization of national existence."[50] There are two views of the government that emerge from completely opposite views of the nature of the politics: one view sees government as an "institution," while the other view sees it as a "corporation" or "cooperative"[51] (elsewhere he calls this distinction one between the "mechanical" and "organic" views).[52]

Institutions are built from the top down. People receive benefits from them, but do not necessarily participate in the formulation of their interests and goals. Institutions are characterized by the passivity of most of their members, and in the final analysis it is they who listen, not they who are listened to in the institution. On the other end of the spectrum of political power is the corporation, composed of "active, delegated and equal (in rights) actors" who unite of their own free will and have a common interest which they are each free to accept or to reject.[53] It is organized from the bottom up, on the basis of free elections. No government is entirely one or the other, but each stands somewhere on this continuum between totalitarianism and anarchy. No government, argues Il'in, will ever become a pure cooperative because government is by its very nature "command-authoritative" and "necessarily coercive."[54]

Il'in argues that the institutional view of government asserts a mechanical balance between its parts based on the compromise of mutually suspicious groups. Thus every citizen suffers from a degree of divided loyalty: on the one hand he must work for the good of all in the state; on the other hand he should intrigue and conspire for his own purely personal concerns. Consequently, the "mechanical, quantitative, formal" understanding of government that has evolved in the West conceals a considerable danger: "it fails to preserve the organic nature of government, it tears the public law away from a person's qualities and possibilities; it does not unite citizens in the common good, but settles their egotistical voices in compromises."[55]

It is a fundamental error, says Il'in, to think that government interest coincides with private interests, and that the health of the state is "guaranteed by the competition and compromise of these conflicting forces."[56] If this were true, then how does one explain the anti-democratic epidemic that plagued many European parliamentary democracies during the interwar period? Il'in accuses the supporters of parliamentarian democracy of being silent about the tendency toward tyranny endemic to their system. In any party system a minority seeks to achieve control of the government and impose its own platform on all. Moreover, party systems lead to egoism and party in-fighting as parties battle it out among themselves to achieve power. Hence, Il'in concludes, "a party is a union of citizens organized in order to seize government power. This is the aim of *all* parties - democratic and undemocratic,"[57] the only difference between them being that democratic parties consider it necessary to respect the constitution while pursuing their aims.

Il'in highlights a basic flaw in parliamentary systems, i.e., that as long as the vying powers reach a compromise there is balance, but if one refuses to compromise, it causes irreparable damage.

The pursuit of a quantitative majority is the crucial goal in parliamentary systems, giving the tactical advantage to party demagogues who would promise anything for the vote of the undecided majority. Can numerical majority really be a valid measure of good government, asks Il'in? "Does history not know enough examples of people who voted for tyrants, adventurists, for totalitarian parties, for the exile of its best people (Aristides), for the sentencing to death of their righteous (360 votes out of 500 were cast for Socrates' death sentence)."[58] It is a rule of party political systems that the greater the number of parties, the more difficult political life is. And when only two or three political platforms exist, does this mean that the rest of political life ceases to exist? Far from expressing the fullness of political thought, Il'in concludes, parties stifle political initiative through the monopoly they hold on political life.

DEMOCRACY AND ARISTOCRACY

Democracies often forget that there is a person behind each vote cast. That person, says Il'in, must be "worthy" of casting a ballot, i.e. he must be fully conscious of his action. "A person participates in the life of the state *as a living organism*. . . . Government is not 'out there somewhere' . . . it lives within us, in the form of ourselves. . ."[59]

Democracy presumes that people are capable of ruling. An essential component of government, therefore, is its aristocracy; or, as Il'in puts it, "every government is called upon to be an aristocracy."[60] Democracy and aristocracy (used in the Greek sense of meaning the best: the patriot who thinks in terms of the general welfare, the politically experienced man of honor and responsibility) are not opposite poles, but are necessarily intertwined in a healthy society. A democracy which is not able to derive the best from its populace leads the entire people to destruction. Consequently, "democracy earns recognition and support only inasmuch as the best forces of the populace enter her ranks."[61]   The crisis of European parliamentarianism showed the limitations of formal democracy and the party system. At the same time it reflected the loss of a sense of right, the loss of religious Christian spirit and the resulting unprincipledness and formalism leading to tyrannies of both the left and the right.[62]

Il'in's solution is two-fold. First, he argues that there is no single guideline or ideal system for all governments and peoples. A political organism is spiritual in nature. Government begins where common principles abide, i.e., in those principles which are important to all, which all have at once or none have at all. Without these principles there can be no consensus in government.[63]

Moreover, in every system, says Il'in, it is always a minority that governs. Even in the most consistent democracies the majority merely selects its elite and gives it general guidelines for how to rule. The fortunes of the nation thus depend on the quality of its leading elite. What Russia needs, argues Il'in, is a new leading elite [sloi], which recognizes and promotes people of "qualitative-spiritual energy."[64] He envisions this "elite" as a group of Platonic dictator-philosophers who go about purposefully christianizing government. At the same time, however, he warns this elite not to overestimate the influence of government, for it is still an "authority approaching from the outside." The elite "is called upon to respect and aid the free creativity of the people it leads, for one can only lead the free; herders are needed only for animals, supervisors only for slaves."[65]

To be sure, Russia needs more than an aristocratic elite. It also needs a strong middle class, a free and enterprising peasantry, and a "brotherly" working class, says Il'in.[66] The operations of government must then be delicately adjusted to the living tradition of the nation, serving to help it grow. A government contrary to this tradition cannot but fail he says, echoing Kartashev. The path to Russian renewal, therefore, lies in "the spiritualization and benevolent enlivening of the Russian national instinct."[67]   Restoring Russia is a task at once patriotic and deeply religious; it is, says Il'in, "doing God's work on earth."[68]

THE BASES OF CHRISTIAN AUTHORITY

For Il'in, a Christian must fully accept the world he lives in; he must love it and his homeland as a "living treasure, the living breath of the spirit of God. *The nation is not God; but its strength of spirit is from God.*"[69] For Il'in, therefore, love of country is an essential component of Christian love, and he would argue that it is impossible to love mankind without first loving and understanding your own people. True love of country teaches humility and repentance.

Il'in prefers a monarch or someone with substantial executive authorities, like the American president, as a national leader. A good monarch is above party factionalism and epitomizes the qualities of a true aristocrat; he embodies national unity and represents the synthesis of society. Il'in favors a monarchy for Russia because he feels that it embodies the Russian ideal of government [*vlast'*] as a spiritual rather than a coercive authority. According to Il'in this ideal posits that a Christian assumes power out of a desire to serve God and man and therefore feels a responsibility in the exercise of power even when no one demands it of him. After a blistering critique of the weaknesses of party factionalism (a critique better known in the United States in the writings of Madison in the tenth Federalist Paper), Il'in appears to settle rather unsatisfactorily for a government of uncorruptable, benevolent dictators.

The church for its part should encourage lay people to exercise their Christian ideals in the lay world, "to shine forth living religiosity in their work, to give it meaning before God and to give people the freedom of inspiration, filling this inspiration with the light of Christian beneficence."[70]   In practical terms Il'in saw this as a return to *consonantia*, the freely chosen spiritual accordance of the tasks of church and state. Both serve the same goal - God's work on earth - but by different means. Hence each should remain independent of the another.

The most controversial of Il'in's pronouncements on Christian ethics was his justification of the resistance to evil by force. According to Il'in, a person has the right to forgive those who have sinned against him, but not those who have caused suffering to others. He can sacrifice his own life and goods, but not the life and goods of others. Hence an individual can, under specific conditions, be called upon to oppose evil and be morally bound to do so. In such instances opposing evil is not limited to personal choice. "In such cases" Il'in writes, "*duty is the measure of justice.*"[71]

Like Kartashev and Fedotov, Il'in created no formal system of thought, but points instead to certain negative characteristics of the present and tries to show how they might be overcome by attempting to christianize society and build the kingdom of God on earth. None of these thinkers were utopians in the sense that they believed that the kingdom of God could ever be approximated on this earth (perhaps for this reason they stopped short of offering specific policies for government). Yet, while each helped to delineate aspects of a specifically Russian concept of politics, their greatest weakness as a group was their inability to give this concept any concrete governmental expression.[72]

Influenced by the crumbling of democratic institutions around them, first in Russia and then in the countries of Western and Central Europe, they sought to determine what would enable democratic institutions to withstand the never-ending onslaughts of usurpers and tyrants. Russian religious philosophers felt that such strength would have to be found within the mechanics of the democratic process, but that these mechanisms could only be relied on if government itself felt committed to the most deeply rooted national aspirations. For them these aspirations were reflected in patriotism (expressed both as public conscience and as service to the nation) and in the christianization of public life (a condition of personal as well as communal salvation). The essential task of democratic government, they felt, was anchoring these aspirations in governmental policy.

From the perspective of most western democracies at the end of the twentieth century, many of their solutions seem distinctly autocratic. But it would not do to forget that these thinkers were reacting to the collapse and abandonment of democratic values and institutions all around them. At a time when many European and American intellectuals were succumbing to the intellectual temptations of fascism and communism, their response was to reaffirm the importance of democracy, abetting it through linkages to the broadest base of popular support they could imagine - patriotism and religious tradition. This unreserved commitment to democracy clearly places Russian religious philosophy in the liberal tradition that has found contemporary political expression in the Christian Democratic parties of Western Europe.

PERESTROIKA AND RUSSIAN RELIGIOUS PHILOSOPHY

The rediscovery of Russian religious philosophy in the Soviet Union has proceeded swiftly along several levels of Soviet society: in the official press, among the intelligentsia, and among informal groups and publications.

One of the most prominent projects to popularize these thinkers is the so-called Russian Encyclopedia, presently involving over three hundred academics.[73] This fifty volume project, under the direction of Academician Oleg Trubachev, is to provide a compendium of all that is known about Russian culture at home and abroad; the editors specifically reject any "administrative, political, or territorial restrictions" between themselves and the Russian diaspora.[74]

The first section the editors set out to complete was the one on Russian philosophy. According to the director of the newly created coordinating council of the Russian Encyclopedia project, L. Bystrov, this section will include information on over 450 Russian philosophers.[75] In addition to gathering information, the Encyclopedia and the All-Russian Cultural Fund will then popularize it by setting up local centers for discussion and information known as Russian Popular Houses. Such a center was established last year in Moscow by writer Tat'iana Ponomareva.[76]

Even before the Russian Encyclopedia project had begun, however, short pieces by selected Russian religious philosophers had begun appearing in the press. These include essays by Lev Shestov,

Father Pavel Florensky, Nikolai Fedorov, Semen Frank, Giorgii Fedotov, Aleksei Losev, as well as articles about Father Sergei Bulgakov. These writings have appeared not only in specialized journals, but even in large circulation newspapers such as *Moskovskii literator, Literaturnaia gazeta,* and *Moskovskie novosti* (in Nikolai Fedorov's case even on television).[77]   Certain journalists, Aleksandr Nezhnyi, for example, seem to have made a vocation of promoting the Church and religion as forces vital to the country's spiritual restructuring.[78]

In recent months a number of journals have inaugurated new sections largely devoted to the legacy of Russian religious thinkers. These include, "From the history of Russian philosophical thought" in *Literaturnaia gazeta*, "Russian ideas" in *Teatral'naia zhizn'*, "Russian Philosophers of the Past" in *Sever*, the "Literature and Culture" section edited by Igor' Vinogradov for *Moskovskie novosti*, and the "Native Thought [*otechestvennaia mysl'*]" column in *Nashe nasledie*, the journal of the Soviet Cultural Fund.   In addition, the Soviet Cultural Fund organizes a series of evening gatherings entitled "Returning Forgotten Names." One of the first of these was devoted to the life and work of Father Pavel Florensky.

The Russian religious-philosophical heritage has been openly advocated by prominent writers and academics, including A. Gulyga, V. Toporov, V. Kurbatov, Iu. Seliverstov, and V. Rasputin, as a place to seek remedies for Soviet social problems. The last three have called on the Soviet Cultural Fund to establish a religious-philosophical society that would examine the contemporary application of Russian religious philosophy. In their words,

> Even today this is not a historical and passe philosophy, but an essentially contemporary, spiritually constructive, and deeply farsighted [philosophy]. The more seriously and appreciatively it is assimilated, the healthier and more confident our intellectual and spiritual foundation will be....[79]

This attitude is shared by a number of informal socio-political groups and independent journals that have arisen since the advent of *perestroika*.[80]   These journals publish a far wider selection of the writings of Russian religious philosophers than their official counterparts; they have not shied away from pieces which openly criticize socialism and the premises of the October revolution and urge a return to Russian patriotism and Christian values.[81] The head of at least one informal group in the Baltic republics, Viktor Popov of the Balto-Slavonic Society, sees the Russian religious-philosophical heritage as offering a possible solution to the nationalities crisis.[82]

Not surprisingly, prominent representatives of the church have on occasion endorsed the reappearance of Russian religious thought.[83] Still, the official church must be circumspect in the social role it assumes. This is not the case with outspoken dissident priests like Father Gleb Yakunin. In the best traditions of Russian religious philosophical thought, Father Yakunin, a well known critic of state policy toward the Church, ran for a seat in the new Congress of People's deputies. Despite his loss, widely ascribed to unfair electoral practices in his district, Yakunin has been embraced by prominent Russian nationalists for his advocacy of the Church's central role in the process of perestroika. Two examples: his signature alongside those of Sergei Averintsev, the Vice-Chairman of the Soviet Cultural Fund, Sergei Zalygin, the editor of the influential *Novyi Mir*, and Academician Tat'iana Zaslavskaia on an appeal to amend the Soviet constitution to grant legal equality to religious believers; and his appearance on the podium alongside People's Deputies Boris El'tsin, Andrei Sakharov, Leonid Batkin, and Iurii Kariakin, at a gathering of one hundred thousand people in Luzhniki Park in Moscow on the eve of the opening of the Congress.[84]

Reinforcing Russian patriotic sentiment and the Church's social and educative role are no doubt issues close to the hearts of a number of newly elected People's Deputies. Deputy Mark Zakharov, for example, who made international headlines with his proposal to bury Lenin, described his agenda as a People's Deputy as follows,

> We must re-evaluate our relationship to universal values and to the moral sources of great Christian culture. We must look around us to see where and in what things we are still pagans, heretics who have forsaken the teaching of our forefathers . . . I will go even further and add that the great cathedrals of the Moscow Kremlin must sooner or later be resurrected, regaining their tattered magnificence and the natural life which cathedrals in Rome, Paris, Madrid and other civilized cities have. I intend to assist in every way [the process of]

distancing ourselves from pre-Christian barbarism and thoughtfully
nurturing the seedlings of spiritual rebirth.[85]

There can be little doubt that the re-discovery of Russian
religious philosophy will lead to increased visibility for the Russian
national and religious revival (what Soviet literary critic Igor'
Vinogradov, borrowing the title of a well known book by Nikolai
Berdyaev, terms "the Russian Idea").[86] By far the most prominent
representative of this revival today and a direct descendent of the
intellectual strand of Russian religious philosophy, is Aleksandr
Solzhenitsyn. Solzhenitsyn has openly acknowledged the influence on
his thinking of the authors of the religious-philosophical manifesto
Vekhi, and has called on today's Russian intelligentsia to conduct a
critical assessment of its beliefs.[87] Solzhenitsyn's socio-political views
coincide remarkably with those of Russian religious philosophers.
Il'in's critique of democracy, Fedotov's skepticism of secular
revolutions, Kartashev's notion of a higher standard for Russia are all
clearly reflected in Solzhenitsyn's writings, although it is not known to
what extent he is familiar with the works of these specific authors. In
addition, a main theme of Solzhenitsyn's writings has been the need to
buttress democratic institutions with religious and patriotic
commitments.[88] Solzhenitsyn's popularity among today's intellectual
elite is additional evidence of the warm reception that the ideas of
Russian religious philosophers are likely to receive more than seventy
years after they were so vehemently rejected. Recently, the U.S.S.R.
Writer's Union rescinded its decision of November 5, 1969, expelling
Solzhenitsyn from the Union, and recommended that the restoration of
the writer's Soviet citizenship be raised at the next session of the
Supreme Soviet.[89]

But while the short-term consequences of the revival of interest
in Russian religious thought are obvious, the long term consequences
are less easy to predict; nonetheless, they point to a possible challenge
to socialism much more far reaching than any "new political thinking"
contemplated by the Communist Party. A showdown looms between
those in society who support the Party's attempts to use the current
reforms to revitalize socialism and those who view Marxism-Leninism
as part of the problem. The challenge to the regime of Russian
religious philosophy is all the more serious because, like Marxism, it

proposes not only a philosophy but a program of political activism. Russian religious philosophy challenges its adherents to social and political activism, admonishing them that Christians should actively oppose anti-Christian governments.

The growing popularity of Russian religious philosophy and the church's greater involvement in social (i.e., political) affairs will in all likelihood radicalize that segment of the Russian intelligentsia which is uncomfortable with communist rule, but has not yet developed any alternative to it. While Russian religious philosophy offers them no immediate solutions, it does offer a road map for reaching such alternatives.

---

1. For more on the evolution of Russian religious philosophy see Nicolas Zernov, The Russian Religious Renaissance of the Twentieth Century, New York: Harper & Row, 1963; Georgy Fedotov, A Treasury of Russian Spirituality, New York: Harper Torchbooks, 1961; and Semen Frank's brilliant introduction to his anthology, Iz istorii Russkoi filosofskoi mysli kontsa 19-ogo i nachala 20-ogo veka [From the History of Russian Philosophical Thought at the End of the Nineteenth and Beginning of the Twentieth Century], Washington, D.C.: Inter-Language Literary Associates, 1965, pp. 5-17.

2. The main works marking the emergence of Russian religious philosophy are Problemy idealizma [The Problems of Idealism] (1902), Vekhi [Landmarks] (1909) and Iz glubiny [Out of the Depth] (1921).

3. Quoted in Zernov, Russian Religious Renaissance, p. 128.

4. David Joravsky, "Cultural Revolution and the Fortress Mentality," p. 99, in Abbott Gleason et al. (eds.), Bolshevik Culture, Bloomington: Indiana University, 1985. Joravsky notes that "The exiles were, and still are, pictured as the last agents of enemy ideology doomed to extinction by the revolution, yet they are also pictured as dangerous people since many Soviet people would respond favorably to the ideology of these enemy agents, if they had not been exiled." Ibid., p. 110.

5. Igor' Vinogradov, "Bezumnaia 'russkaia ideia'" [The Crazy Russian Idea], Moskovskie novosti, June 11, 1989, p. 11.

6. Nikolai Poltoratzky, ed., Russkaia religiozno-filosofskaiia mysl' xx veka: sbornik statei [Russian Religious-Philosophical Thought of the Twentieth Century: A Collection of Articles], Pittsburgh: Department of Slavic Languages and Literatures, 1975, pp. 262-66.

7. Anton V. Kartashev, Vozsozdanie Sv. Rusi [The Recreation of Holy Russia], (Published by the special committee under Silvester, Bishop of Messina and Vicar of the Metropole of Russian Orthodox Churches in Western Europe, Paris, 1956), p. 19.

8. Ibid., p. 27, 30.

9. Ibid., p. 39.

10. Ibid., p. 27.

11. Ibid., pp. 21-22.

12. Ibid., p. 49.

13. Ibid., p. 19.

14. Ibid., p. 17.

15. Ibid., p. 54.

16. Ibid., p. 51.

17. Ibid., pp. 52-53.

18. Ibid., pp. 58-59.

19. Ibid., p. 72-4.

20. Ibid., p. 85.

21. Ibid, p. 98.

22. Ibid., p. 123.

23. Ibid., p. 91, 93.

24. Ibid., p. 148.

25. Ibid., p. 152

26. Ibid., p. 126.

27. Georgy P. Fedotov, Khristianin v revoliutsii: sbornik statei [Christian in Revolution: A Collection of Articles], Paris: YMCA, 1957, p. 46.

28. Ibid., p. 142.

29. Ibid., p. 132.

30. Ibid., p. 19-20, 24.

31. Ibid., p. 21.

32. Ibid., p. 23.

33. Ibid., p. 27.

34. Ibid., p. 27.

35. Ibid., p. 16.

36. Ibid., pp. 14-15.

37. Ibid., p. 80.

38. Ibid.

39. Ibid., p. 75.

40. Georgy P. Fedotov, Novyi grad [New City], edited by Iurii Ivask, New York: Chekhov, 1952, p. 377.

41. Fedotov, Khristianin, p. 135.

42. Ibid. pp. 134-5.

43. Ibid., pp. 74-75.

44. Ibid., p. 151.

45. Ibid., p. 143.

46. Georgy P. Fedotov, Rossiia, Evropa i my: sbornik statei [Russia, Europe and Us: A Collection of Articles], vol. 2, Paris: YMCA, 1973, p. 295.

47. Fedotov, Khristianin, p. 136.

48. Fedotov, Rossiia, p. 289.

49. Fedotov, Khristianin, p. 17.

50. Ivan A. Il'in, Osnovy bor'by za natsional'nuiu Rossiiu [Foundations of the Campaign for National Russia] (NTSNP General representation in Germany, 1938), p. 45.

51. Ivan A. Il'in, Nashi zadachi: stat'i 1948-54 gg. [Our Tasks: Articles from 1948 to 1954], 2 vols, Paris: Obschche-voinskii soiuz, 1956, p. 80.

52. Ibid., p. 280.

53. Ibid., p. 80.

54. Ibid., p. 83.

55. Ibid., p. 281, 286.

56. Ibid., p. 283.

57. Ibid., p. 194.

58. Ibid., p. 196.

59. Ibid., p. 284.

60. Ibid., p. 123.

61. Ibid.

62. Il'in, Osnovy , p. 17.

63. Il'in, Nashi zadachi, p. 285.

64. Ibid., p. 207.

65. Ibid., p. 209.

66. Il'in, Osnovy, p. 14.

67. Ibid., p. 31.

68. Ibid., p. 36.

69. Ibid., p. 40.

70. Il'in, Nashi zadachi, p. 402.

71. Ibid., p. 49.

72. Semen Frank identifies this as a characteristic weakness of Russian religious philosophy. The dominance of eschatological and apocalyptic elements in their thinking, in his words, "often works to the detriment of the sober and responsible

moral task of Christian enlightenment and healing of life here on earth . . ." Frank, Iz istorii, p. 16.

73. Natal'ia Ivina, "Russkaia entsiklopediia" [Russian Encyclopedia], Literaturnaia gazeta, March 22, 1989. L. Ermakova, "Nachinaia s praslavian" [Beginning with the Earliest Slavs], Sovetskaia Rossiia, May 13, 1989. O. Trubachev, "Tysiacheletniaia zhizn' naroda" [One Thousand Years of the People's Life], Sovetskaia Rossiia, January 4, 1989.

74. Ivina, "Russkaia entsiklopediia."

75. Ermakova, "Nachinaia s praslavian," p. 2.

76. V. Surkova, "Russkii tsentr nachinaet deistvovat'" [The Russian Center Begins Operations], Vecherniaia Moskva, December 12, 1988.

77. On Father Pavel Florensky: "Vozrozhdenie" [Rebirth], Moskovskii literator, January 27, 1989, p. 3-4; P. A. Florensky and Father Andronnik (Trubachev), "Pavel Aleksandrovich Florensky" Literaturnaia gazeta, November 30, 1988, p.5; S. M. Polovinkin et al. editors, "U vodorazdelov mysli" [Watersheds of Thought], Voprosy istorii estestvoznaniia i tekhniki, No. 1, 1989, pp. 67-79; "Vozvrashchenie," [The Return], Nauka i religiia, No. 2 (February 1989); S. Trubachev, "Blizhe k zhizni mira" [Closer to a Life of Peace], Sovetskaia kul'tura, November 3, 1988, p. 6.

On Semen Frank: B. Liubimov, "Svet vo t'me" [Light in the Darkness], Teatral'naia zhizn', April 1989; Yu. P. Senokosov, "'Samobytnost'" i 'prevoskhodstvo'" [Originality and Superiority], Voprosy filosofii, October 1988, 156-60; , S. Frank, "Pushkin ob otnoshenii mezhdu Rossiei i Evropoi" [Pushkin on the Relationship between Russia and Europe], Ibid, pp. 147-73.

On Aleksei Losev: Arsenii Gulyga, "Poslednyi iz 'mogikan'" [The Last of the Mohicans], Moskovskie novosti, November 13, 1988, p. 16; Kh. Garber, "Protiv voinstvuiushchego mistitsizma A. F. Loseva" [Against the Militant Mysticism of A. F. Losev], a 1930 lecture, reprinted in Vestnik kommunisticheskoi akademii, cf. USSR Today: Soviet Media Features Digest, November 18, 1988, F-522, pp. 30-49.

On other noted religious thinkers: V. Novikova, "Pritcha o voskresenii" [The Parable of the Sabbath], Govorit i pokazyvaet Moskva, No. 20, 1989 (on Nikolai Fedorov); E. Barabanova, "Lev Shestov: golos vopiiushego v pustyne" [Lev Shestov: The Voice Crying in the Wilderness], Nashe nasledie, No. 5, 1988; Aleksandr Brezhnev, "Russkii myslitel' Sergei Nikolaevich Bulgakov" [The Russian Thinker Sergei Nikolaevich Bulgakov], Moskovskii literator, December 30, 1988, p. 3-4; Vladimir Toporov, "O russkom myslitele Giorgii Fedotove i ego knigi" [On the Russian Thinker Giorgii Fedotov and His Books], Nashe nasledie, No. 4, 1988, pp. 45, 50-53.

78. Articles by Aleksandr Nezhnyi include, "Zakon i sovest' [Law and Conscience], Ogonek, No. 50, December 10-17, 1988; "Razrushennyi khram" [The Destroyed Churches], Izvestiia, September 21, 1988, p. 3; "O chem nam govoriat stoletiia" [What do the Centuries Say to Us], Druzhba narodov, (June 1988), pp. 200-09; and

"Vozmozhnosti dialoga" [The possibilities of Dialogue], Moskovskie novosti, March 20, 1988, p. 13.

79. V. Ia. Kurbatov, V. G. Rasputin, I. Seliverstov, "Ne ocherednoe, a samoe neobkhodimoe" [Not the Usual, but the Most Necessary], Moskovskii literator, February 3, 1989, p. 3.

80. A recent anthology on the independent press notes the existence of over twenty-five religious and philosophical samizdat journals at the end of 1988. Roman Redlikh, comp., Svoimi silami: antologiia nezavisimoi zhurnalistiki, 1987-1988 gg. [By One's Own Powers: Anthology of an Independent Journalist, 1987-1988], (Frankfurt am Main: Possev, 1989). In 1989 the number of independent journals has grown rapidly.

81. Two recent examples are the publication of Ivan Il'in's "O vozrozhdenii Rossii" [On the Rebirth of Russia] in Vybor [A Literary-philosophical journal of Russian Christian Culture], No. 6, October-December 1988, pp. 148-60; and Nikolai Berdyaev's "Khristianstvo i antisemizm" [Christianity and Anti-semitism], in Merkurii, Special edition No, 17, December 1988, pp. 35-43.

82. Mikhail Bombin, "Rossiia: 'Chto delat'"?" [Russia: What Can be Done?], Atmoda, June 19, 1989, p.6.

83. See Aleksandr Nezhnyi's interview with the Metropolitan of Leningrad and Novgorod, Aleksii, "O chem nam govoriat stoletiia," Druzhba narodov, (June 1988), pp. 206-7.

84. A portion of this appeal was published in Aleksandr Nezhnyi , "Zakon i sovest'," Ogonek, No. 50, December 10-17, 1988. The gathering at Luzhniki park received wide press and television coverage, but its speeches were reprinted only in the local Russian language Estonian journal, Tartusskii kur'er, No. 1, June 1-15, p. 6.

85. Mark Zakharov, "Bez programmy" [Without a Plan], Ogonek, No. 16, April 15-22, 1989.

86. Vinogradov, "Bezumnaia 'russkaia ideia'" [The Crazy Russian Idea], p. 11.

87. Dora Shturman, Gorodu i miru [For the City and the World], New York: C.A.S.E./Third Wave Publishing House, 1988, p. 58.

88. Ibid., pp. 76, 119-46.

89. Among the many prominent Soviet personalities supporting Solzhenitsyn's return are historians Ia. Etinger, and Sergei Burin, literary critic Viacheslav Ivanov, mathematician Igor' Shafarevich, and historian Natan Eidelman. "Vernut' Solzhenitsynu grazhdanstvo SSSR" [Return Solzhenitsyn His Citizenship in the USSR], Knizhnoe obozrenie (#32) August 5, 1988; "Uchit'sia terpimosti k zhivushchim" [Learn Patience toward Living Things], Knizhnoe obozrenie (#33) August 12, 1988;

"Zavershaem obsuzhdenie stat'i E. Chukovskoi" [A Discussion of the Articles of E. Chukovsky], <u>Knizhnoe obozrenie</u> (#36) September 2, 1988; Fedor Voronov, "V poiskakh istiny" [In Search of the Truth], <u>Literaturnaia Rossiia</u>, July 7, 1989, p. 16.

Contributors

Mikhail Agursky is Associate Professor and Researcher at the Marjorie Mayrock Center for Soviet and East European Research at the Hebrew University of Jerusalem in Israel.

Vladimir Al'brekht is a Christian religious and human rights activist and a member of the editorial board of the independent religious journal *Bulleten' Khristianskoi obshchestvennosti*.

A. Bessmertnyi-Anzimirov is a noted Christian religious activist and a frequent contributor to independent religious journals in the U.S.S.R.

Libor Brom is Professor and Director of Russian Area Studies at the University of Denver in Colorado.

Douglas Durasoff is Associate Professor of Political Science at Seattle Pacific University in Seattle, Washington.

Oskar Gruenwald is Director of the Institute for Interdisciplinary Research in Santa Monica, California.

Mikhail Heifetz is a Researcher at the Center for Research and Documentation of East European Jewry at the Hebrew University of Jerusalem in Israel.

The Archbishop of Ivano-Frankovsk and Kolymia, Makarii, heads one of the largest Russian Orthodox Church dioceses in the Soviet Union, with over three hundred parishes.

Nicolai N. Petro is International Affairs Fellow of the Council on Foreign Relations. His chapter was completed while the author was Hooper Fellow at the Foreign Policy Research Institute in Philadelphia.

Valery Petrochenkov is Assistant Professor of Russian at Georgetown University in Washington, D.C.

Gleb Rahr is religious radio commentator for Radio Liberty in Munich, West Germany.

Dmitry Shlapentokh was Assistant Professor of History at SUNY College at Oswego, New York. He is now at Michigan State University in East Lansing, Michigan.

Philip Walters is Research Director at Keston College in Kent, United Kingdom.

Index